"I GREW UP IN THE CHURCH"

“I GREW UP IN THE CHURCH”

How American Evangelical Women Tell Their Stories

Bethany Ober **Mannon**

BAYLOR UNIVERSITY PRESS

Cover and book design by Elyxandra Encarnación
Cover photo: Rachel Coyne/Unsplash

Part of chapter 4 appeared as "Xvangelical: The Rhetorical Work of Personal Narratives in Contemporary Religious Discourse," *Rhetoric Society Quarterly* 49, no. 2 (2019), and an early version of chapter 5 appeared as "The Rhetorical Influence of Contemporary Evangélicas," *Rhetoric Review* 42, no. 3 (2023). Reprinted with permission from Taylor & Francis.

Library of Congress Cataloging-in-Publication Data

Names: Mannon, Bethany Ober, 1986- author.
Title: "I grew up in the church" : how American Evangelical women tell their stories / Bethany Ober Mannon.
Description: Waco, Texas : Baylor University Press, [2024] | Includes bibliographical references. | Summary: "Examines the personal narratives that evangelical women writers use to narrow the gulf between feminist and evangelical worldviews and mobilize readers to activism"-- Provided by publisher.
Identifiers: LCCN 2024004222 (print) | LCCN 2024004223 (ebook) | ISBN 9781481318938 | ISBN 9781481318969 (adobe pdf) | ISBN 9781481318952 (epub)
Subjects: LCSH: Evangelicalism--United States. | Women in church work--United States. | Feminism--Religious aspects--United States.
Classification: LCC BR1642.U5 M343 2024 (print) | LCC BR1642.U5 (ebook) | DDC 269/.2092520973--dc23/eng/20240328
LC record available at https://lccn.loc.gov/2024004222
LC ebook record available at https://lccn.loc.gov/2024004223

Dedicated to my mother, Jennifer Gorham Ober

Contents

Acknowledgments

My editor, Cade Jarrell, at Baylor University Press has provided invaluable guidance and clarity. My research and writing came to life when I connected with him and heard his vision for the wide audience my book could reach. Thank you also to Paul Zetterberg, David Aycock, and the team of editors at Baylor University Press who helped bring my writing into the world, as well as to the anonymous reviewers whose thoughtful and insightful readings improved every section.

I clearly remember the 2017 RSA Institute when the Feminist Rhetorical Histories seminar group inspired me to start studying evangelical women. My deepest thanks to Cheryl Glenn and Jess Enoch who ran that seminar, encouraged my research, and celebrated with me as my words found readers. You both have been models of courageous scholarship and wise mentorship. Stephanie Kerschbaum, Charlotte Hogg, and Laura Portwood-Stacer read my book proposal and gave me generous advice. I am deeply grateful to Emily Cope, Curry Kennedy, Elizabeth Kimball, Jim Vining, David Gold, and Sarah Kelm, who read early drafts of these chapters and gave feedback that made me a sharper thinker and writer. Thank you also to Liane Malinowski, Lilian Mina, Amy Ryan, and Ryan Skinnell, the BALLRS who accompanied me on this book writing journey. Our weekly conversations gave me ideas, encouragement, excitement, and endurance for the stages of this project.

Thank you to my colleagues at Appalachian State University, who have been reliable friends and sounding boards for my writing. I also want to acknowledge the College of Arts and Sciences at Appalachian State University, which funded a summer research grant to work on this manuscript. Special thanks to Georgia Privott,

William Knight, Noah Williams, Elliot Froese, Lizzie Bingham, and Shelby Michael, undergraduate and graduate students at Appalachian State University, who all assisted with research and editing. Thank you for the nuggets of research gold you found and for the mistakes and awkward sentences that you caught.

At every point in my education, mentors have taught me that research and writing can be hopeful, lively, and personal. I am grateful to my dissertation advisor, James L. W. West III, committee members Cheryl Glenn and Sandra Spanier, and professors Kathryn Hume and Nicholas Joukovsky. Thank you also to my undergraduate thesis advisor Jonathan Hufstader and University of Connecticut professors Clare Costley King'oo, Gregory Semenza, Lynn Z. Bloom, Gina Barreca, and Sylvia Schafer. You all showed me how to think rigorously and imaginatively about religion, gender, and the significance of personal stories.

My family has been excited about this book from the beginning. Garry Ober, Mary Grace Carpenter, and Claire McCormick—you all gave me ideas and celebrated with me as this project grew. My mother was my biggest supporter, and she deserves credit for suggesting the title "I Grew Up in the Church" before I had even written a word. I wish she were here with me to read the final version.

Finally, thank you to my husband and children. Ander and Ruby, you are the most joyful and loving souls. Ethan, you are the best imaginable partner in writing, parenting, and life-building. I love you all beyond measure.

Introduction

The Scandalous Particularity of Women's Stories

The refrain "I grew up in the church" echoes through North American evangelical writing. For some, the phrase captures how thoroughly their early years attending church molded their adult identities. Martin Luther King Jr. begins his autobiography: "I grew up in the church. My father is a preacher, my grandfather was a preacher, my great-grandfather was a preacher, my only brother is a preacher, my daddy's brother is a preacher. So I didn't have much choice."[1] The phrase also lays claim to immersive knowledge of church doctrine and practice. In an article for *Relevant* magazine, Barnabas Piper writes, "I grew up in the church. No really, I grew up *in* the church. . . . As the son of prominent evangelical pastor John Piper, I not only saw the inner workings of my own church, I was also exposed to church leaders from around the world and saw the good and the bad from their churches, too."[2] The phrase often prefaces personal and self-referential storytelling, which is increasingly an avenue to gain an audience and enter debates in evangelical public spheres. Like the "click!" and #MeToo tropes of women's movements, "I grew up in the church" signals a strategic public revelation of private experiences.

"I grew up in the church" can introduce narratives of conflict and change. The phrase might compare past and present selves or recall friction between individuals and institutions or between faith and secularism. As author Karen Swallow Prior writes in her essay "Practice the Christian Virtue of Reading Promiscuously," "I grew up in the church, but it took an unbelieving, liberal professor at a state university to teach me how reading well could make me a better Christian."[3] Those narratives often entail struggle against church influence and ideology. In an interview on the *Bible for*

Normal People podcast, writer and theologian Carolyn Custis James contrasts teachings of "the church" with the Bible and her parents. James recalls:

> I was raised on the Bible, I was not somebody who colored outside the lines, I was pretty much following what I was being taught and just loved all the Bible teaching I grew up on. I think that set me up for what I'm doing now—a real love of scripture and learning a lot from my parents on that. *But in the church*, the message that I got as a woman, and not just from the church but just from the Christian community as a whole, was that I would find my true fulfillment as a woman when I became a wife and mother.[4]

For James, an education in the Bible instilled a joy in learning theology and scripture. Her education in the church, though, instilled a narrow view of her life purpose. These examples point to the significance of "the church," the powerful human institutions that tell believers how to live out their faith in the world.

These anecdotes reflect a retrospective tendency among evangelicals. Recalling their individual and collective pasts is a common practice with spiritual overtones. Congregations tell and retell their origin stories, members give testimonies of coming to faith, and pastors and politicians craft career narratives that underscore God's call to leadership. Those stories might paint a rosy picture of the past. For several decades after evangelicalism emerged in the 1950s, the movement could see itself as having an important role in United States politics and culture. In *The End of White Christian America*, Public Religion Research Institute (PRRI) CEO Robert P. Jones explains that evangelical churches were able to celebrate steady growth in membership until about 2008.[5] This trend distinguished them from mainline denominations, like Lutherans and Episcopalians, which had seen their numbers dwindle over that same period.

I grew up in an evangelical church that told an origin story with this theme. Our founders had split from a mainline Protestant church in 1982. During their early years, they held services in a member's living room. By the time I was born in 1986, the (mainly white) congregation had grown and begun meeting in a high school auditorium. We went on to build a metal-sided church building in a suburban neighborhood and later expanded that structure into a megachurch with office suites, a coffee shop, and a plush, high-tech sanctuary. The pastor who oversaw this growth derided the shrinking mainline churches around us. I remember hearing him use their liberal theology as a foil for his own sermons built on claims to "objective" truths and literal readings of the Bible. We were proud of our growth, which we took as evidence that we were attracting new believers by faithfully and visibly living out God's word.[6]

In 2008, the year I left the megachurch where I had grown up, the number of white evangelicals in the United States began to decrease. By 2014, white evangelicals had fallen from 21 to 18 percent of the population.[7] A 2018–2019 Pew survey documented a further decline to 16 percent.[8] The PRRI found that these numbers continued to shrink: in 2020, 14 percent of Americans identified as white evangelicals.[9] Evangelicals were alarmed to see this trend, a result of low birth rates among white Americans and the disaffiliation of younger members like myself.[10] Not only did white evangelicals watch their congregations age and decline, they interpreted secularism, liberalism, and multiculturalism as threats to their status in politics and public life. Mark Labberton—president of Fuller Theological Seminary, the largest interdenominational seminary in the United States—describes evangelicalism as evolving into a "theo-political brand" in this period.[11] He observes the consequences of that shift:

> The impression of many on the evangelical left is that the good news of Jesus Christ has been taken hostage by a highly charged, toxic subculture on the evangelical right that—in the name of God—expresses steely resolve to have its own way in the public square. From the evangelical right, the critique is that Christian America is at war with any and all liberalism—evangelical or otherwise—and is in serious danger of losing its conservative virtues and spiritual practices.[12]

Amid this conflict, evangelical rhetoric urges the movement to pursue political power and bolster a distinct identity. This rhetoric supports "an amalgam of theological views, partisan political debates, regional power blocks, populist visions, racial biases, and cultural anxieties, all mixed in an ethos of fear."[13]

Argument

"I Grew Up in the Church" studies evangelical women who confront their movement at a time when it must reckon with declining numbers and take stock of its role in United States politics and culture. I argue that these writers and speakers with diverse backgrounds and theologies address the fractures in evangelicalism differently than many public figures have done. Even as politicians and pastors construct narratives of evangelical persecution and proclaim their countercultural identities, many women recognize a kairotic moment for conversations about faith, politics, and culture. To spark and sustain those conversations, they circulate personal narratives about experiences in the church that balance and often resist the voices and gatekeepers that dominate religious discourse in the United States. Their platforms for those messages—social media posts, podcast appearances, popular memoirs—are small but mighty. This rhetorical work calls audiences to reconsider conservative ideologies in their communities and in culture wars, and then engage both as empowered and thoughtful citizens.

Roiling debates over culture, doctrine, and politics provide the exigence for many of the narratives that women published between 2008 and 2018. For example, in *I'm Still Here: Black Dignity in a World Made for Whiteness*, writer and activist Austin Channing Brown describes her church-based work on racial justice. She recalls learning that in churches, "dialogue functions as a stall tactic, allowing white people to believe they've done something heroic when the real work is yet to be done."[14] Writer Rachel Held Evans, too, uses personal narrative to put her experience and faith in conversation with American politics. In the first of three memoirs that trace her journey out of evangelicalism, Evans narrates how her faith began to fail to provide "an easy, satisfying answer" to every question:

> But then the twin towers fell, and a part of the world I'd thought little about came to occupy my TV screen each night while our country occupied its lands. . . . It occurred to me that the women and children killed in Iraq's civil war were mostly Muslims, not so much by choice, but by birth. They were Muslims because they were born in a predominantly Muslim country to Muslim parents, just as I was a Christian because I'd been born in a predominantly Christian country to Christian parents. Was I supposed to believe the same suicide bomb that sent a terrorist to hell sent his victims to hell too? Because they weren't evangelical Christians like me?[15]

As Evans found that *these* questions did not have easy or satisfying answers, her faith founded on certainty and a conservative worldview began to unravel. So did her affiliation with American evangelicalism. Such stories about identity, lives in and outside the church, and women's leadership seek to shift readers' stances on contentious issues.

Further, I argue that personal narratives narrow the gulf between feminist and evangelical worldviews and mobilize women to reflect on the nature and impacts of mainstream evangelical rhetoric. As they join debates about religion, culture, and politics, women's personal narratives seek to shift the foundations of evangelical argument. They question commonplaces like certainty and individualism or the fear, combat, and authoritarianism that Labberton describes. Their stories use principles of feminist rhetoric: "*logos* based on dialogue and understanding, *ethos* rooted in experience, and *pathos* aligned with emotion."[16] Rather than make claims to objective truth, they attend to "the scandalous particularity" of the writer's moment and place.[17] They embrace the subjective experiences and embodied perspectives that are the building blocks of faith, service, and community.

Such changes in thought and rhetoric have effects beyond their enclave. Evangelicalism, through popular culture and political activity, shapes the public discourse of the United States, as well as laws and media in many states. In "The Last Temptation," Michael Gerson examines the religious rhetoric in the 2016 presidential election to show how evangelical values and rhetoric shaped voters' feelings and decisions. In speeches and articles about Donald Trump's merit, evangelicals used a resentful, insular rhetoric that came to characterize many Trump supporters in and outside the evangelical movement. Gerson, formerly a George W. Bush speechwriter and policy advisor, explains that evangelical resentment and insularity contrasted with the energy for social justice activism that characterized the movement in earlier periods. In the nineteenth century, he writes, evangelicals had "a this-worldly emphasis on social justice." Their influence shaped the broader culture then as well, but did so by propelling abolition, prison reform, and global health work that "helped save millions of lives."[18]

Evangelical rhetoric and belief affect secular America, and contemporary evangelical women show that the converse is also true. In the twenty-first century, secular movements like marriage equality and #MeToo influenced evangelicalism and participated in its renovation. The women I study here often use their personal narratives to bridge the ideological divides between secular movements and conservative Christian faith. For example, in 2016, writer and speaker Jen Hatmaker (with her then-husband) shared on Facebook that through weeks of Bible study and prayer she had come to understand the biblical basis for same-sex marriage.[19] By telling this story of study and revelation, she declared that a Christian could believe in the Bible's authority and reject homophobia. She gave her readers permission to decenter evangelical conceptions of traditional marriage in their voting decisions and political affiliations. That same year, Beth Moore shared her experiences with sexism and sexual assault in the church, arguing, "Scripture was not the reason for the colossal disregard and disrespect of women among many of these men. It was only the excuse. Sin was the reason."[20] In Moore's blog post, the famous Bible study leader showed readers how evangelical leaders used scripture to bolster patriarchal systems. This kind of rhetorical work reverberates beyond these women's immediate church contexts and engages productively with the liberal activism that many in their community reject. For these reasons, evangelical women are a rich site for studying the mutual influences of religion and secular civic life in twenty-first-century America.

Focus and Scope

My emphasis in this book is on the multiple ways evangelical women use personal narratives and the diverse goals this rhetorical practice can realize. Certainly there is much to say about the rhetorical work men undertake in personal narratives.[21] However, I study women in particular because gender ideologies that constrain women—and the literal interpretations of the Bible that support those ideologies—are conspicuous pillars of evangelical identity. As a result, "many women rhetors find that there is no comfortable ethos to employ if they want to shift the dominant discourse on a particular topic."[22] They draw upon rhetorical skill and creativity to establish effective *ethe* within this environment. I limit my study to 2008–2018, a span of time when their rhetorical agency was particularly salient. As Jones documents in *The End of White Christian America* (and as many congregations observed), white evangelicals declined as a percentage of the population during this decade. Evangelicals also saw their movement fracture over Donald Trump's candidacy and administration and began a period of reflection on their values and identity. Women responded to this turmoil with their own stories in print, on podcasts, and in social media.

"I Grew Up in the Church" amplifies the diversity of identity and experience in evangelicalism. Even as white evangelicalism declined, numbers of non-white evangelicals increased. The presence of non-white evangelicals in churches and in public discourse has troubled some established leaders and their personal narratives offer some of the most astute critiques of the evangelical movement and visions for a renovated evangelical rhetoric. The coming chapters also attend to personal narratives that reveal ideological

diversity, absent from some studies of evangelicals.[23] As I planned this book, I selected subversive voices—sometimes radical ones—as well as orthodox writers who are not the usual subjects of feminist rhetorical scholarship. For example, I study women who adhere to complementarianism, others who reject rigid gender binaries, and others who hear and follow divine calls to leadership. Within the faith, we see women of color who confront white supremacist theologies and politics and queer evangelicals who testify to the damage done by rhetorics of certainty. Not all these writers identify as feminists. However, I contend that rhetors who reject purity culture and barriers to leadership are embracing feminist goals, even if they do so tacitly, with qualifications, or with skepticism of women's movements and feminist theory. By studying women who conflict with feminism or who maintain deep allegiance to conservative religion, this project responds to feminist rhetorician Cheryl Glenn's call for her fellow scholars to "move out of our feminist comfort zones" and "initiate hard talks with feminists who hold values and experiences different from our own."[24]

My parameters—personal narratives about the church, written by evangelicals or writers closely tied to that movement, published during 2008–2018—make possible a study of the large and growing field of evangelical women's writing. I omit conservatives who do not engage other positions and liberals who address other liberals so that this study can target rhetors who speak across political, theological, and ideological divisions. I regret that focusing on evangelicals and narratives about "the church" means I omit intriguing rhetors like Nadia Bolz-Weber, Kate Bowler, Brené Brown, Mary Karr, Kathy Khang, Anne Lamott, Patricia Lockwood, Kathleen Norris, Barbara Brown Taylor, Krista Tippett, Tara Westover, and Lauren Winner. Even within my parameters, I found many more texts than I could possibly include. To complete this project, I (often reluctantly) chose not to follow up on leads to some rhetors, texts, or controversies. Evangelical women are a bold, passionate group, and a rich and fascinating topic to research. I hope this study will spark other scholars' interest in the persuasive power of their writing.

Background: Studying Evangelicals

The key terms of this study—*evangelical, women, feminism,* and *personal narrative*—are all contested terms with meanings that have shifted over time. Indeed, their meanings came under scrutiny in the first two decades of the twenty-first century. Researchers have asked whether historical traditions or theological definitions are being replaced by political identity, how adherents to traditional definitions of gender are adapting to an increasingly feminist society, and what role personal narrative plays (or could play) in public discourse. Evangelical women ask similar questions: "Who counts as an evangelical?" "If I call myself an evangelical, who or what am I identifying with?" "What exactly does the Bible teach about gender, virtue, and calling?" and, "How can my personal narrative be rhetorical?" I use *rhetorical* not in the popular sense of manipulative or deceitful, but the philosophical sense of "changing minds, changing motives, and changing worlds."[25]

To understand how evangelical women have engaged these questions, I draw on concepts from several academic conversations. Here, I explain these concepts and introduce several of the scholars who help me to analyze the rhetorical work of evangelical women. First, I consider definitions of evangelicalism, particularly the characteristics that make its twenty-first-century iteration distinct. Second, I review debates about the status and role of women in conservative Christianity and the strategies that women have used to expand those roles. Third, I explain what I mean by personal narrative—both the features of the genre and the significance it holds in feminist and Christian traditions. Parts of this context might be familiar to readers. I anticipate that scholars of feminist rhetoric will know that personal narrative has long been an avenue for public, and sometimes subversive, speech. Likewise, readers who study and observe evangelicals in the United States might already understand how they differ from fundamentalists. My goal here is to show how these three research conversations intersect and inform one another to make possible a nuanced understanding of evangelical women's rhetoric.

Evangelical

My first chapter, "A Rhetorical History of the Evangelical Movement in the United States," develops a thorough definition of *evangelical*, but here I briefly map the nuances of the term. *Evangelical* refers to Protestant denominations like the Southern Baptist Convention (SBC) and the Presbyterian Church in America (PCA). It also has a doctrinal definition. Historian David Bebbington proposes that evangelicals are united in their emphasis on (1) an individual conversion experience, (2) the Bible's authority and inerrancy, (3) the imperative to spread the faith to nonbelievers, and (4) a relationship with God made possible through Christ's substitutionary death (being "born again").[26] Evangelicals themselves sometimes cite these traits, as in this definition by writer Brian McLaren:

> *Evangelical* generally refers to people who (a) highlight respect for the Bible (so that for them, *biblical* is a favorite adjective, being a broad synonym for *good* or *right*), (b) emphasize personal conversion (often associated with terms like being *saved* or *born again*) (c) believe that God can be known and experienced with something like intimacy (expressed in terms like *having a personal relationship with God*), and (d) want to share their faith with others (by being *evangelistic*).[27]

McLaren explains that the term connotes "an attitude toward God and our neighbor and our mission that is *passionate*."[28] In recent decades, the political objects of that passion made *evangelical* a fraught label. In his 2019 book *Who Is an Evangelical?* historian Thomas Kidd argues that the term "has become fundamentally political in popular parlance."[29] He found that *evangelical* "doesn't resonate with many laypeople (especially nonwhites), including those who do appear to be evangelicals according to standard definitions," and many instead choose terms like *Baptist* or *Bible-believing*.[30] Women who call themselves evangelical (or ex-evangelical) must therefore assess how those terms invite or prevent audience identification.

I study evangelicalism as a movement, a label that scholars occasionally use (though without unpacking the implications). For example, Kidd's subtitle to *Who Is an Evangelical?* is *A Movement in Crisis*; rhetoric scholar Stephanie A. Martin calls evangelicalism a "movement" that "rests upon its understanding of truth."[31] In *White Evangelical Racism*, historian Anthea Butler calls evangelicalism "a *political* movement" with racism at the center of its "political, social, and moral stances in the twenty-first century."[32] Evangelicals outside academia also describe themselves as a movement. In *Still Evangelical?* writer Mark Young compares evangelicalism to "most social movements," in that it may be defined as "an identifiable set of groups and individuals with some common history and traits."[33] I find that by conceiving of evangelicalism as a movement, this study accounts for the history and beliefs that link individuals and groups across stark differences. This approach also acknowledges internal disagreement and factions more explicitly than other definitions, like theology or history, can do alone.

Evangelicalism in the United States is primarily a white movement. The 2014 Pew Religious Landscape Study reported that a majority of evangelicals (76 percent) identify as white. Only 11 percent of evangelicals identify as Latino, 6 percent as Black, 2 percent as Asian, and 5 percent as other or mixed.[34] White evangelicals enjoy privilege and power because of their numbers and the history of racism that Butler, Jones, and others recount. White women have been the "best-known stars" in evangelical women's ministry and enjoyed "a much larger print industry to promote them and a marketplace to reward them."[35] But none of this prevents evangelicals of color from being influential voices and active leaders. Their narratives of private lives and public roles in the evangelical movement offer an "alternative to political conservatism as the only Christian way."[36] Evangelicals of color also have much to say about the ways faith grows out of experiences of race and culture. As Brown writes, "I am trying to clarify what it's like to exist in a Black body in an organization that doesn't understand it is not only Christian but also white."[37] These stories prompt some white evangelicals to consider the racism in their history and take seriously the Christian nationalism in their present. And their numbers are growing. For example, as white evangelicals declined from 21 to 18 percent of the population between 2007 and 2014, they grew in real numbers (from 59.8 to 62.2 million) because of growing numbers of Hispanic evangelicals.[38]

Evangelicals differ from Christian fundamentalists, who originated in the twentieth century among churches who sought to isolate themselves from pluralistic modern culture. In the 1940s, a group of white evangelicals came together to reform this shift toward fundamentalism. Billy Graham is perhaps the best-known leader of that faction, which, in the words of religious studies scholar Julie Ingersoll, was determined "to engage culture and transform it."[39] In my own experience in the church, I most often saw the distinction between fundamentalist and evangelical play out in performative stances toward popular culture. For example, the fundamentalist families I knew were vocal about not letting their children read *Harry Potter* because the series portrays witchcraft. Many evangelicals instead made a point to read the books with their children and discuss the themes of love and self-sacrifice—to engage them and then steer the conversation to Christian values.

Women's rhetorical practices respond to these historical divisions, their lingering influence, and the fundamentalist legacy of resentment and fear in white evangelical rhetoric. As Jones argues in *The End of White Christian America*, the Internet and national news in the twenty-first century made it impossible for conservative Protestants "to assume that their own beliefs are universal."[40] Some evangelical leaders have responded to their decline in numbers and perceived decline in influence by casting the group as a persecuted minority. In a May 2019 commencement speech at evangelical Liberty University, Mike Pence warned his audience, "Throughout most of American history, it's been pretty easy to call yourself Christian, but things are different now."[41] The then-Vice President claimed that believers now feared being "shunned or ridiculed for defending the teachings of the Bible."[42] Pence is far from alone in his stance of proud victimhood. A 2017 PRRI study reported, "White evangelicals are more likely to say Christians face a lot of discrimination than they are to say Muslims face a lot of discrimination (57% vs. 44%, respectively)."[43] My analysis of evangelical women seeks to understand the push-and-pull between this resentful mainstream evangelicalism and the marginalized or dissenting—yet hopeful—voices that gained traction during the 2008–2018 period.

Those voices include the outspoken rhetors in *"I Grew Up in the Church."* These women will surprise scholars who know evangelical rhetoric through Sharon Crowley's work on fundamentalism or through political actors like Phyllis Schlafly, Mike Pence, and Franklin Graham. These women surprised me too, because they differ so markedly from the voices that dominated my early life in the church. However, I was not surprised to find evangelical writers paying close attention to the ways texts influence debates and build community. Members of the movement are preoccupied with communication that can persuade audiences and shape worldviews. Policies, debates, or intra-denomination conflicts often reflect their "concerns about presenting a positive picture of the community to outsiders."[44] Evangelicals base these concerns in biblical texts, like the exhortation, "Always be ready to make your defense to anyone who demands from you an accounting for the hope that is in you."[45] Further, the core evangelical beliefs in spreading the gospel and interpreting and applying texts faithfully mean that many evangelicals develop an abiding respect for the power of symbolic action.

While these religious orthodoxies can be restricting forces, adherents also refine and adapt the identities, strategies, and theoretical frameworks of their religious discourse communities. Elizabeth Vander Lei terms this process "renovation," and her collection *Renovating Rhetoric in Christian Tradition* presents case studies of religious rhetors who "experience religious belief as a dynamic process of meaning-making."[46] Martin Camper makes a similar point in his article "The Future of the History of Rhetoric is Religious," which describes the meaning-making practices that rhetoricians can find in religion:

> Throughout human history, religion has been a significant site of rhetorical activity: preaching, meditation, prayer, divination, communication with the dead, initiation rites, temple design, scriptural interpretation, proselytizing, liturgy. These rhetorical activities are oral, material, embodied, spatial, visual, and now even digital. . . . Further, religion has been a key inventional resource in sociopolitical rhetorics that have driven major movements in national and world histories, including abolitionism, anti-colonialism, feminism, and environmentalism.[47]

Members of religious communities routinely participate in these rhetorical activities and imbue them with personal and public significance. Camper brings a historical lens to religious rhetoric, but he names practices that are also fruitful sites for studying contemporary rhetoric. Not only is religion an inventional resource in contemporary social justice work, rhetors also deploy activities like preaching and prayer—and, I add, confession and testimony—in evolving sociopolitical contexts and toward new goals.[48]

Declining influence and internal debates have given evangelicals new exigence for their concern with rhetoric. In recent work like *Winsome Persuasion: Christian Influence in a Post-Christian World* by communication scholars Timothy M. Muehlhoff and Richard Langer,[49] *On Reading Well: Finding the Good Life through Great Books* by Karen Swallow Prior,[50] and *Seasoned Speech: Rhetoric in the Life of the Church* by James Beitler,[51] scholars call believers to engage texts critically and other humans civilly. Some evangelicals are acutely conscious of "Christianese" phrases like feeling "a calling" or being "saved" that are commonplace to insiders but alienating to others.[52] Importantly, evangelicals translate their religious beliefs to rhetoric in varying ways that reflect generational changes and divisions. In *Vernacular Christian Rhetoric and Civil Discourse*, Jeffrey Ringer finds that many college-age evangelicals seek to "adapt, adjust, and interpret their religious beliefs in order to communicate effectively across difference and convey themselves as legitimate members of the pluralistic contexts in which they find themselves."[53] I see this goal in women's writing too. Instead of combat or certainty, their work is based on "an invitation to understanding—to enter another's world to better understand an issue and the individual who holds a particular perspective on it."[54] Evangelicals' deep-rooted interest in rhetoric sets the stage for evangelical women to call their communities to self-reflection on their common practices.

Women and Feminism

Feminist rhetorical scholarship on conservative Christianity has tended to emphasize historical recovery and women who fight to preach or hold leadership positions. We have paid less attention to twenty-first-century women whose religious contexts authorize (and compel) them to speak and write. As I have begun to show, evangelical women navigate a context with ingrained resistance to their leadership and teaching. They do so with strategies—invitational rhetoric, verbal hospitality, and basing knowledge and authority in experience—that originate in feminist theories of rhetoric.

By feminist rhetoric, I refer to the practice of analyzing "the shaping powers of language, gender ideology, and society; the location of subject(s) within these formations; and the ways these constructs inform the production, circulation, and interpretation of rhetorical texts."[55] While contemporary evangelical women might not all *be* feminists, they work within and respond to a "rhetorical ecology that regulates who speaks, who remains silent, who listens, and who acts responsively."[56] They also use the tactics Glenn identifies as feminist rhetoric:

> (1) Disidentification with mainstream (hegemonic) rhetoric; (2) goals that are dialogic and *trans*actional rather than monologic and *react*ional; (3) attention to marginalized audiences who may or may not have the power to address or resolve the problem at hand; (4) use of vernacular and experiences shared with marginalized audiences; (5) redesign of rhetorical appeals, to include *logos* based on dialogue and understanding, *ethos* rooted in experience, and *pathos* aligned with emotion; (6) use of and respect for alternative delivery systems, especially those long considered passive or feminine, such as emotion, silence, and listening; and perhaps most important; (7) a deep commitment to possibility and hope.[57]

Glenn's definition distinguishes feminist rhetoric from the non-feminist or masculine tradition. As the above passages from Evans, Moore, and Brown begin to show, personal narrative is a powerful vehicle for these values and commitments. It is also a form "rooted in equality, immanent value, and self-determination" that invites the audience "to enter the rhetor's world and to see it as the rhetor does."[58] This invitational rhetoric reshapes debates within and about American evangelicalism, particularly for women whose rhetorical agency is constrained in explicit and implicit ways.

By studying women who remain connected to the church and use a vernacular rhetoric that holds conservative and feminist ideals in tension, I work outside what Charlotte Hogg calls "the parameters feminist scholars are comfortable with: radical, sophisticated."[59] However, scholars including Glenn, Hogg, Jessica Enoch, and David Gold have called for feminist inquiry that considers a wide range of "women's rhetorical contexts, practices, and goals."[60] Like Hogg, my study is driven by asking, "What can be learned from rhetorical practices that don't forward the kind of radical women's agendas that have permeated our scholarship?"[61] In line with that goal of widening feminist rhetoric, *"I Grew Up in the Church"* examines women who represent a theological and political spectrum. I study them in their own contexts, which resist feminist/anti-feminist or traditional/progressive binaries. I agree with Butler that studying women of faith this way has "intrinsic value":[62] insight into their tactics for establishing and deploying moral and rhetorical agency within the realities of evangelical culture. For these writers and speakers, "explaining oppression, equality, and civil rights to hostile and/or unreceptive audiences is a challenging rhetorical task that requires ingenuity and skill."[63] Personal narrative is one skillful response to an evangelical movement that is hostile and/or unreceptive to women's leadership and perspectives.

These complex narratives continue a long tradition of women whose religious faith authorizes their public speech and inspires their rhetorical creativity. Feminist scholarship has detailed the way women's rhetoric in earlier periods grew out of religious contexts that both empowered and constrained them. For example, Glenn shows how the mystics Margery Kempe and Julian of Norwich employed a rhetoric of autobiography that "enabled the medieval women to participate in the rhetorical tradition."[64] Patricia Bizzell and Jane Donawerth analyze women's activism and rhetorical development in the antebellum church in the United States. Religious revivals during that time created a realm where women "developed a strand of rhetorical theory related to sermon rhetoric."[65] In her study of nineteenth-century Methodist periodicals, Lisa Shaver argues that feminist rhetoric and reform efforts were motivated by women's convictions "that they were moral agents accountable to God's word rather than man's interpretation of it."[66] Similarly, Lisa Zimmerelli outlines a pattern in women's spiritual autobiographies of the nineteenth century: a "nonthreatening" narrative of God's calling "was the primary mechanism for convincing a congregation to accept her as a legitimate agent of God."[67] In these revivals and in their published writing, women also taught their audiences how to cultivate rhetorical agency. By fostering metacritical awareness of the power (and limits) of writing and speaking from experience, they invited other women to see themselves as rhetors who could influence evangelical culture.

Many of these goals and obstacles remain relevant to evangelical women's writing. However, the women I study also contend with constraints on their writing that stem from the recent history of American evangelicalism. Feminist thought and activism, in particular, sparked bitter debate between and within churches. In response to twentieth-century women's movements, theologians promoted the concept of *complementarianism* to shore up traditional gender roles. This view of gender holds that men and women have different, God-given natures that suit them for distinct roles, and that the Bible mandates women's submission to male authority. Evangelical feminism of the 1970s outlined an opposing stance, *egalitarianism*, which called families and groups to make decisions "based on the specific skill and experience each person brings to the relationship."[68] In 1974, an Evangelical Women's Caucus formed to advance women's leadership and egalitarian biblical interpretation. Theologians like Nancy Hardesty "urged evangelicals to realize that inerrancy and complementarian gender theology were not undisputed biblical truth, but human interpretation."[69] Still, liberals struggled to persuade the broader community. Complementarianism continues to undergird conservative views of gender; the Southern Baptist Convention (SBC), the largest evangelical denomination, prohibits women's ordination based on complementarian reasoning.

In the twenty-first century, evangelical women participate in a rhetorical ecology shaped by these debates and by leaders who, for decades, "enlisted evangelical women on the right side of the culture wars."[70] This relatively recent controversy between egalitarianism and complementarianism is thorny, but it is only one part of the tradition of evangelical women in the United States. Rhetors draw inspiration from women's leadership during the nineteenth century and connect their own work to that earlier time when evangelicalism was "a faith assured of its social position, confident in its divine calling, welcoming of progress, and hopeful about the future."[71] They write stories that circulate through online and face-to-face testimonial networks, "spaces for connection and affirmation" where women are heard and believed.[72] This vernacular feminist rhetoric presents a useful site for studying how patriarchal thought persists in the twenty-first century and how evangelical women navigate that context. It also articulates their vision for renewed church leadership and practice, relationships and identities, and civic life that draw inspiration from the long tradition of evangelical women's rhetoric.

Personal Narrative

Religious and feminist rhetorical traditions give resonance to contemporary evangelical forms of personal narrative. Like *evangelical*, *personal narrative* is a familiar term that nonetheless needs definition. Instead of *memoir* or *autobiography*, which denote extended print accounts of individual lives and signal a "density of language and self-reflexivity about the writing process,"[73] I use the term *personal narrative* for the texts I study. This more capacious term includes texts of varying lengths as well as self-representation, emerging media, and stories across genres.

Personal narratives that make private faith experiences public are one of the rhetorical practices that distinguish evangelicalism. Theologian D. Bruce Hindmarsh shows that antecedents for the "I once was lost but now am found" conversion narrative reach back to Augustine, Julian of Norwich, Protestant martyrs, and Puritan ministers.[74] I discuss this tradition in chapters one and two, where I explain why evangelicals find personal narrative a rhetorically powerful and generative way to communicate. They are not the only religious group to use personal narrative, but the movement has historically used this expected and acceptable discursive practice extensively and, I argue, distinctively. The practice explains theology, exhorts believers, and testifies to unseen or unacknowledged injustices.[75] Evangelical pastor and scholar Eugene Peterson sums up its significance in the phrase "verbal hospitality." He writes, "Stories open doors to areas or aspects of life that we didn't know were there, or had quit noticing out of over-familiarity, or supposed were out-of-bounds to us. They then welcome us in. Stories are verbal acts of hospitality."[76] For many evangelicals, personal narratives carry rhetorical and spiritual value because of their roots in both Christian and secular movements throughout history.

The decade of evangelical decline that I study follows a "boom" around the turn of the millennium, when life writing enjoyed a surge in popularity among writers, publishers, readers, and scholars.[77] Studies of autobiography offer several reasons why this might be the case. Narratives of private lives have "an explicit focus on bringing the voices of ordinary and marginalized people into the public sphere."[78] They tap into a common "desire to confess, to be heard, and to be literate in each other's experiences."[79] A powerful effect of this self-revelation is to "personalize and humanize categories of people whose experiences are frequently unseen and unheard."[80] These factors gave personal narrative cultural currency and created a demand for evangelical memoirs, blogs, and essays. To be sure, before this memoir boom, storytelling was already "one of the most powerful rhetorical vehicles" for women to effect change[81] and build feminist communities.[82] For women in particular, self-narration provides an avenue to construct identities that resist and revise a "historically imposed version of the self."[83] However, in the memoir boom, "memoir has become the central form of the culture: not only the way stories are told, but the way arguments are put forth, products and properties marketed, ideas floated, acts justified, reputations constructed or salvaged."[84] This rhetorical power extends beyond published memoirs. In accessible forms of personal narrative, like the #MeToo social media hashtag and its corollary #ChurchToo, professional and lay writers alike share their stories to remake their culture.

Both feminist and evangelical communities study and value personal narrative as a source of knowledge, but the practice meets with friction in both camps when religious rhetors use it to intervene in public debates. Evangelicals value personal narrative but afford greater authority to arguments built on Bible verses and theological reasoning. Faith remains a blind spot for many feminist scholars who see piety as a lack of agency and critical thinking. Joycelyn Moody prefaces *Sentimental Confessions: Spiritual*

Narratives of Nineteenth-Century African American Women with a sharp admonition:

> I believe that to overlook, to "read around" the spiritual dimensions present in these books is to neglect an essential and vital aspect of them. Readers can learn something from believers even without becoming converted if we so choose, and faith in the mystical need not be seen as an indication of imbecility. Many theorists have cogently shown that such thinking and such fears are white, western, and male in the worse senses of those terms. It is thinking of this sort that perpetuates the myth that black women cannot meaningfully contribute to American society. Any person who values literature should read spiritual texts *as* spiritual texts because we should not disparage or diminish the full complexity of any text.[85]

Moody's rebuke calls feminist scholars to study texts with religious themes rather than write them off as unintellectual or trivial. I underscore that call, and I hope scholars of evangelicalism will likewise see the complexity and rhetorical agency in personal accounts of religious lives.

"I Grew Up in the Church" theorizes personal narrative as a strategic and public practice that facilitates social movements (specifically, in this study, the evangelical movement). Rhetorical scholarship has only begun to examine the ways in which life writing "shapes and directs our attention" to issues and "talks back to dominant cultural scripts."[86] We have much more to consider about the way cultural contexts make personal narratives effective and inspire experimentation with the genre. We also have work to do to account for the role personal narrative plays in social movements and activism. This nascent conversation calls for studies of personal narrative that do not "treat narrative as purely literary, removed from more practical purposes of persuading and informing,"[87] and go beyond uncritical readings of individual experience as "evidence." While criticisms of memoir as "self-indulgent manipulations of sentiment and goodwill" have merit, writers and readers continue to believe personal narrative can do "meaningful work in the world."[88] *"I Grew*

Up in the Church" responds to scholarly and public interest in personal narrative by demonstrating "the rich and varied ways [evangelical women] writers craft narrative to persuade, to justify, to legitimize, to understand, to commune."[89] Amy Robillard's argument for attention to this richness and variety finds a parallel in literary critic Alan Jacobs' call for evangelicals to learn to tell "better and more responsible and more coherent personal stories" that don't force the complexity of human experience into straightforward conversion formulas.[90] While a testimony can work to simply align the testifier with cultural narratives or reiterate received knowledge, stories of experiences in the church illustrate the shifting, multifaceted ways individuals relate to religious institutions and ideologies.

By documenting the presence and work of personal narrative in emerging evangelical rhetoric, this book addresses a problem Michael-John DePalma and Jeffrey Ringer identify in *Mapping Christian Rhetorics*. In this field, "religious rhetorics tend to remain invisible, buried within fuzzy categories that conjure radicalism and intolerance."[91] Analyzing these writers reveals that they are not new "incarnations of the Religious Right or Moral Majority."[92] Instead, they intervene in evangelical debates about gender, sexuality, race, economic inequality, and social justice. The genre is a skillful response to a resistant culture because it resonates with evangelical beliefs even as it calls attention to the systemic oppression evangelicals avoid discussing. This vein of contemporary religious rhetoric improves scholarly understandings of the rhetorical practices of evangelical women and makes visible the changes they bring about in the evangelical movement.

Plan of the Book

I began this project by reading widely to locate evangelical texts that feature personal narrative and reflect diverse perspectives and identities. Each chapter introduces a cohort of women writers, the style and focus of their personal narratives, and their influence in evangelical culture. I then connect their work to histories of feminist rhetoric and evangelicalism, showing how they engage those traditions and renovate established practices for new audiences and goals. Sections of chapters two, three, and four examine specific controversies from the 2008–2018 decade when rhetors came face to face with evangelical views of gender. The controversies illuminate patriarchal constraints on evangelical women; their responses show their rhetorical dexterity. Moreover, the attention their work receives offers evidence that their calls for new rhetorical practices struck a chord with readers.

"I Grew Up in the Church" is not an apology for evangelical women; I hope to explain, not to advocate. Many of these writers have at times dismissed feminist theology, misrepresented critical race theory, or used abortion as a litmus test for supporting politicians. Even though I found myself clenching my jaw as I read confident defenses of complementarianism or disparaging remarks about feminism, I recognized the agency rhetors exercised in making those arguments and the reality that some writers inhabit contradictory positions. Glenn, Hogg, and Saba Mahmood persuaded me to sit with these contradictions and study across these "lines of division"[93] for a full understanding of evangelical women's rhetoric. Feminist rhetorical history and theory are my primary lenses for interpreting these texts, but through that interpretation this project also outlines a distinctively evangelical rhetoric. I analyze how texts follow the contours of Bebbington's definition of evangelicalism (conversion, biblical authority, atonement, and activism), including the ways women reenvision this quadrilateral in twenty-first-century contexts. Each chapter shows that evangelical theology and culture create the exigence for personal narratives and their strategies.

Chapter 1, "A Rhetorical History of the Evangelical Movement in the United States," makes a case for studying evangelicalism as a movement with a distinct rhetoric. I build an extended definition of evangelical rhetoric by synthesizing histories of the movement and tracing how that history gave rise to the commonplaces and practices it uses today. Based on this history, I argue that evangelical rhetoric took shape at pivotal points like the Second Great Awakening or the Progressive Era when evangelicals had to contend with other social movements. I then identify eight commonplaces that coalesced in these moments: individualism, conversion, fear, divine providence, biblical authority, white supremacy, certainty, and combat. These "signal chains of argument"[94] contribute to group identity and imbue contemporary evangelical discourse with generations of theological debate and historical events. This chapter then theorizes five practices—evangelism, preaching, biblical hermeneutics, apologetics, and testimony—that carry the weight of Christian tradition and doctrine and structure communication in the twenty-first-century iteration of the evangelical movement.

This history and definition of evangelical rhetoric contextualize the influence that women wield. Chapter 2, "A Generous Evangelical Orthodoxy," applies this history to writers Wendy Alsup, Hannah Anderson, Trillia Newbell, and Karen Swallow Prior, whose personal narratives defend traditional doctrine. I show how their beliefs inspire activism, especially in response to abuses of power within the church. One case study in particular—the revelations of misogyny and spiritual abuse by celebrity pastor Mark Driscoll—illustrates how personal narratives create church cultures and can also be a necessary, effective strategy to make injustices visible. By separating orthodox[95] faith from conservatism, these writers and their "generous orthodoxy" try to extricate evangelicalism from modern-day ideologies and political rhetoric.

Chapter 3, "Storytelling as Verbal Hospitality," introduces the prolific memoirist Rachel Held Evans, whose books recount her journey out of a culture "only interested in winning arguments, converts, and elections."[96] Evans, after leaving the conservative evangelical church she attended (and "the church" of American evangelicalism writ large), remained an influential voice. Her memoirs use an ecological *ethos* to argue that culture wars and combative rhetoric alienate even committed Christians. This is particularly true of young believers, and those with identities the church marginalizes, who are most in need of hospitality. I briefly analyze a second ex-evangelical writer who joins her in this project. In *Rescuing*

Jesus, journalist Deborah Jian Lee testifies to the racism she experienced as an Asian American woman in evangelical spaces. Through knowledgeable outsider perspectives, Lee and Evans call attention to the violence and fear that shape evangelical politics and culture.

Chapter 4, "The 'Resisterhood' of Progressive Evangelical Women," studies evangelical women who explicitly and vocally denounce conservative views on gender, sexuality, and race. Sarah Bessey, Austin Channing Brown, and Jen Hatmaker all build readerships by remaining within evangelicalism while calling for its renewal. These writers carve out progressive evangelical identities that destabilize rigid gender hierarchies and biblical literalism, two conservative emphases. Through narratives like Hatmaker's discovery of a biblical basis for same-sex marriage or Brown's account of the commitment to whiteness she witnessed in churches and nonprofits, these women advocate for doctrinal positions on race, gender, and sexuality that respond to secular activism. Their commitment to faith as a basis for feminist and antiracist work renews nineteenth-century activism and asks the evangelical movement to invest in conversations it often avoids.

Despite opposition, many women achieve positions leading evangelical institutions. To explain how their presence changes evangelical rhetoric and culture, chapter 5, "The Rhetorical Leadership of Contemporary *Evangélicas*," analyzes the book *Hermanas: Deepening Our Identity and Growing Our Influence*. In this book, coauthors Natalia Kohn (Rivera), Noemi Vega Quiñones, and Kristy Garza Robinson testify to the effective leadership of women—particularly women of color—and the realities of evangelical power structures that center white male voices. The text enacts an apostolic *ethos* that is pragmatic, concerned with the lives of congregations and individuals, in contrast to the prophetic *ethos* focused on reform or a combative *ethos* focused on winning culture wars.[97] Using the practices of testimony, *testimonio*, and analogical imagination, Kohn, Vega Quiñones, and Robinson recount how they each negotiated patriarchal white evangelical spaces and encourage Latina Christians to follow them in these paths.

"I Grew Up in the Church" concludes by reflecting on the role of hope in evangelical women's rhetoric. These writers and speakers have every reason to expect their words will be ignored, drowned out, or suppressed in a noisy and fractious environment. Still, they persist in writing against institutional power structures and dominant political values in the movement. Instead of earthly evidence, faith in divine providence and *kairos* (God's timing) motivates their work. That belief is not discouraging or disempowering. Rather, it emboldens speech and writing in difficult or inhospitable environments.

I follow this conclusion with an epilogue that considers changes in evangelicalism after 2008–2018. In the subsequent five years, 2018–2023, white Christian nationalism exploded, evangelicals attacked the Black Lives Matter and #MeToo movements, the Supreme Court overturned Roe v. Wade protections for reproductive rights, and the SBC tried (and largely failed) to hold congregations accountable for hiring or shielding sexual abusers. I watched these events unfold as I researched and drafted this book. I also watched evangelical debates that continued to revolve around women's writing. Rachel Held Evans passed away and evangelicals revisited her work; Kristin Kobes Du Mez and Beth Allison Barr published bestselling books on biblical manhood and womanhood that inspired many evangelicals and angered others; Beth Moore announced she could no longer belong to the SBC and wrote a memoir about her experiences. Perhaps the seeds planted in the decade of evangelical decline grew, flowered, and bore fruit we can see in these texts.

This book offers a hopeful argument, propelled by my reading of feminist and religious rhetoric. Glenn frames feminist rhetoric as a hopeful project, which holds out hope that feminist rhetorical inquiry can make a difference in the world. Crowley ends *Toward a Civil Discourse* optimistically: "Story is, perhaps, the most efficient means of garnering attention" to counter fundamentalisms.[98] Jones concludes *The End of White Christian America* on a confident note too: "In the soil fertilized by White Christian America's remains, new life is taking root."[99] In personal narratives, I see evangelical women proclaiming faith in the possibility of renewal after years of division and decline. Sandra Maria Van Opstal, a pastor who calls herself a Latina born to immigrant parents, proclaims, "There is hope for evangelicalism, and that hope is us."[100]

For Van Opstal and others, clear-eyed recognition of the violence and "anemic faith"[101] of theopolitical evangelicalism still tempers that hope. In "Remaining to Reform," Van Opstal describes the betrayal that evangelicals of color felt when 81 percent of white evangelicals voted for Trump in 2016. She explains her reaction:

> I'm often ashamed and angered by my evangelical family in the United States but it doesn't cause me to leave—it causes me to speak up and speak out. Evangelicalism is about conversion, reform, transformation, and repentance. If I'm going to remain, I'm going to use my voice for reform. I'm going to take seriously how the authoritative Word of God speaks to the racism and xenophobia of our evangelical family.[102]

Despite shame and anger with the evangelical movement, Van Opstal says, "I am evangelical because this was the expression of faith that nurtured and raised me."[103] Such roots mold identity and bring conflict, but they also inspire boldness. Evangelical women confront the tension between their convictions, the beliefs and practices of their churches, and their commitments to civil discourse and human dignity. That confrontation creates powerful rhetoric and nurtures new life in the religious culture of the United States.

1
A Rhetorical History of the Evangelical Movement in the United States

The commonplaces and practices at the core of the evangelical movement are ripe for women to use and reform. This chapter begins by mapping the complicated nature of evangelical identity during its four-hundred-year history in the United States. Definitions of *evangelical* based on doctrine, culture, history, affiliation, and politics all highlight vital features of evangelicalism. I don't try to adjudicate which is most accurate. Instead, I contend that studying evangelicalism as a movement is valuable because it directs us to ask how members grapple with core beliefs, other factions, and other movements as they construct their identities and goals. I then trace the history that created the evangelical commonplaces of individualism, conversion, fear, divine providence, biblical authority, white supremacy, certainty, and combat. These commonplaces spur and direct public engagement, unite and divide groups, and reinforce and undermine power structures. Last, I describe rhetorical practices that characterize evangelical faith: evangelism, sermons, biblical exegesis, apologetics, and testimony. Evangelicals use these forms of speaking and writing to negotiate the values and ideologies they learn from churches, families, schools, and media. In that negotiation, they create identities within and apart from those institutions and discourses.

The rhetoric that evangelical women critique, deploy, and transform is neither a transcendent feature of the faith nor a current trend. Commonplaces like combat and practices like testimony took root in past events. *"I Grew Up in the Church"* is not an historical project, but starting with a rhetorical history has value, as scholars like

Kathleen J. Turner and Robert E. Connors argue. Such a history of evangelicals shows how wrestling with power, identity, and social responsibility has been central to the movement from its emergence in the Great Awakening and through events like the Civil War and Conservative Resurgence and introduces "the ways in which rhetorical processes have constructed social reality at particular times and in particular contexts."[1] Turner distinguishes rhetorical history from criticism: "Broadly speaking, whereas rhetorical criticism seeks to understand the message in context, rhetorical history seeks to understand the context through messages that reflect and construct that context."[2] Her definition describes how this chapter sets the stage for the next four. Chapters two through five seek to understand evangelical women rhetors in the context of the decline of white Christian America. First, though, I consider how the history of American evangelicalism gives personal narratives persuasive and spiritual power in this community.

Readers might be familiar with evangelicals from books like Sharon Crowley's *Toward a Civil Discourse*, *The Faithful Citizen* by Kristy Maddux, or *Believe Me* by John Fea. Some might have spent time in evangelical communities. This chapter still has much to teach those readers, since the movement is more complex and rhetorical than even insiders and knowledgeable outsiders realize. Moreover, rhetorical studies have just recently begun a sustained conversation about evangelicals and their strategies for "changing minds, changing motives, and changing worlds."[3] We have much to learn from scholars like Beth Allison Barr, Anthea Butler, Julie Ingersoll, Robert P. Jones, Kristin Kobes Du Mez, Mark Noll, and others in history, religious studies, and sociology who have built a body of research on evangelicals. As Connors writes, "Rhetorical history, like all history, provides those who study and read it with a certain necessary kind of hard knowledge."[4] This chapter provides that hard knowledge of periods when evangelicalism encountered other movements and the rhetoric that emerged.

Who Is an Evangelical?

Doctrinal definitions focus on beliefs, an appealing approach that seems to articulate the unchanging core of the faith rather than worldly cultural and political contexts. Rhetoric scholars who study evangelicals often use historian David Bebbington's doctrinal definition from *Evangelicalism in Modern Britain*. For example, Emily Murphy Cope and Jeffrey Ringer cite Bebbington's "quadrilateral," four evangelical priorities that have persisted since the eighteenth century:

(1) Conversionism, the understanding of conversion as a personal experience that significantly transforms each Christian's life;

(2) Biblicism, the premise that the Bible is the ultimate authority for Christian living;

(3) Activism, the impulse to spread and enact faith through relief/social work; and

(4) Crucicentrism, a focus on the substitutionary death of Christ.[5]

Historians cite Bebbington's quadrilateral[6] and evangelicals do too; contributors to *Still Evangelical?* ground their discussions in the quadrilateral. Bebbington's definition has staying power among scholars and evangelicals because of its simplicity and apolitical focus on beliefs, though that focus means it comes up short in describing twenty-first-century evangelicals.

Scholars have expanded upon the doctrinal definition to describe how evangelicals act in the real world. Even though writers in and outside academia cite Bebbington's quadrilateral, historian Kristin Kobes Du Mez notes that many believers "would be hard pressed to articulate even the most basic tenets of evangelical theology."[7] Instead, she argues, "What it means to be an evangelical has always depended on the world beyond the faith," especially popular culture.[8] In her bestselling *Jesus and John Wayne: How White Evangelicals Corrupted a Faith and Fractured a Nation*, Du Mez explains that evangelicals who know little about doctrine have

> raised children with the help of James Dobson's Focus on the Family radio programs or grown up watching *VeggieTales* cartoons. They rocked out to Amy Grant or the Newsboys or DC Talk. They learned about purity before they learned about sex, and they have a silver ring to prove it. They watched *The Passion of the Christ, Soul Surfer*, or the latest Kirk Cameron film with their youth group. They attended Promise Keepers with guys from church and read *Wild at Heart* in small groups.[9]

This consumer culture wields more influence over white evangelical identity than do pastors or the Bible. Religious studies professor Julie Ingersoll likewise defines evangelicalism as a culture, "a set of symbols that act as a rubric for ordering life and providing meaning."[10] For Ingersoll, "an evangelical is someone who understands its argot, knows where to buy posters with Bible verses on them, and recognizes names like James Dobson and Frank Peretti."[11] That popular culture had a destructive influence, too: it spreads militarism and Christian nationalism, a larger cultural identity that Bible verses cannot dislodge.

Evangelical cultural identity hinges on gender. Ingersoll writes that "gender is a central organizing principle and a core symbolic system"[12] that evangelicals constantly negotiate and construct. Historian Kate Bowler sees evangelicalism as a subculture that defines itself against wider American culture, in part by policing traditional gender roles. At the same time, the "evangelical commodities and industries that boomed from the 1970s onward" opened doors for women. Those who could adhere to evangelical gender norms found celebrity through "television, radio, books, magazines, speaking tours, and endless value-signaling products from Tshirts to license plates."[13] Evangelicalism takes its widely visible, public form through these symbols, commodities, and industries that both constrain women and offer them opportunities.

Defining evangelicalism as a popular culture overlooks the centuries that came before Focus on the Family or women's conferences. Molly Worthen proposes that history "is the most useful tool for pinning down today's evangelicals" and tracing a genealogy of American evangelicalism does highlight core features of the movement. Worthen finds their origin in Europe, in Reformation-era revivals that rejected church authorities and hierarchies. American evangelicalism shared "European Pietists' zeal for private Bible study and personal holiness" and Worthen notes that "evangelical catchphrases like 'Bible-believing' and 'born again' are modern translations of the Reformers' slogan *sola scriptura* and Pietists' emphasis on internal spiritual transformation."[14] In *Who Is an Evangelical?* Kidd (an evangelical) finds a founding moment later, in the mid-1700s. At revivals led by New England minister Jonathan Edwards and English clergymen John Wesley and George Whitefield, crowds of non-Christians converted, and believers renewed their faith. This Great Awakening birthed denominations like the Presbyterian Church of America and Southern Baptist Convention. Studying evangelicalism in the young United States, Mark Noll sees a tendency to sermonize about the duties of citizens and the state and a practice of tying political positions to scripture.[15] These histories show that twenty-first-century evangelicals share a denominational genealogy with their forebears and inherited a love for public participation, individual belief, and democratic church structure. History does not account for differences in thought or the partisan politics and popular culture that wield influence in the twenty-first century. Still, history and doctrine set the terms for evangelicals' internal debates and their conflicts with other movements.

Pollsters like Pew or Gallup use a fourth definition: self-identification. Pew counts respondents as evangelical if they select "Protestant" as their religion and answer "yes" when asked "*Would you describe yourself as a born-again or evangelical Christian?*"[16] Gallup asks, "Would you describe yourself as 'born-again' or evangelical?"[17] That self-identification might reflect religious affinities and attitudes rather than (or along with) explicit creeds. The Institute for the Study of American Evangelicals (ISAE) explains that *evangelical* "denotes a style as much as a set of beliefs, and an attitude which insiders 'know' and 'feel' when they encounter it."[18] These affinities and coalitions are rooted in history, popular culture, and theology. As I alluded to above, and as the next section explains, they are also rooted in politics.

Definitions based in affinity and self-identification have troubling implications. The pollsters' yes/no questions and the notion of "feeling evangelical" (and, for a rhetorician, "sounding evangelical") all set aside doctrinal or historical definitions. Self-identification brings in people who do not necessarily attend evangelical churches, adhere to traditional evangelical morality, or profess Bebbington's core beliefs. If they call themselves evangelical because they feel affinity with their conservative white churchgoing neighbors, they count. The absence of an external standard for belonging leads evangelicals to argue over who is inside the fold. Even insiders feel self-conscious about how well they perform evangelicalism. This broad cultural evangelicalism includes what Russell Moore calls "blood-and-soil Christianity." In "When the South Loosens its Bible Belt," Moore describes a "sense of belonging and obligation not to a church but to a particular brand of white political and cultural identity" and writes that these cultural evangelicals are combative and feel like "a besieged minority."[19] These cultural but "unchurched" evangelicals conflict with church attendees who might identify more with historic evangelical morals and beliefs (as expressed in Bebbington's quadrilateral). Even if such traditional adherents think the grievance and rhetoric of blood-and-soil Christians do not represent "real" evangelicalism, they can't ignore their real influence on culture and politics.

Definitions based in doctrine, history, culture, and affinity belie the outsize role politics play in American evangelicalism. Robert P. Jones of PRRI notes that white evangelicals consistently voted for Republican presidential candidates starting in 1980.[20] In 2016, a stunning 81 percent surprised the country by voting for Donald Trump; by contrast, 96 percent of African American Protestants and 62 percent of white voters with no religious affiliation voted for Clinton.[21] The political valences of *evangelical* also show up in activism. "Evangelical beliefs have always had political applications," Kidd explains, whether protesting "injustices like slavery" or "trying to impose a de facto or de jure establishment" like Prohibition.[22] Noll also describes an activist ethos among evangelicals. Before the Civil War, faith motivated people to heighten conflicts over slavery (but not to confront racism). After the war, religion lost influence in national politics but remained powerful for individuals and regions. For example, it helped to "subvert the possibility of reconstruction and the possibility of a racially just society."[23] For Noll, politics is at the core of evangelicalism, not a recent change.

Both forms of politics, voting and activism, divide white and non-white evangelicals. Jones argues that white evangelicals' consistent political behavior is a response to "the perceived external threat of racial and cultural change in the country."[24] Kidd separates historical and contemporary evangelicalism to argue that partisan and racial divisions are recent—a result of "Republican insider evangelicals" who "abetted the politicization of the movement."[25] Political scientist Ryan Burge argues that the term is so politicized in the twenty-first century that it has no stable theological meaning "and has now morphed into a social, cultural, and political term that stretches far beyond the boundaries of Christianity."[26] Evangelicalism of the eighteenth and nineteenth centuries might be best defined by its historical roots, but in the twentieth century, political identity and white identity became at least as salient as theology, history, or affiliation.[27]

I propose that rhetoricians study evangelicalism as a movement. This focus looks at the interaction and influence of evangelical factions, and the texts where those interactions play out. I don't mean to argue that this is a better definition than previous scholars offered. Rather, I propose that this is a productive approach because of where it directs our attention. Defining evangelicalism as a theology, historical tradition, culture, coalition, or political identity looks at belief, heritage, consumer markets, self-identification, and voting patterns—all certainly important. Yet studying the rhetoric of a movement turns to the commonplaces that evangelicals employ when they argue over positions and ideas, or the practices with which they construct individual and collective identity and values.

To study evangelicalism as a movement, I examine (1) the clashing of discourses; (2) collective identity; (3) rhetorical form and style; and (4) the ends of social change. These four major research problems in the study of social movement rhetoric and counterpublics[28] are interrelated in evangelical women's writing. In its emphasis, *"I Grew Up in the Church"* has more in common with "text-oriented counterpublic scholarship" than scholarship on the ways groups "organize instrumentally and constitutively."[29] Put simply, I focus on texts rather than organizations. I am interested in women's activism that takes place through personal narrative, which emerges out of an evangelical tradition but not a defined or organized group. I also study evangelical women as a counterpublic within the wider evangelical movement. Karma Chávez discusses how coalition-building takes place off the public stage: activists might retreat to separate spaces to interpret the messages created about them or to "invent rhetorical strategies to publicly challenge oppressive rhetoric or to create new imaginaries for [their] groups and issues."[30] Evangelical women do both in personal narratives, a space that evangelical leaders cannot really control. Within this space, women develop their own interpretations of their needs, interests, and identities, and engage wider publics to advance these alternative perspectives. Using an evangelical vernacular, print and digital personal narratives shift public evangelical discourse by creating coalitions, voicing critiques, and making space for "new beliefs, identities, and experiences."[31] In some cases, this oppositional discourse influences the policies of evangelical churches and governing bodies and can be a tool for material change.[32]

Studying evangelicalism as a movement also directs our attention to the relationship between its margins and center. I mean this in two ways. First, evangelical women historically and presently occupy marginalized positions in the evangelical public. When they are excluded from leadership and asked to submit to male authority, women need to be creative and strategic in seeking to shift evangelical discourse. Second, mainstream evangelicals and their leaders are always in relationship with fringe or extreme ideologies even as they might try to distance themselves from those controversial positions or discourses (which, like blood-and-soil Christianity, have little to do with church or faith). For example, in her study of evangelical militarism, Du Mez argues that "those who occupy what center there is have largely failed to define themselves against the more extreme expressions of 'biblical patriarchy.'" The culture wars of the 2000s "bound together 'normative complementarians' and 'biblical patriarchs,'"[33] so moderate evangelicals cannot easily disentangle their complementarian rhetoric and doctrine from the overtly sexist and white nationalist factions they endorsed and platformed. Rather than ask whether extremists still "count" as evangelical, a social movement approach traces how extreme and mainstream discourses influence one another.

Evangelical History and Rhetoric in the United States

Evangelicals celebrate their history but in doing so they downplay significant points when the movement wrestled with its doctrines, political alignments, and relationships to secular social movements. This section details eight key moments when responses to movements like abolition or feminism—often antagonistic responses—formed evangelical identity and rhetoric. During the First and Second Great Awakenings, Civil War, Progressive Era, fundamentalist-modernist controversy, civil rights movement, rise and fall of evangelical feminism, and Conservative Resurgence, evangelicals cohered as a movement, albeit one with multiple competing voices. In these moments we also see the "human producers, audiences, and physical systems of circulation"[34]—that is, the organizations, policy and belief statements, and publications—that contribute to evangelical rhetoric.

These historical moments gave rise to eight *topoi* or commonplaces: individualism, conversion, fear, divine providence, biblical authority, white supremacy, certainty, and combat. Such commonplaces "create knowledge by fostering connections or specifying relationships between a community's values, beliefs, and experiences."[35] They represent the "situated cultural values" of evangelicals and "constitute rhetoric [of this movement] in ways that organize or guide [members'] feelings, opinions, and actions."[36] I explain each one, often beginning with definitions in the *Evangelical Dictionary of Theology* that show how evangelicals understand and use their commonplaces. I elaborate on these definitions with texts by Butler, Jones, Noll, Worthen, and Du Mez for a layered definition of evangelical rhetoric.

I bring my own perspective to naming these eight commonplaces. As I read evangelical scholarship and personal narrative, I noticed this vocabulary as the discursive backbone of the movement. Thinking further back, that observation began with (but does not rest on) hearing and reading these terms when I was growing up in the church. I believe most evangelicals would recognize them as centerpieces of their rhetoric. However, even as they use or hear terms like *authority* or *worldview*, they might not realize the tradition or rhetorical force they carry. Crowley explains that commonplaces presuppose and encapsulate extensive arguments; they are not often uttered but they can be deduced and reconstructed. A commonplace can remain "unspoken by a given individual who nonetheless accepts it, and people can be surprised to learn of their subscription to this or that common belief."[37] Those definitions and histories might be submerged in layers of euphemism or new historical contexts, but, as with a commonplace like white supremacy, that does not lessen their power or relevance.

First Great Awakening

The Great Awakening (approximately 1735–1743) established evangelical rhetoric and identity based on preaching, dramatic conversions, and a democratic style of religion. In the *Evangelical*

Dictionary of Theology, theologian D. Bruce Hindmarsh defines the Great Awakening as a time of dramatic spiritual revivals propelled through open-air meetings. Preachers like Wesley and Whitefield "witnessed large numbers of men and women experience personal conversion in a short period of time," which they attributed to the "remarkable 'work' of God."[38] The movement centered on spontaneous personal conversion and deeply felt individual faith rather than liturgy or church affiliation. Whitefield preached that "all people—regardless of church membership, ethnicity, or social standing—needed the 'new birth' of salvation through Jesus Christ."[39] These religious revivals reached enslaved African Americans who responded to "the evangelical rejection of earthly status and authority, coupled with the emphasis upon an intense personal conversion experience" and formed independent Black Baptist congregations.[40] Even though preaching and conversions focused on the individual, Hindmarsh cites "small-group fellowship, extempore prayer, personal testimony, and hymn singing" as communal practices in these revivals.[41] These persisted as important rhetorical practices for churches, but personal religious expression took precedence over church structure and liturgy.

Revivals established *individualism* as an evangelical commonplace. The modern emphasis on individuals during the 1600s and 1700s and belief that "even the lowliest people could become children of God through Christ" reached "full bloom" in North America.[42] This personal view of morality and salvation led some white evangelicals "to turn a blind eye to the manifest injustices around them, most notably the enslavement of African Americans."[43] The individualist mindset continued to characterize later evangelical rhetoric. In her study of twenty-first-century megachurch sermons, Stephanie A. Martin sees pastors rejecting social engagement. She summarizes their narrative: "Life's most vexing problems would never find solutions through politics. Individual conversion was the only source of hope."[44] In *White Too Long*, Jones explains that evangelical individualism comes from a "personal Jesus paradigm" in which "Jesus did not die for a cause or for humankind writ large but for each individual person"; humans can respond—again, individually—by answering a "knock at the door" or "letting Jesus come into your heart."[45] Individualism emerges from evangelical beliefs about the Bible as well. The doctrine of "sola scriptura"—that the word of God is a sufficient authority for Christian life—tells lay Christians that they can understand the text of scripture without direction from the church or tradition. Scripture is the authority, but individual readers should determine what the text means, apply it to their lives, and reject interpretations that clash with their worldviews.

The Great Awakening also established the *commonplace of conversion* as central to evangelical rhetoric. On one hand, conversion has a simple meaning. Evangelicals understand being "born again" as both a discrete event and an ongoing process of transformation. Kidd cites Wesley's definition of conversion as "a thorough change of heart and life from sin to holiness: a turning," and adds, "this turning, to evangelicals, is enabled by God's power." That is, conversion is a conscious decision made possible by God's revelation and God's intervention in human lives. The significance of conversion as a commonplace in evangelical rhetoric goes beyond this definition. Kidd places conversion at the center of his definition of evangelicalism and calls being "born again" the "experience that defines what it means to be an evangelical."[46] The first tenet of Bebbington's quadrilateral is conversionism, "the understanding of conversion as a personal experience that significantly transforms each Christian's life."[47] Conversion gives evangelicals a countercultural identity that they celebrate. Being born again and walking in the Spirit (maintaining a life of faith) distinguish them from non-Christians and nominal Christians. And white evangelicals typically define conversion in individual terms that preclude reckoning with racism. For them, conversion is not a matter of collective repentance and change, but each individual person's realization of their sinfulness, subsequent repentance, acceptance of Christ's forgiveness, and growing relationship with God. As Jones says, the "personal Jesus" paradigm leaves no room for collective sin.

Conversion also provides an appealing narrative arc. The structure of many evangelical personal narratives (and many secular ones) can be summed up with John Newton's lines from his hymn "Amazing Grace": "I once was lost, but now am found / Was blind, but now I see." However, as I show in the chapters of this book, this individualized and overdetermined narrative arc can be a template evangelical women use to renovate the practice of telling conversion stories. Their narratives explore doubt, complexity, ambivalence, collective sin and repentance, and conflict with other factions of the movement.

Second Great Awakening

From 1790 to 1860, another wave of revivals made churches dynamic, influential actors in public life. The number of Protestant churches grew exponentially[48] and "gave direction, purpose, meaning, and stability" to the lives of Americans, including Black, white, male, and female believers. "Only because they were so important religiously," Noll writes, "did the churches also become so important politically."[49] Historian Benjamin Lynerd makes the point even more bluntly: "Civil and private religion practically operated as one."[50] Moral reform societies emerged to oppose "national sins" like "Sabbath-breaking, vulgarity, intemperance, and the 'love of money.'"[51] Together with churches, these reform societies promoted "the mutual dependence of individual liberty, moral virtue, and Christian faith."[52] In this way of thinking, the fate of the nation depended on the moral choices of individuals. Sociologist Michael P. Young calls this era "the first national wave of social movements in the United States."[53] This great height of evangelical social engagement contained a nativist impulse. Some evangelicals who called for sanctifying the nation were responding to an influx of immigrants. In *Believe Me: The Evangelical Road to Donald Trump*, historian John Fea cites New England minister Lyman Beecher as an evangelical who called for restrictions on

Catholic immigrants. The revivals of this time held "a potent mix of spiritual dynamism, moral reform, and newly fueled suspicions of religious outsiders."[54] The Second Great Awakening furthered evangelicalism as a movement that brought religion to bear on national politics, solidified an individualist view of faith, and placed politics firmly at the core of evangelical rhetoric.

White evangelicals' perceptions of themselves as threatened by secular culture and other ideological enemies makes the *commonplace of fear* central to their discourse. In *Believe Me*, Fea traces the role of fear in evangelical political activity and relationships with other groups and movements. His chapter "A Short History of Evangelical Fear" begins with the Puritans and their fears of a wrathful God, religious diversity (in the form of Catholics and Quakers), and Native Americans. In the nineteenth century, evangelical leaders mobilized believers around fear of Catholics, abolition, and racial equality. These fears later propelled the fundamentalist movement of the 1920s. Clergymen like Bob Jones "gained followers, built large congregations, and gained national reputations by . . . cultivating anxieties among the faithful about the potential movements of the Antichrist, and sounding the alarm of the modernist threat."[55] Fea, Worthen, Butler, and other historians trace the fearful responses to these intellectual and social upheavals and, later, to the decline of white Christian America. This is not to say that all evangelicals display this fear.[56] For example, the contemporary women I study critique its pervasive power. They center their rhetorical work on uncovering the damage that commonplaces like fear can do when they structure thought and action.

Civil War

Civil War-era debates among evangelicals remain relevant because they were never resolved. Some antebellum evangelicals in the North (both Black and white) argued that slavery was against God's will. This does not mean they advocated for equality; Jones points out that even abolitionist Charles Finney defended segregation and race-based prejudice.[57] The majority of white Southern evangelicals were pro-slavery and "consigned the slavery issue to the realm of politics, not church."[58] Both sides could quote the Bible to support their positions and accuse the other of "failing to obey what they saw as the Bible's teaching on the slave question."[59] And many white evangelicals in both regions were silent on the issue. After the war, "with the question of slavery off the table, the distance between many southern and northern white Christians actually closed, bridged by the continued shared commitment to white supremacy and segregation."[60] Before the war, Christians had debated biblical teachings on slavery. However, these debates "did not persuade most Caucasian Americans that African Americans were on their level of humanity."[61]

The war also caused rifts over biblical interpretation. Proslavery advocates had straightforward support: specific passages in the Old and New Testaments, like Genesis 9:25–27 or 1 Timothy 6:1–2, sanctioned and regulated slavery.[62] Anti-slavery arguments were more nuanced. Rhetors like Henry Ward Beecher and Daniel Coker cited Exodus 21:16, which condemned slavery, and cited the Bible's "'spirit' of universal liberation."[63] Other rhetors placed verses in historical context and argued that the Bible never legitimated the hereditary, racially-defined slavery that existed in the South.[64] This debate over textual interpretation was formative for evangelical rhetoric around race and also for evangelical ways of using the Bible in argument. The nuanced biblical attacks on slavery "faced rough going precisely because they were nuanced,"[65] a pattern that repeats in later debates about gender roles. Conservatives dismissed arguments that limited texts to their historical context, saying that those interpretations denied the authority of scripture. They favored literal readings of specific passages over the overarching narrative of liberation and human dignity. The debate over slavery also shook Protestants' belief that the Bible could guide politics. The text "was not nearly as univocal, not nearly as easy to interpret, not nearly as inherently unifying for an overwhelmingly Christian people, as they once had thought."[66] This conflict over the authority and role of the Bible later resurfaces when evangelicals respond to movements for racial, gender, and economic equality.

The Civil War had lasting effects on white and Black evangelical churches. White evangelicalism "receded as a dominant force in national politics" but maintained power over the former Confederate states.[67] It also gave rise to the Southern "Lost Cause" narrative. White ministers showed their audiences how to map Confederate defeat in the Civil War onto the New Testament stories of the wrongful imprisonment of an apostle and even the crucifixion of the Messiah, implying that just as Jesus was resurrected from the dead and will ultimately come again to rule the earth in righteousness, there will yet be a time when the noble ideals of the Confederacy, even if not the practice of chattel slavery itself, will rise again.[68]

Independent Black churches and denominations formed after the Civil War. These congregations were centers of Black religious life, civil society, education, and publishing in the late nineteenth and early twentieth centuries. Within these counterpublic institutions, writers, preachers, and lay members sustained "a lively black discourse for an expanding black audience."[69] This separation is one reason why many twenty-first-century Black Christians do not describe themselves as "evangelical." Even when their doctrine and democratic style of worship seem "characteristically evangelical,"[70] their churches and denominations grew from an explicit post-Civil War break with white evangelicalism.

Evangelicals invoke the *commonplace of divine providence*, God's will for his people, when they call for activism or try to discern God's purpose. The history of the movement includes several points, like the Civil War, when evangelicals made such appeals. Noll shows that Christians who spoke about the Civil War often used providential reasoning. When the Bible revealed no clear unified teaching on race and slavery, they tried to interpret "what God was 'doing' in and through the war."[71] This commonplace of "providence" echoes the rhetorical concept of *kairos*, which itself appears in Christian texts. In "*Kairos* and the Rhetoric of Belief,"

Dale Sullivan analyzes Old Testament uses of *kairos*, which usually indicate "that there is an opportune time for something to occur, that there are special times determined by God, shown by God, and filled with God."[72] This notion persists in the language of American evangelicals, like Great Awakening preachers who believed they were living in a moment of opportunity to spread the kingdom of God. Evangelical rhetoric, in both its mainstream and dissenting forms, assumes that "spiritual power and the Word of God can and do break into human affairs."[73] This is a liberating notion for many women. Even if they never see their messages take hold or effect change, they can be encouraged by knowing these things happen in God's time.

This providential reasoning is notable not only for its expression of faith in God's control and power but for Christians' confidence "that they could understand clearly why God was acting the way he did."[74] Interpretations of God's plan depended on the rhetors' standpoints, of course. Some Christians argued that God had provided the institution of slavery for the South to flourish; others saw the war as God's intervention on behalf of his people who were enslaved. These themes reappear in twenty-first-century evangelical discourse: God uses destruction to "chasten his people," God brings about good out of evil, and God chooses political leaders. Evangelicals who call on providential reasoning might believe God uses people individually through a divine revelation or calling. Their reasoning can betray "a simplistic trust in immediate divine causation"[75] that means Christians no longer need to think hard about what is happening and the systemic or cultural factors at work.

The Progressive Era Social Gospel

Religious activism flowered in the aftermath of the Civil War. Christians of the time "aimed for social and cultural activism, and believed that saving souls was related to saving the whole of society."[76] This period saw groups like the Salvation Army form and saw evangelicals like Charles Finney preach against wealth and against the "poverty, disease, and filth that were endemic to industrial slums."[77] Church historian Norris A. Magnuson summarizes this Progressive Era social gospel and its distinctive ideas about the Bible and economics:

> Opposing the dominant laissez-faire individualism in economic life, with its sanctioning of unrestrained competition, social gospelers pressed for cooperation between management and labor. They saw in the OT prophets' denunciation of injustice, in Jesus's life and teachings, and in the immanence of a God of love in human society the sanctions for a contrasting human order.[78]

This social and cultural activism articulated a biblical basis for challenging power structures in the United States and vigorous arguments for expanding women's roles in the church. Phoebe Palmer and Frances Willard gained reputations as speakers who advocated for women's right to preach, as well as suffragist, antipoverty, temperance, and abolition movements.[79] David Gerson has called this a "great height" of evangelical engagement with American society.[80]

The social gospel has a mixed legacy in American evangelicalism. On the one hand, its influence dissolved after this peak in social engagement, while capitalist, patriarchal, and white supremacist ideologies continued to hold sway over the movement. Advocates for the social gospel based their arguments in the Bible but many were open to modern theology and nonliteral interpretations. This stance made them vulnerable to attacks from conservatives defending biblical literalism and capitalism. Still, the goal of "applying Christian principles to social problems and human need"[81] persisted (though conservative factions would co-opt the idea). The social gospel also had an ongoing influence through the women's movement. Feminist theologian Nancy Hardesty argues that evangelical women's activism motivated even those nineteenth-century feminists who did not identify with the social gospel.[82] This period set a precedent for the feminist, activist rhetoric we see among contemporary evangelical women. Many of the writers that I examine in this project can locate their progressive, socially engaged expressions of faith as part of this longer tradition.

I have referred to *biblical authority* several times in this chapter; the commonplace is central to almost every conversation in evangelicalism. Evangelicals wrestle over the meaning of that authority. Worthen explains one interpretation—inerrancy—and its origin:

> The basic idea—that scripture is free from all error—is an ancient one. The earliest Christians had little notion of the scientific method or modern standards of historical inquiry, but they were keen to defend the Bible as the record of God's word and a perfect source of truth. Christians intent on asserting the Bible's authority through logical argument quarreled with mystics and prophets who claimed to know God's will through their own experience, and with doubters who found inconsistencies in the biblical text.[83]

Inerrancy is not the only way of reading the Bible, but Worthen shows that this particular quarrel would "dog and divide American evangelicals" through their history.[84] It would be more accurate to say that this conflict was mainly prevalent in white churches. In his history, Sernett notes that "the white fundamentalist preoccupation with the question of inerrancy made the Bible a cultural icon. In contrast, Black Christians, while appealing to biblical authority, rarely have developed rigid doctrines of inerrancy."[85] Theologian Marcus Borg, in *Reading the Bible Again for the First Time*, explains white evangelical preoccupation with inerrancy and with the Bible as a cultural icon. Since they hold that the Bible is "true because it comes from God," any other interpretations are affronts to God.[86] They recognize problems with literal readings of passages like Jesus' miracles but insist that "believing things hard to believe" is possible through faith.[87]

This conscious literalism works rhetorically to mark a distinction from progressive evangelicals and mainline Protestants who entertain historical or metaphorical interpretations. Historian Pamela Cochran explains that in the absence of authoritative church bodies, inerrancy is a "theological, almost creedal guideline to help evangelicals determine their membership and guide their behavior."[88] In the twentieth century, Worthen writes, "inerrancy came to represent not only a set of beliefs about the reality of Jesus's miracles, but the pledge that human reason must always bow to the Bible."[89] This commonplace is important to maintaining evangelical solidarity and its encounters with disbelief, which require robust defenses "to ward off the possibility of the group's dissolution."[90] In their activist work, white evangelicals apply this discourse of biblical authority and literal truth beyond the bounds of religious spaces. This strategy gives their arguments "particular intensity—both when it takes place as Scripture battling against Scripture and when it occurs as Scripture battling against those who vehemently dispute the relevance of Scripture."[91] Persistent conflicts over the nature and scope of the Bible's authority explain much evangelical hostility to social issues like slavery and feminism. For some, literal readings were the theological *reasons* for hostility to abolition or women's preaching. For others, biblical authority was a permission structure for hostility.

Fundamentalist-Modernist Controversy

In the early twentieth century, a fundamentalist evangelical movement sought to reaffirm orthodox Protestant Christianity in the face of liberal theology, German higher criticism, and Darwinism—modernist ideologies that they saw as undermining the Bible's authority. Historian C. T. McIntire attributes the beginning of this "fundamentalist-modernist controversy" to the publication of *The Fundamentals*, volumes of essays widely distributed from 1910–1915. These essays by Christian ideologues across North America and the United Kingdom initiated "an urgent battle to expel enemies of orthodox Protestantism" that played out in universities, seminaries, churches, and ordination boards.[92] Ultimately, neither side won that battle. The fundamentalists who insisted on reading the Bible literally were unable to expel the modernists who read the text historically or metaphorically. Instead, fundamentalists formed a separatist movement with their own denominations, churches, revival ministries, and seminaries.

The fundamentalist-modernist controversy, which became a public issue in the 1925 Scopes Trial, "fixed in the popular mind a sharp distinction between rural, evangelical, traditional America and an urban, educated, and secular counterpart."[93] It also made evolution a lasting ideological and cultural enemy for conservative Christians.

The fundamentalist-modernist controversy was a turning point that gave rise to *evangelical* as a self-conscious identity. Beginning in the 1940s, a subgroup of fundamentalism rejected the idea that separatism was the best way to defend traditional interpretations of Christian doctrines. In his introduction to *Still Evangelical?* Mark Labberton describes the split:

> Fundamentalism tends to see itself as a bastion of faithfulness defending the faith against secular opponents and Christian compromisers (evangelicals and liberals both).
>
> In contrast to this is the rise of a more distinct evangelicalism that maintains Christian orthodoxy but does so with a greater engagement with and receptivity to culture and to critical self-reflection.[94]

Evangelicals resisted liberalism but they sought to connect with non-Christian America. Leaders like Billy Graham and Carl Henry aspired to intellectual and cultural influence on the wider culture and claimed the name "evangelical" to distinguish themselves from fundamentalists. The controversy is also one reason why evangelicalism is largely white. Black churches were theologically conservative but not particularly involved in debates like the historicity of Christ's virgin birth, the veracity of miracles, or Jesus' bodily resurrection. Because the divide took place within white denominations, "the emergence of neo-evangelicals [led by Graham and Henry] out of the fundamentalist fold since World War II has been predominantly a white phenomenon."[95]

The modern, mainly white American iteration of evangelicalism grew from this fight between fundamentalists and modernists. This moment solidified evangelical rhetoric that was preoccupied with defenses of belief and keenly aware of public perception.

Fundamentalism did not disappear, though, even as evangelicalism superseded it. Some fundamentalists continued to embrace the term and claimed to represent "true, Bible-believing Christianity"; Jerry Falwell and Pat Robertson continued to fight all "offspring of secular humanism."[96] Evangelical discourse also retains the combativeness, whiteness, affinity for politics, and hyperawareness of distinctions between "true" and "false" Christianity that animated the fundamentalist-modernist controversy. Contemporary evangelical women writers are mindful of this history and legacy when they analyze evangelical ways of knowing, arguing, and relating to other movements.

The *commonplace of worldview* became vital to evangelical intellectual life in the early twentieth century. In *Naming the Elephant: Worldview as a Concept*, theologian James Sire defines *worldview* as "the fundamental perspective from which one addresses every issue of life."[97] A worldview is based in "basic presuppositions, more or less consistent with each other, more or less consciously held, more or less true" and Christians might not realize them until they encounter a challenge "from another ideological universe."[98] The history of worldview predates American evangelicalism, but Worthen explains why the concept became particularly valuable for them in the twentieth century. Evangelicals not only embraced worldview to express their own faith, they saw it as a powerful weapon in debates with liberals:

> Deciphering an opponent's worldview meant unlocking their unifying theory of everything. It meant refuting the claims of liberal empiricists and pragmatists like John Dewey and William James—who suggested that our knowledge about the world is a changing mass of provable and useful facts—and exposing instead the semiconscious and unverifiable assumptions that shape a person's perception of reality.[99]

After the fundamentalist-modernist split, this powerful tool became central to evangelical intellectual life. By the 1990s, seminaries offered Worldview Studies certificates. Universities and homeschool networks created biblical worldview curricula, and parachurch organizations like Focus on the Family developed small group studies.

Worldviews are not just intellectual exercises; they divide the world into (in Sire's words) "ideological universes." The commonplace is key to evangelical identity and public engagement. As Worthen says, a worldview is a tool to prepare for fights with nonevangelicals. Defining sides in a cultural or political debate in terms of Christian and non-Christian (or biblical and nonbiblical) worldviews assures evangelicals that "the right ideas can change the world" and casts American politics "as a battleground of good and evil."[100] By thinking in terms of worldview, an evangelical can also understand how liberals, atheists, or members of other faiths see the world, and attack their beliefs at the foundations. Reflecting on one's own worldview serves a regulatory purpose. The commonplace directs evangelicals to evaluate how well their own beliefs and language and those of others reflect a Christian or biblical worldview, as described and modeled by established powers in the church.

Definitions of worldview like Sire's do not account for the cultural contexts that create them. For example, white evangelicals claim that their "theological conclusions are derived directly from an inerrant Bible" but history shows that "white Christians' cultural worldview, with an unacknowledged white supremacy sleeping at its core, has been read back into the Bible."[101] Jones gives the example of Dylann Roof, whose "identity as a white Christian was central to his worldview."[102] Roof was a practicing Christian when he killed nine worshipers at the Emanuel AME church in Charleston. He went to church regularly growing up and was a baptized member in good standing. Roof's journal had detailed sketches of a white Jesus and declared that "Christianity can be a warrior's religion."[103] Jones concludes, "Clearly, Roof's worldview was anchored in his self-understanding as a white Christian in relationship to a white Jesus."[104] He calls white Christians not to "flinch from the clear evidence that Roof's Christianity wasn't incidental to his motivations and his racist views."[105]

Evangelicals call upon worldview and biblical authority to shore up the *commonplace of certainty*. In *The Sin of Certainty*, Bible scholar Pete Enns explains how belief in biblical authority manifests as an insistence on being certain about what you believe:

> Like a lot of Christians, I was taught—from a young age all the way through seminary, and in most every church I've ever been to, book I've read, or sermon I've heard—that having strong faith depends on "knowing what you believe." And people of true faith will be able to articulate what they know to a lost and blind world that just doesn't get it. It was all very logical and clear. Having that kind of sure knowledge of the mysteries of life is promoted as one of the major perks of being an insider to God.[106]

Enns argues that "'knowing what you believe' is a major, almost universal preoccupation" for evangelicals.[107] This commonplace tells audiences that doubt means "faith is on life support at best, dead and buried at worst."[108] For many, having or professing absolute certainty signals strong faith and places a believer firmly in the evangelical community. Deep questions signal wavering faith and weaken the doubter's identity within the movement.

Historians, particularly Worthen and Fea, have shown that preoccupation with certainty is a hallmark of evangelical thinking in the United States. Worthen describes a "prickly certainty" in evangelical history. Conflicts like the fundamentalist-modernist controversy arose not just because of their worries about "how scientific discoveries or historical investigation might change the Bible's role in society, but because they declared that the Bible's authority would never change."[109] Twentieth-century pastors calmed their listeners' fears of communists, minority groups, and other perceived outsiders by modeling a sense of certainty about God's work through and among his people. Figures like Reverend Jerry Falwell offered "certainty at a time when the consensus on the Bible's status in American culture was shakier than ever."[110] In these cases, certainty is not just a matter of strong or weak individual belief. It is essential to evangelicals' asserting an identity and exerting influence on a diverse culture.

In the following chapters, I say much more about the role and consequences of the commonplace of certainty. Here, I will note two critiques that evangelicals voice. Enns articulates how this mindset is antithetical to evangelical beliefs and an obstacle to genuine, resilient faith. When believers who cling to certainty are "confronted with the possibility of being wrong, that kind of 'faith' becomes all about finding ways to hold on with everything we've got to be right."[111] It creates a brittle, defensive faith rather than a curious, resilient one. Second, Jones argues that the commonplace of certainty furthers white supremacy in engagement with American culture. He writes, "The mythology—really, the lie—that white Christians tell ourselves, on the few occasions we face our history, is that Christianity has been a force for unambiguous good in the world."[112] Certainty about this fact hurts individual believers and their communities because it is a hindrance to honest reckoning with past and present injustice.

Civil Rights

We have seen that no genuine commitment to racial equality followed abolitionism, and evangelicals were largely absent from the civil rights movement. Kidd summarizes the white evangelical response to movements for racial equality:

> Some white evangelicals expressed sympathy but worried about radical influences in the civil rights movement. Many remained silent, or reminded fellow whites about the spiritual nature of the church and the necessity of sticking to the gospel. (This principle did not seem to apply when white Christians were advocating for prohibition, anticommunism, or prayer in schools.) Overall, most white evangelicals did nothing to assist the civil rights movement.[113]

For example, at a 1953 revival, Billy Graham, by then a famous leader, made gestures toward racial equality like removing ropes between segregated sections. However, when he and other national evangelical figures supported civil rights, "they did so guardedly, pinning their hopes to a slow and voluntary integration that would emanate from the church rather than from the federal government."[114] Historians have pointed to the contrast in examples of Black evangelicals whose faith motivated their activism. Fannie Lou Hamer's work to register Black voters in Mississippi was driven by her evangelical faith.[115] Butler cites Tom Skinner and Bill Pannell, writers and speakers who were two examples of "major Black Evangelicals of the 1960s [who] directly engaged white believers on their racism."[116] Frustration over white inaction further alienated African American Christians from the evangelical movement and prompted the formation of the National Black Evangelical Association in 1963.[117]

White evangelicals were ambivalent about or hostile to the civil rights movement in part because of these fundamentalist influences and in part because leaders cast activism as a distraction from the call to share the gospel. Jerry Falwell exemplifies this anti–civil rights discourse in a 1964 sermon, "Ministers and Marchers," where he urged Christians not to get involved in politics. He declared that he found it "impossible to stop preaching the pure saving gospel of Jesus Christ and begin doing anything else—including the fighting of Communism, or participating in the civil rights reform."[118] One line is ironic in retrospect: "Preachers are not called to be politicians, but to be soul winners."[119] Jones calls this declaration "a powerful way of delegitimizing the work of black ministers working for black equality."[120] Butler argues that school integration was the issue that led evangelicals like Falwell—who had once set up a dichotomy between activism and sharing the gospel—to enter politics. After the Brown v. Board of Education ruling, public figures like W. A. Criswell, Billy Graham's pastor at First Baptist Church in Dallas, called ministers to "resist government mandated desegregation because it is a denial of all that we believe in."[121] This is when Falwell reversed his stance on activism. In "I Love America" and "7 Things Corrupting America," two sermons from the 1970s, he urged Christians to get involved in politics. The idea of not doing so, Falwell claimed, was a lie (though one he had promoted) "invented by the devil to keep Christians from running their own country."[122] When the IRS enforced integration laws by revoking the tax-exempt status of segregated schools like Bob Jones University, white evangelicals doubled down on their worldview that "their own country" was being taken from them.

By 2008, evangelicals might have seen Falwell as an archaic or fringe figure. However, I cite his sermons here because they so clearly reverberated in evangelical rhetoric. When Falwell died in 2007, an article in the *Nation* said that "under Falwell's guidance, the Christian right subsumed much of the Republican apparatus."[123] His public statements on religion in politics shaped the movement into an entity that would selectively embrace and reject political action and justify that choice by creating a dichotomy between preaching the gospel and fighting injustices. Jemar Tisby cites this dichotomy as one example of an argument "that perpetuated racial inequality in decades past" and gets "recycled in the present day."[124] Young evangelicals might have grown up with grandparents who listened to Falwell's radio program. They might have inherited his beliefs (cloaked in updated rhetoric) that churches should eschew activism and preach "the pure saving gospel." They might have absorbed his belief that the United States belongs to Christians.

Most evangelicals would not recognize *white supremacy* in their vocabulary for debate, community building, and reflection. However, the commonplace historically appeared in the evangelical practices of preaching and biblical exegesis. Jones summarizes theology that taught white supremacy was a divine mandate:

> White Christian ministers and churches can assert inerrant biblical teachings that people of African descent are, a few thousand years removed, the descendants of Cain in the Old Testament who was punished by God for disobedience with a physical mark; that the God of the universe has chosen whites to civilize and dominate the earth; and that the separation of the races, particularly white and black in this middle part of North America, is unquestionably God ordained.[125]

Kidd is more forgiving toward evangelicals. He writes, "White evangelicals have often been reluctant to let their spiritual beliefs [that all people are equal before God] inform their views of racial oppression and inequality."[126] Jones might argue that Kidd lets evangelicals off the hook. In *White Too Long*, he argues that white evangelical theology went far beyond passivity to actively perpetuate racism. Well into the twentieth century, white evangelical Protestants "cast [Blacks] as descendants of Cain, whom the book of Genesis describes as being physically marked by God after killing his brother, Abel, and then lying to God about the crime." The narrative implied that Black Americans inherited Cain's physical distinctiveness and "his inferior moral character."[127] White evangelicals resist this fact about their theology. They attribute racist beliefs and teachings to culture and individual sin rather than Christianity.

Contemporary evangelicalism has an uneasy relationship with its racist past, including support for slavery, complicity with violence after the Civil War, and opposition to civil rights. Believers struggle with the fact that founders of the movement like Whitefield and Edwards owned slaves; Whitefield was even influential in bringing about the legalization of slavery in Georgia in 1751. In *White Too Long*, Jones pairs historical and demographic research with his own story of growing up in the SBC, attending seminary, and discovering that Christianity has been "the central cultural tent pole" upholding white supremacy.[128] Unlike biblical authority or divine providence, which evangelicals celebrate, he realized that "the norms of white supremacy have become deeply and broadly integrated into white Christian identity, operating far below the level of consciousness."[129] I hesitate to reiterate these ideas, as I do when quoting Jones, but his project is an important one. He confronts fellow white evangelicals with the commonplace of white supremacy that remains unspoken by many individuals who nonetheless accept it. Jones aims to raise this fact to the level of consciousness. For many readers, hearing from a researcher with a Baptist theology degree and a religious and cultural background like their own could make these ideas newly visible and give them a starting point for critical reflection.

White Too Long also introduces readers to antiracist writing by Black Christians. Twenty-first-century rhetors like pastor Thabiti Anyabwile and historian Jemar Tisby profess orthodox beliefs but challenge conservative politics in the church. Tisby turns a biblical lens on contemporary racism in his book *The Color of Compromise* and in his podcast *Pass the Mic*. Anyabwile is the author of *The Faithful Preacher* and *Reviving the Black Church*. His work also circulates among conservatives on the Gospel Coalition website. There, he sets out a biblical case for reparations, argues that calls to "only preach the gospel" ignore central teachings of the Bible, and counters critiques of social justice. Predictably, white evangelicals find reasons to dispute or dismiss their research and teaching. However, evangelicals who become curious about the racism threaded through their movement will find Anyabwile and Tisby speaking to this issue.

Evangelical Feminism: 1970s and 1980s

In the 1970s and 1980s, a persuasive biblical basis for gender equality gained a toehold in the church. Historian Pamela Cochran delves into this period in *Evangelical Feminism*. In 1974, theologians Nancy Hardesty and Letha Scanzoni published *All We're Meant to Be: A Biblical Approach to Women's Liberation*. The book marked a starting point for evangelical feminism as a movement within the larger evangelical movement. *All We're Meant to Be* uses historical-cultural interpretation to show that passages traditionally used to limit women's roles reflected their cultural context and should not be taken as universal teachings. For example, they explain that when *helpmeet*, the word used for Eve in the book of Genesis, appears elsewhere in the Bible, it never refers to subordinate roles and most often refers to God. They also argue that Genesis gives men and women equal responsibility for human sin.[130] These interpretations briefly gained traction. In 1973, attendees at the Evangelicals for Social Action conference drafted and circulated the Chicago Declaration, stating that men and women are called to mutually submit to one another. Hardesty chaired a women's task force that produced a set of proposals including a call to churches to evaluate sexism in their teaching and a call for the conference to approve women's ordination. The task force went on to form an Evangelical Women's Caucus (EWC) with newsletters and regional chapters to teach feminist hermeneutics and social critique.

More important than the details of these organizations are what this short movement tells us about gender in evangelicalism. First, the EWC and evangelical feminist movement parallel the wider twentieth-century feminist movement in the United States. Both attracted educated, upper-middle-class women "who believed that women suffered injustices and discrimination because of their sex," though evangelical feminism argued "that the Bible offered a viable solution."[131] Second, while evangelical feminism shows us the capacity for feminist activism in the evangelical movement, it reinscribed evangelical racism and homophobia. Like the secular feminist movement, its single-minded focus on gender did not extend to or include other forms of justice. Evangelical feminism largely ignored race and, in the 1980s, the group fractured over sexuality. EWC members who argued that homosexuality was compatible with Christianity cited "the authority of reason and experience"; others thought this stance denied "the unique authority of scripture in determining doctrine."[132] By the time Cochran wrote her history in 2005, the EWC had left the evangelical coalition and had ceased to be an influence on evangelicalism.

Conservative Resurgence

In 1979, a conservative faction in the Southern Baptist Convention (SBC) sought to reverse three previous decades of moderate leadership. In the mid–twentieth century, the SBC (which at the time rejected *evangelical* as a "Yankee word") tolerated "theological variety" on issues like abortion, the literal truth of the Bible, and women's roles.[133] In the 1970s, though, a group of SBC pastors and politicians alleged that progressive theology was making its way into its seminaries and churches and coordinated a push to restore conservative leadership. Led by Paige Patterson, president of Criswell College, and Paul Pressler, a Houston judge, the group sought to reshape SBC seminaries and thereby influence congregations. They recruited conservatives to run for SBC leadership and pushed out liberal and moderate seminary faculty, using biblical inerrancy and women's ordination as litmus tests. Like evangelical feminism, this Conservative Resurgence was a point when evangelicalism shifted in response to other cultural and political movements in the country.

An event like the Conservative Resurgence is inside baseball, but it trains a spotlight on the SBC. This largest Protestant denomination is a major player in the evangelical movement; in fact, public perception and media coverage often conflate the two. Its size means that Southern Baptist culture creates evangelical norms. In the Conservative Resurgence, that culture included an insistence on purity of beliefs, especially biblical literalism and traditional gender roles. Later accounts of this resurgence recall it as a holy war with lasting damage. Opponents describe it as a radical, divisive turn to overt politics. Carl L. Kell, a professor of communications who compiled *Exiled: Voices of the Southern Baptist Convention Holy War* in 2006, describes it as "an unbroken succession of conservative-fundamentalist presidents" and their "considerable rhetorical effort to move the Convention to a sure and steady rightward course." Twenty-five years later, Kell writes, the SBC was "a purified denomination, but not without considerable collateral damage."[134] In contrast, proponents and many participants describe the Conservative Resurgence as a return to biblical orthodoxy. Patterson and Pressler both wrote books that celebrate their strategy and success in returning conservative theology and values to the SBC.

The SBC is also significant for my study of evangelical rhetoric because of its institutional organization, which makes it a focal point for beliefs and debates. Journalist Michael Foust explains the structure of the SBC in a *Baptist Press* article:

> In Southern Baptist polity, the president appoints several committees, although one—the Committee on Committees—has the most power. That committee nominates the Committee on Nominations, which in turn nominates the members of the boards of trustees for all the entities (including the seminaries). By carefully appointing likeminded individuals to the committee on committees, the president can—over time—impact nearly every element of Southern Baptist life.[135]

Among evangelicals, who generally prefer autonomy and local leadership, that explicit governance structure is unusual. The Conservative Resurgence shows how savvy leaders take advantage of this structure to move the entire denomination. The SBC president does not create doctrine, but as a figurehead and administrator he sets the tone and terms for discussions of topics like women's ordination, critical race theory, or sexual abuse within the church. In the SBC, we see how the institution of "the church" steers evangelicalism.

The Conservative Resurgence vilified feminism and promoted traditional doctrines and practices, two lasting influences on evangelical rhetoric. After evangelicals briefly aligned with women's movements in the 1970s, the debates about gender cohered in opposing camps: complementarian and egalitarian.[136] As Du Mez argues, the Conservative Resurgence "battle over inerrancy was in part a proxy fight over gender."[137] Previously, women had claimed SBC leadership positions and called for interpreting the Bible in historical context. Conservatives instead insisted on a literal reading of the text and held up that hermeneutic as masculine and faithful. Du Mez paraphrases their position: liberals and moderates waffled over interpretation while conservatives "stood firm in their quick grasp of the obvious, literal truth of Scriptures."[138] These battles over inerrancy and gender roles gathered steam with the founding of the Council on Biblical Manhood and Womanhood (CBMW) by John Piper and Wayne Grudem in 1987. The lines of debate solidified in policies like an SBC statement on complementarianism and Piper and Grudem's collection *Recovering Biblical Manhood and Womanhood: A Response to Evangelical Feminism*. The CBMW denounced feminists and egalitarians for following secular culture rather than God's word, creating the evangelical movement of recent decades that largely rules out any confluence of faith and feminism.

The *commonplace of combat* pervades evangelical rhetorical history. In *Jesus and John Wayne*, Du Mez details how twentieth-century evangelical leaders and popular culture portrayed Bible-believing Christians as warriors in a cosmic battle.[139] This led them to condone aggressive, violent, allegedly "biblical" masculinities that claimed to hold the line against secularism. Evangelicals use pointedly combative language when they confront social change. For example, when editor Curtis Lee Laws introduced the term *fundamentalist* in 1920, he defined this group as those ready to do "battle royal for the Fundamentals [of the Christian faith]."[140] Since neither side "won" that battle, a propensity for conflict shaped the evangelical movement perhaps more than either philosophy did. Studying the 1970s, Bowler tells of college ministry leader Helene Ashaker "begging her all-female audience to volunteer immediately to join her in combating the 'braless college chicks' and their women's lib philosophy." Ashaker called for women to write defenses of Christian beliefs, saying, "Armies are building on both sides, and ours [had] better be bigger."[141] The line between combat as spiritual metaphor and as actual violence is thin. In 2015, Dylann Roof saw himself as "a white Christian warrior who consciously launched his attack on sacred ground, targeting a historic black church in the hopes of encouraging his fellow white Christians to rise up."[142] Du Mez details how evangelical leaders have loudly supported the U.S. military. She also shows that evangelicals' sense of themselves as an embattled, righteous minority led them to revere political and cultural figures—like John Wayne or Donald Trump—who have little regard for Christian beliefs and ethics but represent a defense of white male identity and traditional power hierarchies.[143]

Practices

Evangelical rhetoric appears in identifiable forms throughout evangelical writing and speaking, both public and private. Along with the commonplaces I describe above, these include the distinct genres of sermons and apologetics and the more diffuse practices of evangelism, biblical exegesis, and testimony. I focus on these five practices, but evangelical rhetoric includes others. James Darsey and Joshua R. Ritter name the genres of religious rhetoric in the United States as sermons, jeremiads, prophetic rhetoric, and apocalyptic rhetoric.[144] In his personal narrative in *White Too Long*, Robert P. Jones alludes to other practices: "At church, I learned how to sing, write, date, give a persuasive public speech, and run an efficient meeting using *Robert's Rules of Order*."[145] As with my discussion of commonplaces, I focus on the rhetorical practices that, my research and experience show, are prominent in evangelical women's rhetoric.[146] I observed these, too, while I participated in evangelical communities. Readers might point out other terms that are foundational to evangelical rhetoric, and I hope these gaps inspire future research.

Evangelism

When I was twenty, a college classmate tried to convert me. Leaving our "The Bible as Literature" seminar one day, this boy I barely knew launched into his testimony of how Jesus changed his life. I remember being fascinated when I recognized a familiar narrative arc. He told me about the meaninglessness of his old sinful life, an unexpected encounter with Jesus, and the new hope and purpose he felt after converting to Christianity. His story was concise, passionate, and rehearsed, a textbook example of a formula my church had also taught. I could picture his Bible study group practicing their testimonies and resolving to each share the gospel with a nonbeliever on campus that week. He never asked about my own faith or experience until he closed with an awkward, "So, what do you think?" I registered both curiosity and discomfort as I thought, "This is how it feels to be evangelized."

Closely tied to the notion of being "born again" is the practice of evangelism. Evangelism motivated the revivals of the First and Second Great Awakenings and repeated calls for believers to share the gospel rather than advocate for justice. As with many of these rhetorical practices, evangelism has a simple explanation and a nuanced one. Religious historian Timothy P. Weber offers a straightforward definition: evangelism is "proclamation of the good news of salvation in Jesus Christ to bring about the reconciliation of sinners with God the Father."[147] Weber unpacks the nuanced components of the practice:

- *Message*—Evangelism must be based in the Bible and convey its message of good news: the sinfulness of humans, the love of God, the sacrificial death of Jesus, and the promise of forgiveness and new life.
- *Method*—Christians, Weber writes, have "devised" varying ways of spreading this message, including preaching, revivals, mass media, and friendship.
- *Goals*—The purpose is "the conversion of the sinner to a radically new way of life," or leading listeners to be born again. That initial repentance should lead to growing faith, obedience to God's commands, and "participation in Christ's body, the church."[148]

Weber's definition, and the history and commonplaces of evangelicalism, show where this practice of sharing the good news becomes complicated. Is the "good news" only a message of spiritual salvation, like my classmate shared, or does it have material implications? Which styles and methods carry "overaggressiveness, manipulation, intimidation, and well-intentioned misrepresentation [that] actually subvert effective evangelism"?[149] Who gets to be a full participant in "Christ's body, the church"? What does "a radically new way of life" mean? These questions are crucial for the women I analyze, who probe questions of ethical and effective rhetoric to see how personal narrative might convey the many understandings of the "good news."

Preaching

Public preaching has a central place in evangelicalism, even as the movement proclaims that every believer can read and interpret the Bible privately. Sermons are a distinctive feature of evangelicalism and part of what makes it highly rhetorical. Historian Randall

Balmer writes that evangelicals "mastered the fine art of oral discourse, especially persuasive rhetoric."[150] Balmer traces "the centrality of discourse—of preaching—in American evangelicalism" to the Protestant Reformation when Luther recognized "the power of the spoken word to educate, to communicate, to mobilize":

> The extent to which evangelicals have appropriated that lesson is reflected in both their architecture and their order of worship. In high-church traditions the altar is central, and the entire liturgy leads up to the Eucharist. In most evangelical churches, on the other hand, the pulpit is at center stage, and the service reaches its crescendo in the sermon, the spoken word.[151]

A sermon is not only the centerpiece of worship, it is authoritative teaching. In her study of Beth Moore's teaching, Cope explains the formula that gives sermons their authority. They are "delivered by a single, authoritative rhetor (usually a man)"; they "rely heavily on appeals to Scripture, often interpreted through a grammatical-historical hermeneutic"; and they "attempt to persuade the audience to accept correct beliefs and 'biblical' practices or reaffirm the audience's beliefs and practices."[152] Similarly, Pete Enns describes the evangelical sermon as built on verse-by-verse expositions that aim to "explain what is there so you can know what is right and what is wrong to believe."[153] That "biblically-based 'expositional' theology" is only one sermon style and it differs from other styles like "culturally-based black 'experiential' theology."[154] In each case, though, sermons teach both doctrine and rhetoric. When I interviewed college students about the rhetoric they observed in their religious backgrounds, many said that sermons showed them how to build evidence for claims, engage listeners through delivery, and deploy rhetorical appeals.[155] In the United States, that model can serve political ends. Martin describes how megachurch pastors reach large audiences with sermons that emphasize "the Protestant work ethic, American exceptionalism, [and] personal responsibility."[156] By prescription and example, pastors teach evangelicals to educate, convince, and motivate listeners using commonplaces like worldview or certainty.

Evangelical preaching is a male arena in policy and practice. The SBC explicitly prohibited women's ordination in 2000. Even in denominations that do ordain women, many members are skeptical of their authority. Further, Roxanne Mountford shows male preachers enact a "muscular Christianity" with traditionally male metaphors and masculine delivery.[157] Women who don't see themselves represented in those speakers or messages are not the primary audience of much evangelical preaching.[158] However, the rhetorical practice of preaching is not static. Women like Beth Moore, who found opportunities to teach in spaces other than the pulpit, recognized this lack of attention to women as an opportunity for rhetorical creativity. Others achieved ordination in some denominations. The megachurch where I grew up ordained a female pastor (she officiated my wedding and my mother's funeral). Communication scholars Lindsay Hayes and Sarah Kornfield describe an emerging style of story-sermon that uses strategies like narrative, inductive reasoning, and nonauthoritative style long associated with women rhetors. The story-sermon, a contrast with expositional preaching, "seeks to move the congregation through the work of the imagination" rather than explicit arguments about correct beliefs and "biblical" practices.[159] In official and unofficial spaces, these changes in the meaning and style of preaching foster women's rhetorical work.

Women's right to preach has not waned as an issue, but I find that sermons and preachers are losing sway among evangelicals. In a lively religious marketplace of books, radio, podcasts, YouTube channels, and conferences, individuals can attract audiences outside of churches. As Du Mez writes, many evangelicals have "learned more from Pat Robertson, John Piper, Joyce Meyer, and The Gospel Coalition than they have from their pastor's Sunday sermons."[160] That evangelical marketplace also expands women's avenues to speak and write with authority in person, in print, and online. As personal narrative becomes an especially popular form, it challenges sermons as "the primary genre of contemporary evangelicalism" and lessens its role as "the organizing event of evangelical culture."[161]

Biblical Exegesis and Hermeneutics

An emphasis on certainty and biblical authority places textual interpretation at the heart of evangelicalism, but also complicates that practice. Sermons and writing about the Bible center on exegesis (unpacking the meaning of a text) and hermeneutics (theories guiding interpretation) as tools to arrive at the truth. Both raise questions: "What does an author mean to communicate? To which historical events does a text refer and how does it represent them? How does the very structure of the text construct its meaning? How does this text speak into my and others' cultural situations? How are these texts representative of ideological structures?"[162] To address these questions, some evangelicals apply metaphorical, historical, or experience-based ways of reading. Others cling to "conscious literalism"[163] and accuse other reading practices of eisegesis (reading one's own biases into a text). We have seen how, rather than tolerate multiple reading practices, the evangelical movement has angrily debated which hermeneutic or which exegeses reflect the correct view of God and of scripture. Worthen describes evangelicals as "a community that extols individualism but ensnares every individual in a web of clashing authorities."[164] In other words, evangelicals have to wonder what to do when they arrive at different understandings than their pastors. When Bible passages give contradictory guidance on, say, slavery, who or what ultimately carries authority over their thoughts and actions?

The complicated nature of biblical interpretation lies at the heart of internal conflicts and friction with other movements. Du Mez argues that debates over inerrancy were really debates over gender roles; Noll shows that biblical defenders of slavery "perceive[d] doubt about the biblical defense of slavery as doubt about the authority of the Bible itself."[165] In recent history, "White Christian selectivity harnessed the Bible in service of maintaining the current status quo, which, conveniently, was structured to maintain white supremacy."[166] Evangelical history underscores the (obvious, yet subversive) observation that any biblical exegesis reflects cultural context and often political motivation. This is true even, and maybe especially, for interpretations that claim to be objective.

Apologetics

Religion scholar J. G. Stackhouse defines apologetics as discourse "that shows and tells why the gospel deserves respect and, ultimately, allegiance."[167] That discourse might answer questions or ward off attacks, or it might proactively assert the Christian message. Stackhouse distinguishes internal apologetics (which strengthens faith, presents grounds for belief, and clears up theological confusion and error) from external apologetics (which removes obstacles, clarifies issues, and offers "winsome inducement to those who are not yet Christians").[168] Both forms claim to make rational arguments and marshal objective evidence, and they have wide appeal to evangelicals. Professors or seminarians might specialize in apologetics as an academic field, but evangelicals encounter the practice outside academia. They might hear pastors present "rational" evidence for the Bible's claims, read arguments in blogs, or discuss books like Lee Strobel's *A Case for Christ* or Tim Keller's *The Reason for God* with their small groups. The practice filters down to youth too; Rachel Held Evans recalls attending an apologetics camp for teenagers.

Apologetics developed in response to Enlightenment-era desires for a Protestant theology that would "stand up to rational inquiry just as well as the new science and philosophy did"[169] and to Scopes-era fears about the intellectual legitimacy of Christianity. Jerry Root, professor of evangelism, describes apologetics as a tradition "continuing on from the second century writings of Justin Martyr through to the more recent writings of G. K. Chesterton, C. S. Lewis, and William Lane Craig." He summarizes their work: these apologists "show how the Resurrection, Old Testament prophecies, the archeological data, the evidence for miracles, the dramatic nature of changed lives (people hostile to the faith actually becoming believers and bearing witness to the faith), and many other evidences support the Christian claims." An advocate, Root presents apologetics as historical, high-minded, and unoffensive.

The practice can "help seekers and doubters to get over the intellectual barriers keeping them from embracing faith in Christ" or give believers "confidence and assurance for [their] own faith."[170] Feminist rhetoricians might instead recognize apologetics as an "uncompromising, confrontational" masculinist discourse.[171] Evangelicals like Evans express similar critiques and ask whether such one-sided arguments are effective, ethical ways to communicate about the Christian faith.

Testimony

I end with the practice of testimony, my primary focus in *"I Grew Up in the Church."* Chapters 2–5 go on to examine how personal narratives foster an alternative evangelical rhetoric, but here I situate the practice of testimony in the history of evangelicalism, its commonplaces, and the other practices I identify. Personal narratives that make private faith public are a distinct social practice and aspect of evangelical culture. Hindmarsh traces a "pattern of heartfelt individual conversion" in the movement "since the transatlantic revivals of the eighteenth century."[172] John Newton's "I once was lost but now am found" conversion narrative continues the pattern set by Augustine, Protestant martyrs, and Puritan ministers. Hindmarsh shows that rhetors in each era shaped spiritual autobiographies to respond to the "religious and political strife of the era."[173] As theologians Stanley Hauerwas and L. Gregory Jones write in *Why Narrative? Readings in Narrative Theology*, personal narrative is "a crucial conceptual category for such matters as understanding issues of epistemology and methods of argument, depicting personal identity, and displaying the content of Christian convictions."[174] Even apart from the content of their stories, authors who engage in "the narrative display of Christian convictions" join in a practice that evangelicals and other Christians have venerated for centuries.[175]

Personal narrative is also part of the public rhetoric in evangelical institutions, which, going back to the Great Awakening, value transformative conversions and relationships with Christ. Joined with the priority placed on spreading the faith, this high regard for personal faith invites members to tell their communities about God's work in their lives. In his *Time* article, "The Unmaking of the White Christian Worldview," Robert P. Jones recollects testimonies in his childhood church. Whether they were spontaneous, "a member rising to break the prayerful silence," or scheduled moments "marked 'Testimony' in the bifold church bulletin":

> Critically, what stitched these private and public practices together was an emphasis on personal sin. Common themes were failures in roles and priorities. The grown-ups promised to be more honest in their business dealings and to be more godly parents and spouses—husbands better leaders and wives more pliant to that leadership. When youth were invited to testify, we were often given guidance about how to be honest but appropriate—typically an expression of regret coupled with a promise to reform from running with the wrong crowd.[176]

Jones illustrates how personal narratives are not always organic or authentic self-expressions. Stories can enforce norms and tie personal experiences to metanarratives that reinscribe evangelical beliefs. In his description, testimonies deploy commonplaces like individualism and conversion. Divine providence is another commonplace that rhetors draw on when, looking back at their lives, they see God's hand at work. Providential reasoning is also a reason why testimony and personal narrative carry persuasive power among evangelicals. For members steeped in the belief that God has a plan for each life, discerning that plan by recounting past experiences and constructing a narrative is a spiritual practice that leads to deeper faith.

Personal narratives can have more complex goals and meanings, though. In her essay "Testify!" Kristen Scharold observes, "Personal tales of transformation are a conduit of theology; they are what sets theology into motion."[177] Theologian Mark Teasdale advocates for evangelism that "trades in stories more than propositions," since stories invite people to engage "their own richly textured life stories" and foster joy rather than moralism.[178] Scharold and Teasdale hint at a reason for the popularity and power of testimonies: subjective and invitational personal stories stand in productive contrast to the certainty and combat of the evangelical movement. Through this practice women can gain authority in publishing, social media, podcasting, and conferences; readers and listeners seek them out for their specific perspectives. In this marketplace, consumer products like popular books form a "powerful system of authority—an evangelical popular culture that reflected and reinforced a compelling ideology and a coherent worldview."[179] The writers I study walk a fine line between market-friendly and subversive messages. They derive authority from being relatable and appealing while offering strong critiques.

Evangelical women join a tradition of female rhetors in western Christianity who find persuasive and liberatory possibilities of life writing. In *Rhetoric Retold*, Cheryl Glenn shows that Julian of Norwich's *Revelations of Divine Love* and *The Book of Margery Kempe* are foundational works of feminist autobiographical rhetoric. *The Life and Religious Experience of Jarena Lee* likewise uses a personal narrative rhetorically, detailing Lee's call to ministry and the ways she served God through public speech to support women's right to preach. These examples point to storytelling as a form of persuasion "congenial to women" who learn rhetoric as a craft rather than a formal discipline.[180] Despite being expected, and accepted, personal narrative still meets friction when it conflicts with traditional biblical readings. Evangelicals allow that experience can be "the sphere in which we encounter a revelation from God" but they do not constitute "saving knowledge of the true God" as the Bible does.[181]

Conclusion

Several discursive patterns connect evangelicals' four-hundred-year history and appear in speech and writing during the 2008–2018 decade. Debates again and again hinge on tensions between individual and collective faith or responsibility, superficial readings of the Bible that vilify other movements, deep yet ambivalent investment in politics, and fractious negotiations of authority. I describe this history, including times like the Conservative Resurgence that might not be well known to my readers, to define evangelicalism as a movement with distinctive ways of creating and communicating knowledge. Evangelical identity is a "thick knot of meanings emerging from a snarl of cultural contexts";[182] this chapter untangles some of those meanings and contexts. I build upon these threads in the analysis of women's writing that follows. As they renovate evangelical rhetoric, contemporary women identify the ideologies bound up in these commonplaces and practices and they envision new purposes and meanings.

Recounting evangelical history is an essentially rhetorical process. When self-identified evangelicals like Kidd or Root study the Great Awakening or the apologetics tradition, they place evangelicalism in an historical and intellectual lineage apart from partisan politics. They see evangelicalism as created by men whose primary motive was to know and follow God's will. I also engaged in a rhetorical project when I presented evangelicalism as a movement rather than a theology or a historical tradition. My narrative removes a sense of spiritual purity from evangelical identity. I present evangelicalism not as a "densely articulated belief system"[183] rooted in divine revelation and a relationship with God, but as a movement that humans created through language in response to the material conditions and intellectual currents around them. Analyzing evangelicalism in this way foregrounds the rhetoric that took hold when factions confronted one another or came to terms with other movements seeking to shape politics and culture. As I researched this history, I did see social influence, intellectual rigor, and moral clarity. I also saw petty conflict, rhetoric that upheld injustice and violence, and willingness to compromise beliefs for political and economic gain.

This history gives urgency to women's interventions. The writers I study wrestle with questions like: What goals do evangelicals pursue when they refer to their history? What are they eager to celebrate or ignore? What rhetorical practices construct those memories? How did ideas like "biblical womanhood" take hold? What rhetorical work do those traditions continue to do in contemporary writing? These questions are sometimes explicit in personal narratives and sometimes provide the backdrop. Each presents an opportunity for evangelical women to engage their history critically and create new narratives for the movement. The following chapters examine this rhetorical work and the changes they have, at times, achieved.

2
A Generous Evangelical Orthodoxy

The 2016 election sparked a surge in public testimonies to women's discomfort with evangelical politics. Writer and acclaimed teacher Beth Moore deplored Trump's "disesteem and objectifying of women" and described how she had been the target of similar rhetoric from evangelical men.[1] Trillia Newbell, then a leader in the SBC, responded to Trump's insulting comment about developing countries. She tweeted, "Because racism is on display from national leaders, no one can now say 'racism would go away if you'd stop talking about it.' Perhaps now, especially for the church, we can face realities, confess, repent, and actually move towards true harmony and reconciliation."[2] This call for a renovation of the kind of evangelical rhetoric that justified the Trump candidacy continued to unfold in publications like *Christianity Today*, in conventions and conferences,[3] in personal essays and memoirs, and in social media posts. Orthodox evangelical women insisted that the movement examine the conservative politics that many saw as incongruent with their faith.

Writers like Newbell, as well as Wendy Alsup, Hannah Anderson, Aimee Byrd, and Karen Swallow Prior occupy a complicated role in the evangelical movement. On the one hand, they uphold evangelical orthodoxy, or "right thinking." They recount their experiences of faith with the goal of explaining beliefs like complementarianism and biblical authority and helping readers incorporate evangelical tenets into their lives. On the other hand, their reputations as women of faith make them persuasive critics of evangelical rhetoric and politics. Stephanie A. Martin claims that the release of the *Access Hollywood* tape "marked the beginning of a discursive split between the [evangelical] movement's most prominent men and some of its most admired women."[4] In reality, that discursive split has deeper roots and wider implications. These admired women use evangelical rhetorical practices to dissociate orthodox beliefs from contemporary politics and identify where conservative evangelicalism merely reflects right-wing ideologies.

A stance that I describe as "generous orthodoxy" emerges in their books, articles, and testimonials. Their personal experiences with evangelical rhetoric, faith, and institutions make a case for beliefs that are orthodox without being conservative. I borrow the term *generous orthodoxy* from theologian Hans Frei. In "Response to 'Narrative Theology, an Evangelical Appraisal,'" Frei responded to the critiques of his work voiced by *Christianity Today* founder Carl F. H. Henry. Frei writes, "My own vision of what might be propitious for our day, split as we are, not so much into denominations as into schools of thought, is that we need a kind of generous orthodoxy which would have in it an element of liberalism—a voice like the *Christian Century*—and an element of evangelicalism—the voice of *Christianity Today*."[5] The phrase "generous orthodoxy" later gained wider usage. Popular writer Brian McLaren describes his own combination of traditional and liberal beliefs in *A Generous Orthodoxy*; the phrase appears in blog posts by dozens of pastors and seminarians; Malcolm Gladwell used "Generous Orthodoxy" as the title of a 2016 episode of his *Revisionist History* podcast. In these popular texts, the term names an evangelical discourse that embraces historic Christian doctrines without insulting or dismissing emerging and liberal doctrines. I argue that we can also apply this phrase to political and gender differences, where it may be most helpful and relevant today.

I should be clear that even though the "generosity" of these rhetors separates them from many in the evangelical movement, the content of their beliefs does not. They reject many parts of feminist and social justice movements. Their personal narratives support doctrines like complementarianism that many feminists and Christians would argue are inherently oppressive, no matter the generosity of the rhetoric that articulates them. Others mischaracterize secular feminism or fixate on its conflicts with a biblical worldview. And yet, they work to amplify women's voices, assert women's spiritual and rhetorical agency, and affirm experience as a valid source of knowledge. All three are feminist projects rooted in evangelical orthodoxy. This chapter studies women who are caught between conservative communities and liberal scholarship, ideas, and movements. To "bring their arguments into wider circulation and alter ecosystems"[6]—here, the ecosystem that includes conservative, liberal, and feminist evangelicals who all have reasons for dismissing them—orthodox evangelical women have to establish an ethos that maintains relationship and mutual regard with each. Cultivating public reputations as "true believers" who offer critiques from a place of love for the Bible and the church is a precarious, uncomfortable tactic with which these women seek influence in their communities.

I begin by introducing five orthodox-but-not-conservative women and outlining a conceptual framework for studying texts from this perspective. I then turn to the rhetoric of pastor Mark Driscoll and women's responses to him. This case study illustrates how the decline of white Christian America led to authoritarian and sexist rhetoric in twenty-first-century evangelicalism and the personal narratives that named and critiqued the mounting reliance on fear and combat. I then zoom out to explain how personal narratives enable evangelical women to do rhetorical work from inside evangelicalism—in particular, how "generous orthodoxy" shifts dominant discourses in the movement.

Wendy Alsup

Wendy Alsup began ministry as deacon of women's theology and teaching at Mars Hill Church in Seattle, which she attended from 2002 to 2008. The megachurch became famous first for its growth in numbers in a region not known for churchgoing culture, then for the aggressive personality and rhetoric of pastor Mark Driscoll, and finally for abruptly closing in 2014. Alsup is the author of *Practical Theology for Women*, *The Gospel-Centered Woman*, and *Is the Bible Good for Women?* She writes about spiritual formation and church culture for the Gospel Coalition, *Modern Reformation*, and the Pelican Project, an online community that describes itself as "a guild of women fostering commitment to Christian faith and practice across cultural, denominational, and racial lines."[7] In her writing, Alsup meditates on what the Bible can teach women about trauma, divorce, breast cancer, and single parenting—experiences in her own life that are unusual topics in evangelical women's culture where a winsome, uplifting tone is the norm.

Hannah Anderson

Unlike the other women in this chapter, Hannah Anderson built a career as a writer without having any role in public ministry. Her three books—*Made for More: An Invitation to Live in God's Image*, *Humble Roots: How Humility Grounds and Nourishes Your Soul*, and *All That's Good: Recovering the Lost Art of Discernment*—are narratives of her spiritual growth, the physical landscape and rural culture of Southwest Virginia, and the culture of her husband's small church (a contrast to the megachurches that characterize much of evangelicalism). Anderson also writes articles on culture, ministry, vocation, and family and relationships for publications including *Mere Orthodoxy* and *Christianity Today*.

Trillia Newbell

Evangelicalism is a predominantly white movement, for historic and current reasons I discussed in chapter one, and the same is largely true of these orthodox evangelical writers. Trillia Newbell is one exception, and her writing speaks to being a woman of color in the evangelical movement. Her book *United: Captured by God's Vision for Diversity* asks why churches "too often remain separate but equal."[8] Besides authoring her own books, Newbell amplifies other women writers in collections she edits, like *Women on Life: A Call to Love the Unborn, Unloved, & Neglected* and *Beautifully*

Distinct: Conversations with Friends on Faith, Life, and Culture. Her articles for *Christianity Today* and the Gospel Coalition address women's leadership, interracial marriage, unique challenges facing Black women, and intersections of Black and Christian identities.

From 2013 to 2020 Newbell worked for the Ethics and Religious Liberty Commission (ERLC) of the Southern Baptist Convention. She began as the consultant for women's initiatives and became director of community outreach. In those roles, she developed women's ministry resources, wrote for the website, hosted a podcast, and organized and spoke at ERLC conferences. In 2020, she became an acquisitions editor at Moody Publishers, a less visible leadership role but one that still supports women's voices and education.[9]

Karen Swallow Prior

Karen Swallow Prior taught literature and writing at Liberty, one of the largest evangelical universities in the United States, from 1999 to 2019. In a *Christianity Today* article, Kate Shellnutt describes the changes at Liberty during those two decades: "[Prior] has watched the school transform as its leadership transitioned from late founder Jerry Falwell to son Jerry Falwell Jr.; its enrollment multiplied through pioneering online education platforms; and ultimately its reputation became further aligned with President Donald Trump, a friend of Falwell Jr.'s."[10] Even before making waves as a Never Trumper and a critic of the profit-driven corporate model at Liberty, Prior was known for being a pro-life activist and a writer. She is the author of *Booked: Literature in the Soul of Me*, *Fierce Convictions: The Extraordinary Life of Hannah More—Poet, Reformer, Abolitionist*, and *On Reading Well: Finding the Good Life through Great Books*. With Alsup, Prior founded the Pelican Project.

In her writing, teaching, and social media, Prior advocates for separating biblical values from cultural practices. A *New Yorker* article on Prior from January 8, 2019 places her "at the vanguard of a new movement of Christians looking to reclaim their faith from the regressive racist and misogynistic politics that have co-opted it."[11] Prior rejects the label "conservative" in favor of "orthodox," underscoring this distinction. Her writing prompted me to center this chapter on the crucial distinctions between these two terms, and the rhetorical possibilities that "orthodox" presents.

These biographies show that evangelical women do not separate into clearly demarcated categories. Some, like Newbell, have held leadership positions. Some have political and theological convictions that overlap with progressives and ex-evangelicals. However, the figures I study here form a distinct group of rhetors because of their *ethe* and goals. First, they explicitly adhere to orthodox theology. Second, they publish in establishment venues like *Christianity Today* or the Gospel Coalition, a stamp of approval from the male evangelical power structure. Finally, these rhetors locate themselves in conservative denominations. Evangelicals don't usually define themselves by affiliations, instead prioritizing individual faith, but a person's choice to join an SBC or Presbyterian Church in America (PCA) congregation contributes to their *ethos* as a true believer. Whereas progressive writers might identify with a collage of doctrines or theologies, orthodox writers tend to claim denominational and institutional alliances.

Conceptual Framework

Scholars who are interested in the subversive, radical voices in religious communities tend to overlook these true believers and their measured critiques. This blind spot is unfortunate. Writers who largely uphold patriarchal institutions are not only essential for a study that considers the diversity of evangelical women; this group also has much to offer feminist rhetorical study. They have the *ethos* to sway believers loyal to evangelical power structures and traditional doctrine, which those outside the movement—whether by choice or because the establishment labels them heretics—lack. Conservative Christians can easily dismiss their progressive counterparts or knowledgeable outsiders by saying they don't have a biblical worldview. In contrast, they take orthodox writers like Prior and Newbell more seriously. With this audience among conservatives, orthodox women propel many of the most interesting evangelical debates over social justice, gender, and biblical interpretation.

Feminist Rhetoric

Feminist rhetorical scholarship has found that religion in the United States creates fertile spaces for women to develop and deploy rhetorical skill and agency. In *Conversational Rhetoric*, Jane Donawerth shows that conservative Protestantism fostered and shaped North American feminist rhetoric. Margaret Fell, Jarena Lee, Lucretia Mott, Ellen Stewart, Catherine Booth, and Frances Willard redefined preaching as "testimony or holy conversation."[12] They all start with biblical interpretation but use different forms, like Jarena Lee's spiritual memoir and Ellen Stewart's conversion narrative. Donawerth argues, "It is in this religious strand of rhetorical theory, rather than in secular textbooks, that the language of women's rights enters rhetorical theory, for these women base their arguments on the right to religious freedom and liberty of conscience for women."[13] Fell, Lee, Stewart, and Willard base their rhetorical work in biblical interpretation; Lee and Stewart also use spiritual narrative. However, the field of feminist rhetoric does not offer many theoretical tools for studying rhetors who demonstrate only selective interest in challenging and dismantling power structures and ideologies of dominance.

To analyze avowedly orthodox evangelical rhetoric and understand how it enters into conversation with feminist projects, I draw on Charlotte Hogg's "An Ethics of Hope and Care." Hogg argues that conservative women "vary widely in their beliefs, and more study can illuminate the rhetorical moves created within and perpetuating dominant ideologies, providing productive insights central to a feminist mission of analyzing structures—from the systemic to the daily—that influence power in a variety of ways."[14] More study could also show how conservative or orthodox women propel activism and change in evangelical culture. Their "conceptions of self, moral agency, and politics"[15] have consequences beyond individual faith; the rhetorical work of orthodox evangelical women sparked outraged commentary from their male and female counterparts and caused realignments among previously like-minded believers. Because they work to establish their reputations as traditional, Bible-believing Christians, their writing carries distinct persuasive power.

Additionally, I use research on conservative women taking place in other fields, such as Ingersoll's *Evangelical Christian Women* and anthropologist Saba Mahmood's *The Politics of Piety*. To study orthodox and conservative evangelicals on their own terms, I try to avoid imposing a "feminist critique from outside the tradition" or "search for hidden forms of empowerment."[16] Mahmood's wish to move past "the simple binary of resistance/subordination" also informs my analysis of conservative women who describe gender roles, religion, and their rhetorical work using terms other than *resistance*, *equality*, and *liberation*.[17] These four studies chart a way to analyze how orthodox evangelical women instruct other women in the rhetorical practices that can build spiritual and intellectual identity. This act is not necessarily subversive or radical, as feminist rhetoricians have typically used those terms, but it enacts rhetorical agency.

Studying the rhetoric of evangelical orthodoxy is important in a project that aims to understand the debates taking place in evangelicalism and the different ways that evangelicals use the feminist practice of personal narrative. To focus only on the explicitly progressive voices challenging conservative doctrine and politics would be to omit this set of voices contributing to the lively debate within this subculture. Those orthodox evangelical voices provide insight into the range of evangelical rhetorical practice. That group also provides an opportunity to better understand the ways conservative doctrine and politics persist in certain communities. I follow Mahmood in seeking to study conservative rhetors on their own terms, without searching for liberal conceptions of agency and resistance in their writing. Mahmood describes her goal as "restoring agency to religiously devout Muslim women hitherto denounced for their patriarchal proclivities."[18] In her research into the Egyptian piety movement, in which women teach and study Islamic scriptures together, she resists "the supposition that women Islamist supporters are pawns in a grand patriarchal plan, who, if freed from their bondage, would naturally express their instinctual abhorrence for the traditional Islamic mores used to enchain them."[19] She frames her research as a counterpoint to studies of women and religion that focus on liberation:

> Nor is it my aim to recover a "redeemable element" within the Islamism movement by recuperating its latent liberatory potentials so as to make the movement more palatable to liberal sensibilities. Instead, in this book I seek to analyze the conceptions of self, moral agency, and politics that undergird the practices of this nonliberal movement, in order to come to an understanding of the historical projects that animate it.[20]

With Mahmood in mind, I am curious about the conceptions of self, moral agency, and politics that undergird evangelicalism and women's participation in the movement. If freed from conservative religious subculture, they still might not express an instinctual abhorrence for complementarianism. Instead of searching for latent liberatory potentials, this chapter analyzes the conceptions of moral agency, rhetorical agency, and politics that emerge from—and motivate—the rhetorical practices of conservative evangelical women.

Case Study: Mark Driscoll

Wendy Alsup begins her 2008 book *Practical Theology for Women* with a personal narrative of God calling her and her husband Andy to move from South Carolina to join a successful, growing church in Seattle. She tells the story in a way that impresses upon readers (and herself) that God's providence made this possible. Planning the cross-country move had exhausted their savings and they had no new jobs lined up. Leaving South Carolina, she prayed "that God would not allow us to leave the state if he didn't want us in Seattle."[21] As they crossed into Georgia, Andy got a call from his future employer. "All of a sudden, I felt like God rolled back the clouds for a moment and gave me a glimpse of himself I had never seen before," she writes.[22] Alsup crafts these events into a narrative of God's hand giving them the material needs to participate in a divine plan. Her story makes God's will seem concrete and discernible.

Alsup's experience of divine intervention has personal and public purposes. Her specific details make real "the splendor of God, his sovereign control over the details of life, and his intimate awareness of our lives."[23] Reiterating that evidence is both a personal spiritual practice and a witness to others—specifically, a witness to being called to a specific place and ministry. When Alsup writes, "I knew beyond a shadow of a doubt that God wanted us in Seattle," she reaffirms her faith in God's power and models how readers can find providential signs in their own lives.[24] Alsup went on to become deacon of women's ministry at Mars Hill Church in Seattle, working under pastor Mark Driscoll's leadership. Writing in 2008, Alsup presents her own calling as even more powerful because it was part of the church's success.

Mark Driscoll is a case study of the conflation of orthodox belief and conservative culture. Based on reading Prior and other women who take on this problem, I see orthodox beliefs as following Bebbington's quadrilateral: (1) personal, transformative conversion; (2) the Bible's authority; (3) the call to spread and enact faith; and (4) the substitutionary death of Christ. Driscoll's story illustrates how these tenets were refracted through a combative, misogynist strain of conservatism in 2008–2018. Analyzing this case study advances my argument that women's personal narratives reshaped evangelical rhetoric during a period of evangelical decline for three reasons:

- Driscoll's rise and fall illustrate how evangelical commonplaces affect church culture and constrain individual believers.
- The personal narrative genre brought about material, demonstrable change. These narratives also bring

ambiguity to clean narratives about the church's rise and collapse.

- Women's critiques held Driscoll accountable for misogynist rhetoric. After his resignation, they probed the difference between orthodox belief and cultural or political conservatism.

Driscoll's rise and fall continue to haunt evangelicals. His gendered rhetoric and celebrity status tell evangelicals a lot about their movement. Driscoll and his work represent destructive elements in their rhetoric and culture, and women in particular take that lesson seriously.

I was not aware of Driscoll before I began studying evangelical women in 2017 and I had no firsthand experience of his preaching or the culture he created. To learn about those, I use anthropologist Jessica Johnson's ethnographic account in *Biblical Porn: Affect, Labor, and Pastor Mark Driscoll's Evangelical Empire*. I also refer to the *Rise and Fall of Mars Hill* podcast, with its recordings of Driscoll's sermons and its interviews with orthodox evangelical women. Du Mez also documents events I did not witness firsthand. *Jesus and John Wayne* lays out Driscoll's militarism and violence, and connects these aspects of his ministry to other events and figures in evangelical culture. These accounts provide content and context for my rhetorical analysis of the contemporaneous texts that documented Driscoll's rhetoric, influence, and conflation of "orthodox" and "conservative" in his teaching. These primary sources include Alsup's *Practical Theology for Women*, with her account of joining and working at Mars Hill, and interviews and articles from *Christianity Today*. I also use texts written or published after Driscoll's empire started to dissolve. These include an online testimonial by Jonna Petry, wife of an elder at Mars Hill, and Rachel Held Evans' blog posts summarizing and preserving passages of Driscoll's online writing. Their retrospectives show how orthodox women critiqued Driscoll and located his arc in a broader narrative of the evangelical movement.[25]

Mark Driscoll's Rhetoric and Evangelical Commonplaces

In 2021, *Christianity Today* podcast *The Rise and Fall of Mars Hill* described two decades when Driscoll's church was a major force in evangelicalism. Driscoll founded Mars Hill (named for a location in the New Testament book of Acts) in 1996 and the church grew to include fifteen satellite congregations, a global ministry, and an online presence. Driscoll boasted thousands of attendees at services, even in "the least churched city in the US" (a phrase he often used). Johnson attended Driscoll's Sunday services while she researched *Biblical Porn*. She describes his preaching as "theologically hardline but culturally hip, appealing to arty urbanites in their twenties and thirties with its raucous music, savvy employ of visual and digital media, and edgy sermons delivered in the sarcastic patter of a stand-up comedian by a brash pastor who was generationally and culturally aligned with his congregation."[26] This style and quantifiable success made Driscoll an evangelical celebrity. He further built his personal influence by founding Resurgence, an organization to train church leaders, and the Acts 29 church planting network, which gave seed money to men who felt called to start new congregations. Driscoll became popular by attacking feminism, defending traditional beliefs, and modeling cultural relevance in those "edgy sermons." He was an exception to the trends that scared evangelicals during the decade of decline from 2008–2018.

On the first episode of *Rise and Fall*, journalist Kate Shellnutt describes how Driscoll's empire unraveled in 2014. Websites had circulated evidence of Driscoll's authoritarianism, plagiarism, and unethical decisions, like using church funds to inflate sales of his book *Real Marriage*. Shellnutt remarks, "The blogs are where all this went down."[27] Personal writing online detailed his misogyny and the tactics of intimidation and social isolation that suppressed information and stifled dissent in the church. Even after Driscoll resigned and the church closed, personal narratives continued that conversation about church growth and celebrity. Evangelicals looked back at this glaring example of their movement's dangerous affinity for savvy branding and hardline theology; they also revisited Driscoll's misogynist rhetoric. While his combative, sexualized rhetoric was extreme, he was nevertheless embraced and amplified by moderate, mainstream leaders.

Driscoll's sermons, books, and online writing use evangelical commonplaces to support aggressive, misogynist rhetoric. In particular, he asserts that Christians are locked in combat with secular culture and portrays himself and his church as a part of God's divine plan. All three of these commonplaces are rooted in orthodox beliefs and they added to Driscoll's credibility and appeal. In a September 2014 blog post, Rachel Held Evans summarized how he presented these orthodox beliefs through antagonistic content and style:

> Driscoll has long been known for his authoritarian leadership over Mars Hill Church, and for his controversial teachings regarding gender and sexuality. He made national news in 2006 when he blamed Ted Haggard's affair with a male escort on Haggard's wife for "letting herself go" and has often repeated the teaching that women who fail to please their husbands sexually (by providing regular oral sex and maintaining their attractiveness) bear some responsibility for their husbands' infidelity.
>
> Driscoll refers to pacifists as "pansies," the emerging church as "homo-evangelicals" who worship a "Richard Simmons hippie queer Christ," and churches with women in leadership as "chickified," warning that "if Christian males do not man up soon, the Episcopalians may vote a fluffy baby bunny rabbit as their next bishop to lead God's men."
>
> He has long spoken out against the supposed "feminization" of the church and argued in support of a more violent, macho-man Christianity, stating "I cannot worship the hippie, diaper, halo Christ because I cannot worship a guy I can beat up." In 2011, he issued a call on Facebook for his followers to share stories about and ridicule "effeminate anatomically male worship leaders."[28]

In writing this section (in fact, this whole chapter) I try to convey conservative evangelical rhetoric but give as little oxygen as possible to the insulting, damaging, and dishonest claims and language that I find there. To that end, I include summaries like the one Evans writes rather than extensive passages of Driscoll's text. The above overview (which is itself vivid) reflects Driscoll's ideology and his media reach. Evans documents her summary with links to coverage in the *Seattle Times*, *Christianity Today*, and *Salon*, as well as original content on Driscoll's own website. These were not remarks made in sermons at his own church and received by an audience who endorsed his beliefs and style. Driscoll's claims about gender, sex, and sexuality were public and they circulated far beyond his immediate readers and listeners.

In one example, Driscoll used an online forum hosted by the church website to voice his disdain for anything other than rigid, traditional gender roles. Evans quotes a section of a post in which he ranted about feminism and secular culture:

> And so the culture and families and churches sprint to hell because the men aren't doing their job and the feminists continue their rant that it's all our fault and we should just let them be pastors and heads of homes and run the show. And the more we do, the more hell looks like a good place because at least a man is in charge, has a bit of order and let's (sic) men spit and scratch as needed.[29]

Driscoll names predictable villains of conservative evangelical culture: women who lead in church and at home, men who "aren't doing their job" by not asserting power in those spaces, and the damaging effects this climate has on young men (like "Johnny"). His sexism is even more explicit when he responds to a woman on the discussion board:

> I speak harshly because I speak to men. A woman might not understand that. I also do not answer to women. So your questions will be ignored. I would however, recommend to you a few verses to memorize: I Timothy 2:11–15 I Corinthians 14:33–35.

> To learn them, ask your father or husband. If you have neither, ask your pastor. If she is a female, find another church. If you are the pastor, quit your job and repent.[30]

Driscoll layers evangelical theology with disdain for women who don't see the merit of harsh speech and to whom he owes no explanation for his conduct. His use of scripture and complementarian gender ideology lend legitimacy to aggressive and manipulative rhetoric. These excerpts also reflect his characteristic tone, which some audiences loved. Johnson writes, "Mark's employ of hyperbole and humor to excite and seduce audiences were renowned and considered among his gifts and strengths as a communicator."[31] Fans received Driscoll's abrasive language as an unapologetic declaration of evangelical beliefs, even the work God had called him to do.

Divine Providence and Narratives of Calling

One root of Driscoll's persuasive power was his narrative of God calling him to ministry. In an episode of *Rise and Fall*, host Mike Cosper plays over a dozen recordings of Driscoll narrating his call to ministry at different times in his career. This example sums up the pattern, which he repeats in sermons, conferences, and interviews: "I was called into ministry through a prophetic word. I was praying and God spoke to me. He said 'plant churches, study the Bible, marry Grace, train young men.'" Driscoll said this instruction required him to make a complete about-face in his life. He had no interest in God or church, but he read the Bible because his girlfriend (Grace, whom he later married) had given him a copy. He tells his audience: "I remember the spirit of God absolutely flipping a switch in me, and I believe that is when God regenerated me." This was a specific, constructed story of his call to ministry. Early in his career, Driscoll had told versions that had no voice of God and no grandiose vision for church planting. In these other accounts, his gradual conversion was influenced by reading St. Augustine's *Confessions* in college and debating faith with a fellow student. Over time, though, he distilled that narrative to a tidy story of God calling him for a singular purpose.[32]

This is how the rhetorical commonplace of divine providence can animate evangelical personal narratives. Driscoll's story presents God's plan as a concrete, even audible, phenomenon, intensely personal but meant to be retold and acted out in public. He constructed and then used this story of divine intervention for personal and public purposes. His "plant churches, study the Bible, marry Grace, train young men" narrative became the language of faith at Mars Hill. That rehearsed account of his individual calling bolstered his celebrity status but also gave the church a sweeping purpose: to revive Christianity, including a biblical view of gender and marriage, in Seattle and the entire country.

Authority

This origin myth introduces Driscoll's belief in biblical authority, which he performed in his forum posts, sermons, and books. Driscoll's narrative evolved in a key way: he placed the Bible (specifically, Paul's letter to the Romans) at the center of his story. He cited Bible verses as self-evident support for his calling but did not quote or unpack the actual texts, a habit visible in the "I speak harshly because I speak to men" forum post I quoted above. Johnson notices a similar strategy in a chapter Driscoll wrote for the 2007 collection *Listening to the Beliefs of the Emerging Church.* Driscoll "supports his theology with more than seven hundred verses of Scripture"[33] to signal the validity of his argument and the authority or authenticity of his exegesis. Here, "by structuring the entirety of his chapter with numeric references to the Bible rather than actual verses—page after page and comma after comma—Driscoll forecloses any interpretation beyond his own."[34] He deploys those citations to shut down arguments and assert his identity as a Bible-believing Christian.

Driscoll's simplified narrative of his calling also reinforced his pastoral authority. As Cosper remarks, such origin myths have emotional and theological appeals to Christians (and others), who "love the sense that someone is following a bold dream, or a divine inspiration."[35] Beyond building a leader's charismatic appeal, stories of divine calling place "an almost apostolic amount of authority in the hands of the person who is hearing directly from God."[36] Driscoll leveraged that calling to consolidate his power in the church. Criticizing his choices or questioning a policy meant a person was "off mission," and he used that as grounds for verbally abusing and firing copastors and staff.

Claiming a biblical basis for his calling and his culturally conservative positions let Driscoll claim authority based on his faithfulness to scripture. His rhetoric might have been more extreme than other pastors, but, like them, he preached in a "verse-by-verse style of systematic theology, cleaving to a 'literal' reading of the Bible and a conservative social doctrine."[37] This style aligned him with mainstream leaders like Al Mohler and John Piper. Even if these older men in the evangelical establishment disapproved of Driscoll's crudeness, they praised his boldness in preaching the gospel.[38] Driscoll thereby gained access to a network of conservative evangelical male leaders who "shared stages, blurbed each other's books, spoke at each other's conferences, and endorsed each other as men of God with a heart for gospel teaching."[39] They could overlook differences in doctrines and styles because "they were united in a mutual commitment to patriarchal power" that they located in the Bible.[40] When Driscoll displayed overt misogyny or homophobia, this network excused that harmful rhetoric as a defense of the gospel.

Combat

Driscoll enacted a combative form of masculinity and then spelled it out in books and sermons. Du Mez quotes the model of masculinity he laid out in his 2008 book *Vintage Jesus*: Jesus was "a man with calluses on his hands and muscles on his frame" and "an aggressive, anger-filled leader who picked fights with religious authorities, slaughtered thousands of pigs, ordered his disciples around, and didn't mind causing offense."[41] This definition sanctioned Driscoll's own penchant for aggressive and anger-filled sermons, picking fights with what he saw as a feminized church in America, and ordering around other leaders. In public speech and writing, "Driscoll thrived on manufacturing a sense of threat posed by outsiders" like unorthodox theology, Islam, or feminism, and he "incited fear in order to maintain control."[42] He promoted doctrine in language that seems calculated to cause offense and defended that tactic by claiming it was necessary for a people under attack. Driscoll's brash style reiterated familiar evangelical rhetoric. He built his arguments on references to combat, biblical authority, and divine providence, signal chains of argument that tied him to the Bible and evangelical tradition. All three reinforced his insistence that God was using him to revitalize evangelicalism and make it relevant to a new generation who needed to be confronted with biblical truth.

"The blogs are where all this went down"

In my introduction and chapter one, I describe the significance autobiographical rhetoric holds for evangelicals. Personal speech and writing resonate with their belief in an individualistic faith and echo practices like confession and testimony. The Driscoll case study shows how evangelical commonplaces of authority, divine calling, and combat can give spiritual significance to personal narrative and how the form can normalize extreme and alienating rhetoric based in those beliefs. However, his story also shows that personal narrative can compel material change in evangelical culture, bring nuance to metanarratives, and teach theology by grounding abstract concepts. These texts seek to hold the broader evangelical movement accountable for the rhetoric that enables this manifestation of the faith.

Driscoll's authority started to fray when former members and elders publicly spoke and wrote about their experiences. The personal narratives brought about material changes by directing attention away from the abstraction of "the church" and toward the individual lives affected. The website *Joyful Exiles* collects firsthand accounts of how Driscoll's rhetoric supported authoritarian tactics. One account comes from Jonna Petry, whose husband, Paul, left his law practice to become a salaried Mars Hill pastor in 2005. Jonna recounts that when Paul refused to sign new bylaws that "gave Mark control without any secure mechanism for accountability," Driscoll fired him from his staff position.[43] Church leaders then convened a "trial" that found Paul guilty of "lack of trust and respect for spiritual authority and improper use of confidential information"[44] and removed him from the body of elders. The remaining elders published a letter on the church website instructing members to shun him and the whole family. Over fourteen single-spaced pages, Jonna Petry details these actions and the emotional and economic consequences her family endured.

Petry's story was odd for me to read as an outsider with no connection to Driscoll or his church. I had a hard time understanding the gravity of her account, especially compared to the accounts of sexual abuse that have come out of other churches.[45] The answer to this might lie in her assertion that Driscoll's actions were spiritual abuse: "When someone uses their power within a framework of spiritual belief or practice to satisfy their own needs at the expense of others." Driscoll's insults and retaliation weren't illegal, but they were "a breach of sacred trust" and went against Jesus Christ's command to love one another.[46] While not equivalent to sexual abuse or to conservative preachers advising women to submit to violent husbands, Petry's definition explains why spiritual abuse ruptures evangelical communities.

Jonna Petry's narrative is significant for detailing this wrong in painfully concrete terms and because of the role she attributes to public storytelling. She quotes Acts 20, where the Apostle Paul "pleaded with the Ephesian elders to pay attention and guard the flock."[47] To share her story is therefore an act of obedience. While Petry doesn't explicitly cite allegations that she is telling these stories to ruin a good man, she defends her decision not to keep the spiritual abuse private. "We believe that to remain quiet now would be unloving and disobedient to God," she writes.[48] In an evangelical culture that directed attention to church growth or sermon clips that went viral, her story is a call to pay attention to Driscoll's history and pattern of abuse toward his flock instead.

Former members can tell stories of spiritual abuse but can also tell nuanced stories of the joy and growth they experienced as members of the church. In *Practical Theology for Women*, Alsup recounts how the congregation supported her during a painful inflection point in her life. Soon after moving to Seattle, her husband needed open-heart surgery. She recalls that as she sat in the waiting room, couples from her small group joined her to provide food, company, and prayers. "At any one time," she writes, "we probably had at least four people from our church talking and laughing with Andy's parents and me during the entire surgery."[49] Mark Driscoll visited and invited her to come to his house near the hospital any time she needed a shower or nap. Alsup accepted the offer:

> I humbly fished out the cell phone number for the pastor who lived around the corner from the hospital, though I was formerly too proud to even contemplate inviting myself over. I was barely coherent as I sobbed my need for a place to sleep. He had me walk to their house. It was the night before Thanksgiving. He and his wife put a fire log in the fireplace and made up their sofa bed with lots of comfortable blankets. They made me a cup of tea, put their arms around me, prayed with me, and tucked me into bed.[50]

She tells this story again on *Rise and Fall* (where she adds that the tea had a soothing splash of rum). She explains, "I'm not the only person who has a story like that with Mark."[51] The podcast details many others, like instances when Driscoll covered rent for single moms. Cosper also observes that members were loyal to Driscoll because Mars Hill was "where they grew into their calling, and their sense of purpose."[52] He summarizes the deep-rooted connections many describe:

> Mars Hill was where they learned to give their lives away in service to something bigger than themselves, and where they saw unbelievable things happen as thousands of people flocked to Jesus. It was where so many young men heard the call to embrace the

> responsibilities of adulthood, to revere marriage and pursue it. It's where they got married and had babies. It's the place they watched their kids grow up. . . . You can imagine how many inflection points, how many moments of suffering when the community gathered around you, how many moments of deep and shared joy took place within the context of that community.[53]

These experiences in the church partially explain why staff and members tolerated Driscoll and his rhetoric. But these reflections speak to another reason why many people excused and even defended him, rooted in the unique importance of the church and the preacher. These testimonials show that even as the evangelical movement embraces the individual "I," "the church" still holds emotional and theological power in the movement and individual lives. For many evangelicals, church is the organizing structure for friendships, identity, and community service in a way that other civic groups or religious spaces can't equal.

For evangelicals, church can also be the site of rhetoric that equates biblical beliefs with conservative ideologies and enforces or normalizes conservative politics through superficial or manipulative uses of scripture. Many defenses of Driscoll—that he was a bold fighter for the gospel, that even though his style wasn't orthodox his doctrine was, that in private life he was different than his onstage persona—resemble political arguments. These reasons find echoes in the calculated defenses that men like Mohler and Piper offer when politicians exhibit behavior that contradicts their professed beliefs in the Bible or the Constitution. Perhaps this pattern prepared evangelicals to accept similar rationalizations in conservative politics. We also see how Driscoll promoted a gender hierarchy (as in his "I speak harshly" post) with proof texts, cursory citations of Bible verses that lack context or analysis. He also enacts and articulates the combative, authoritarian masculinity that, Du Mez argues, is the foundation of evangelical alignment with conservative politics in the United States. Driscoll made these values and tactics appealing to his listeners by presenting them as countercultural and subversive, rooted in the authority of scripture, and indispensable for a people called to bring the gospel truth to a secularizing country.

Responding to Conservatism with a Generous Orthodoxy

The "generous orthodoxy" that evangelical women envision requires rhetorical dexterity. After all, they have to enter a discursive landscape with combative and authoritarian rhetors like Driscoll. Theologians who explained and elaborated on the concept of generous orthodoxy point to the balance of conviction and flexibility needed to pursue this goal. In his introduction to the collection *Generous Orthodoxies: Essays on the History and Future of Ecumenical Theology*, Paul Silas Peterson writes:

> Hans Frei was the first to use the term "generous orthodoxy" to describe this sense of *mediation and openness* ("generous"), on the one hand, and, on the other, to describe the sense of *connection to doctrinal tradition* ("orthodoxy"). This general trend followed from the belief that the diverse expressions of the Christian faith should be in conversation with one another in order to generate a positive relationship of dialog and cooperation. Many of the theologians associated with this sentiment of theology did not attempt to overcome doctrinal positions by eliminating particularity or their specific confessional tradition. They rather undertook the challenging task of making them fit together in a dynamic tension with the various particularities. Something emerged that was neither "my way or the highway," nor "anything goes."[54]

Many of Peterson's terms—dialogue, cooperation, conversation, and dynamic tension—run counter to the commonplaces I identify in evangelical rhetoric. They represent a shift away from combat, fear, and certainty. When women respond to conservative rhetors with generous orthodoxy they use tactics that are likewise rooted in the authority of scripture but offer alternatives to combativeness and superficial biblicism. Driscoll is one very illuminating case study, but this goes beyond his controversy. Generous orthodoxy describes an important current in evangelical women's personal narrative that takes on conservative factions in the movement.

Evangelical women articulate a generous orthodoxy through their readings of the Bible. This philosophy works to find points of agreement and dynamic tensions between denominations and schools of thought, as scholars like Frei and Peterson envision; it is also pertinent to contemporary evangelicalism when it bridges differences in rhetoric and worldview. Narratives of encounters with the Bible offer generous orthodoxy as an alternative to the evangelical rhetoric that hinges on certainty and authority. Orthodox writers don't dispute the authority of scripture—and some uphold the doctrine of inerrancy—but they intervene in these debates by testifying to the damage this rhetoric causes. In her 2017 book *Is the Bible Good for Women?* Wendy Alsup describes and critiques the "ungenerous" orthodox reading she learned as a young person in the church:

> I have a history of both prescriptive and descriptive passages used arbitrarily against me in ways that made me nervous about approaching Scripture for a while. You might have as well. I was raised in fundamentalist Christian churches with long lists of rights, wrongs, dos, don'ts from the Bible that were confusing and often contradictory. Preachers applied the Bible haphazardly and seemed to emphasize the parts of the Bible that best suited their personal agendas. I remember being taught, for instance, that women should not wear pants because, according to Deuteronomy 22:5, women were not supposed to wear "that which pertaineth unto a man" (KJV). Yet I noted the inconsistent way Scripture was used, for these same preachers did not have a problem with church members wearing cotton/polyester blend clothing despite similar warnings against mixed fabrics just six verses later in the same chapter of the Law.[55]

Alsup highlights a site where fundamentalism persists in contemporary evangelicalism: in promoting a literalist rhetoric of the Bible that has more to do with politics and biases than with reflective study of the text. Readers might identify with this story because they recognize parallels to their own backgrounds, or they might receive this story as a blunt portrayal of conservative rhetoric they have not personally encountered. The latter is an important function of this kind of testimony. Extreme or fringe beliefs—including fundamentalist or conservative rhetoric—are not always visible to evangelicals who consider themselves moderates or who are immersed in the rhetoric and practices of their own middle-of-the road churches. As a result, those evangelicals might overlook that rhetoric or minimize its influence in the movement. I recall members of my family waving aside beliefs like opposition to women's preaching or Christian nationalism by saying, "I don't know anyone at our church who believes that." For readers who might be similarly blinkered, Alsup's recollection illustrates the presence of this fundamentalist rhetoric.

Alsup also uses personal experience to highlight and critique the corrosive effect of ungenerous, fundamentalist rhetoric. She shows how this discourse supports conservative politics and culture with her example of women's clothing that explicitly ties this literalist rhetoric to evangelical gender ideologies. In this fundamentalist context, Bible verses are evidence for positions and the Bible's authority is a warrant for "haphazard" and "contradictory" arguments. She also seems to suggest that not all scripture is relevant to modern Christians, an assertion that would rankle some literalists. Alsup offers her experience not as authoritative but as illustrative. This memory, paired with her present-day critique, gives examples of the kinds of distinctions an orthodox evangelical might make without denying foundational doctrines.

The drive toward certainty, or black-and-white interpretations, spilled over into the broader rhetoric of those churches. Alsup recalls: "On top of the random and inconsistent use of Scripture, youth-group leaders regularly taught prohibitions 'from the Bible' that I figured out later weren't actually in the Bible at all. . . . They were so afraid the kids would violate black-and-white commands that they turned the gray areas around such commands into black as well."[56] The correction conservatives need, Alsup suggests, is a new approach to reading and applying the Bible. She describes the reading practice she adopted as an adult:

> I took a break from the theme of preachers from my youth, over-the-top self-examination for whether or not I was obeying the intent of every command of Scripture. I bathed in the teachings of irresistible grace, unearned mercy, and unconditional love for a decade or so. They were like a warm Epsom salt bath for my weary spiritual body. My muscles relaxed. I could breathe again. I didn't have to earn my righteousness to be approved by God. Christ had earned it, and that was enough.[57]

These emphases—rigorous self-examination and obedience on the one hand, and "irresistible grace, unearned mercy, and unconditional love" on the other hand—do not belong to specific denominations. Alsup traces a trajectory from argument-driven, literal readings of the Bible to meditative readings of the Bible as a message of grace, mercy, and love. This is a change in emphasis rather than in doctrine. However, with that shift in emphasis, Alsup tempers the historical Christian doctrine of biblical authority with an element of liberalism.

Karen Swallow Prior articulates this balance of traditional doctrine and liberalism overtly, including through her teaching. In her *New Yorker* article, Griswold describes one of Prior's classes at Liberty University, where Prior read aloud a passage from "The White Man's Burden." Griswold quotes Prior disentangling biblical teaching from cultural projects:

> The aggressive spread of the faith was an ideal of the Victorian age, she went on, but that doesn't mean that the Bible supports imperialism. During the nineteenth century, Christianity was used as a justification for secular political projects, and this collapse continues today. "So much of what we think is Biblical Christianity is really Victorian," she said. For example, contemporary Christians often claimed that traditional notions of proper gender roles—such as that a woman's place was in the home—came from scripture, when, in fact, they were largely products of nineteenth-century European thought. "It's super important to learn to distinguish between Victorianism and Biblical Christianity," she said.[58]

In this moment of her class, Prior separates conservatism from evangelicalism to reorient their readings and interpretations toward a generous orthodoxy. She does not argue against biblical authority or inerrancy, but she asks students to consider how their notions of biblical teaching are, in fact, extrabiblical. She argues that historical contexts determined many biblical interpretations, a concept from liberal theology, to prompt students to build more accurate understandings of both their religious history and their orthodox beliefs.

Generous Orthodoxy and Secular Movements

This anecdote about Prior illustrates how a generous orthodoxy engages both conservatism and secular movements. Her discussion of "The White Man's Burden" and Victorian ideologies argues that evangelicals should see imperialist acts of "spreading the faith" as secular projects, not biblical ones. In other writing, she argues that secular spaces led her to deeper faith. In an article for the Gospel Coalition, Prior recalls her experience in college:

> I grew up in the church, but it took an unbelieving, liberal professor at a state university to teach me how reading well could make me a better Christian.
>
> I had been led by the pastors, revivalists, and Sunday school teachers of my youth to believe that if one really loves God, one demonstrates it by one's willingness to be a pastor (or, in my case, a pastor's wife) or to travel as a missionary to a faraway land—the more desolate the better.
>
> But I didn't want to be these things. (I suppose it's more proper to say I "didn't feel called," but it's more honest simply to say I didn't want to.) I wanted to be a student, a reader, a writer, and, eventually, a professor.
>
> I didn't know how to reconcile my love of literature and learning with my love of God. So for a while, I gave up God.[59]

Her early education in the church set faith and secular education in opposition to one another; in reality, she had much to learn from secular professors and writers. For Prior, a Christian worldview had devalued reading and critical thinking, while this secular space helped her "understand that reading need not be merely an interesting pastime or secular scholarly pursuit, but has significant theological implications and practical applications for the Christian."[60] Personal narratives need not attack orthodox beliefs to broaden the realm of accepted discourse.

In a similar vein, Alsup models critical self-reflection about secular feminism and humanitarian activism that is rooted in spaces and schools of thought outside the church. In a passage of *Is the Bible Good for Women?* published after her experience with Mark Driscoll and after she left his Seattle megachurch, she traces this intellectual and spiritual journey:

> Is the Bible good for women? Growing up in the conservative South, I never considered that question. I didn't understand anything of women's rights except the caricatures I saw on the news during attempts to pass the Equal Rights Amendment. But I was one of three daughters, no sons, born to a Christian dad who valued his girls well. Though I experienced my fair share of struggles growing up, female oppression in a patriarchal society did not seem to be one of them. As I grew older and watched the news with a more critical eye, a different view of women came into my line of sight. There were countries where women couldn't vote? There were cultures that would put victims of rape to death in honor killings?
>
> Then I moved to Seattle, where women's rights and feminist issues are often center stage in local news and conversation. I couldn't hide from these issues anymore. Female mutilation, legal oppression, and culturally accepted rape were much bigger issues affecting many more women worldwide than I had ever understood. And domestic abuse, the blaming of sexual abuse survivors, and discrimination in the workforce occurred closer to home. My experience of being valued as a female by the men in my life was not the norm worldwide, but I also came to realize it wasn't the norm in the conservative South either. I was bombarded by women's issues. As a believer in Jesus since childhood, and one who loved and valued the Bible, I was barraged with criticism of the Scripture around women's issues as well. Does the Bible address

> oppression of women in helpful ways? Or does it only perpetuate such oppression among its followers? In a world that is quite often very bad for women, does the Bible help or does it make it worse?[61]

Driscoll, and authoritarian evangelical rhetors like him, linger in the background of Alsup's closing questions. When she asks, "Does the Bible address oppression of women in helpful ways? Or does it only perpetuate such oppression among its followers?" Alsup redirects the debates about biblical manhood and womanhood. Instead of bringing a biblical worldview to gender, these questions bring a feminist worldview to the Bible. The important question to ask in a world with undeniable violence and discrimination against women is not, "How do we delineate and promote biblical gender roles in a secular culture?"—as conservative leaders like Driscoll or Grudem have asked. Instead, feminist movements that start from a commitment to analyzing and fighting oppression pose more urgent questions about the text's implications.

Orthodox evangelical women were not as reflective about race and sexuality in the church as they were about gender during the 2008–2018 decade. During this decade, responses to movements for social justice and the LGBTQ movement appear more in writing by the ex-evangelical, progressive, and non-white evangelical writers of my next three chapters. This relative silence might reflect their relative lack of experience with social justice movements or LGBTQ activism. It might be a strategic choice to avoid these topics in order to maintain precarious relationships with conservatives and liberals (though some readers might say that choice shows a degree of spinelessness).

One exception, though, is Trillia Newbell's *United*. Her account of being a Black woman in a white Tennessee church narrates that experience using the commonplaces of white evangelical rhetoric and the winsome tone many women feel obligated to adopt. She frames her story warily:

> I hope you'll pull up a chair next to me as I share my personal journey, reveal the hope I have, and reflect on the goodness and

> grace of God. This is not another browbeating about the past. I won't be rehashing all of the history that we already know about. And neither will I discount the difficulties of genuine diversity. If diversity was easy, we wouldn't have the problems that we're confronted with today.
>
> I'll share about the beauty of diversity that can be on display to a broken world. We will look at my life as a black female and how God fulfilled a desire of my heart through friendships. I will encourage you to know the benefits (oh, there are so many!) of being united in Christ both practically and relationally and the mutual growth acquired through fellowship with those different from you.[62]

Newbell distances her narrative from any discussion of systems and structures, instead focusing on relationships; she presents diversity in the church not as an issue of confronting racism but of realizing God's blessing. This individualism shapes her story when she describes her struggles with identity as a teen. She writes that she experienced "reverse racism" when classmates accused her of sounding "like a white girl" but healed from that rejection and confusion when, as an adult, she began going to church with a (white) friend.[63] Her story has repeated examples of becoming close friends with other Christian women who were different from her. She applies the personal Jesus paradigm to the experience of being a racial minority in the United States and in the church, casting that experience as one of individual transformation.

As Newbell tells her experiences, she makes a point to attribute goodwill to her white peers. At college, white students were confused and unsure about race but willing to ask questions and gain understanding. When she immersed herself in a white church, friends' questions about her hair and her politics ("some assumed I was a Democrat because I am black") made her feel uneasy about her obvious difference, but those questions were "innocent and well-intentioned."[64] She at times felt "lonely, isolated, and even fearful" because "there was something missing in [her] fellowship," but not because of actions or attitudes of the people there.[65] She seems to say something needed to be added, not changed. And she describes church leadership making an effort with meetings to talk about how to better serve non-white members and gospel music in Sunday worship. Becoming a Christian supplanted her anger over racism in the past and present, because she realized "that our hearts are hardwired for sin, so apart from Christ we are capable of all sorts of evil."[66] Throughout the story she repeatedly argues that bonds of shared faith are more powerful than culture or ethnicity. Change is needed, but will come from a deeper understanding of the Bible and openness to God's vision for a diverse church.

Newbell writes this at a time when evangelical churches were willing to discuss race, particularly the makeup of church congregations and leadership. The SBC has elected its first African American president, Rev. Fred Luter Jr., in 2012. Newbell reflects on her experience in the SBC and a local SBC church: "There seems to be an open dialogue about race, particularly as it relates to blacks and whites worshiping together."[67] In an October 9, 2023 episode of the *Holy Post* podcast, Jemar Tisby also looked back at this decade and commented that in the early 2010s churches seemed willing to discuss race in America and expressed a desire to have multiethnic congregations.[68] Still, as Newbell's writing of the time shows, that discussion centered on building community within the church and recovering a biblical call for diversity. An observation by Tisby suggests another reason for Newbell's tentative discussions of racism and difference. Tisby argues that "Black Christians in evangelical churches and organizations must always face the issue of limits and control based on how explicitly they address the issues—such as racism, police brutality, economic inequality, and access to quality education—in their ministry and how comfortable the white majority is with their message."[69] Newbell perhaps tempers her writing to build and maintain relationships in her church and the broader SBC. She is certainly not alone in making that rhetorical choice. Her later social media posts suggest a change, though. In 2016 she wrote, "Actually in tears after seeing someone I love post that they are voting for Trump. I can take the Christian celebrities but friends are hard."[70] In 2018 she called out Donald Trump's racist rhetoric and the claim that racism would go away if people stopped talking about it.[71] The events of 2016 and later led some women to lean further into the dynamic tension between their beliefs and conservative evangelicalism.

A Tool for Renovating Evangelical Rhetoric

Elizabeth Vander Lei's renovation metaphor feels more and more apt the longer I spend with evangelical women. The evangelical movement, with its history and rhetoric, is the "house" orthodox writers seek to renovate. Rather than tear it down or abandon it altogether, they undertake the hard work of making the structure safe and hospitable. They assess which walls are load bearing and which can be removed to create a more open floor plan; they repair leaking roofs and remove tattered carpet to reveal the original wood floors that are sometimes still in good condition.

Why is personal narrative a fitting tool to do this work? The answer differs among varying groups of women, and I parse these differences in each chapter. I argue that women who articulate an "orthodox but not conservative" evangelicalism find the genre particularly useful because it articulates knowledge alongside questions and locates both in Christian tradition. By joining a spiritual practice of "thinking narratively about individual lives,"[72] Alsup, Prior, Anderson, Byrd, and Newbell pursue a "sense of mediation and openness ('generous'), on the one hand, and, on the other . . . describe the sense of connection to doctrinal tradition ('orthodoxy')."[73]

Personal Narratives Value Experience as a Source of Knowledge

Up to this point I have highlighted the ways personal narrative can critique or hold to account conservative evangelical rhetoric and the power structures it supports. Some examples implicitly defend and promote orthodox beliefs, but personal narratives can do that explicitly too. For example, in *Housewife Theologian*, Aimee Byrd uses narrative to defend the idea of wives submitting to their husbands. She and her husband (Matt) each have a God-given mind and brain, with different gifts and thoughts. She describes what it looks like for them to complement each other: "Matt knows what my strengths are, and depends on my help in those areas. There are many daily decisions that I need to make without Matt around. Whenever I decide or do anything, I should be thinking of how this represents my husband and questioning if he would approve. And he trusts me to do this."[74] In Byrd's account of her home life, submission is neither oppressive nor unjust, and it does not devalue women's intellect. Rather than cite the Bible to defend or explain complementarianism and submission, she tells readers how she applied this teaching. The personal account does serve as evidence in the complementarian/egalitarian debate (refuting the notion that submission means passivity or the devaluing of women's minds), but it has a more powerful function in presenting complementarianism as an appealing and healthy relationship.

Telling personal narratives also teaches theology through a process called analogical imagination. Alan Jacobs defines analogical imagination as "the discovery of how different lives in different times and places belong nonetheless to the same genre."[75] Jacobs claims that the "ongoing health of Christianity" depends on this facility—the ability to, for example, "see that when Mother Teresa of Calcutta speaks to the graduating students at Harvard she is doing something very like what Paul did when he spoke in the Areopagus of Athens."[76] Personal narratives model this imaginative reading practice and teach readers to feel connections to God and to the stories of the Bible. After God gave Alsup a glimpse of his will and presence by providing Andy with a job, she wonders, "Was that how Abraham felt when he found the ram in the bushes and became the first to call God Jehovah-jireh, God-provider?"[77] This comparison sounds grandiose, and it is, but such language helps readers locate themselves in the grand narratives and capital-T Truth of evangelicalism.

Alsup's stories in *Practical Theology for Women* extrapolate theological concepts from moments in her life. When Alsup writes, "I knew beyond a shadow of a doubt that God wanted us in Seattle,"[78] she reaffirms her faith in God's power and models how readers can find providential signs in their own lives. The generosity of Driscoll and other evangelicals showed her that the "body of Christ" is made up of equal parts who suffer and rejoice with one another. Alsup offers these personal narratives to counter a common Christian belief: "that the deep things of God—doctrine and theology—are not practical, and that the practical things of the Bible are not deep."[79] Her story enacts "practical theology," her term for her conviction that "what God teaches about himself in his Word" is essential to "personal daily life."[80] For evangelical women, vivid stories of encounters with God can bring biblical concepts or passages to life. Such personal narratives transplant theology from an academic, pastoral realm closely guarded by evangelical men to a personal and subjective realm accessible to a wider readership.

Orthodox evangelical writing deploys personal narrative as a witness to God's goodness. This is a traditional use of personal narrative, as Hindmarsh explains, and orthodox writers conform to some patterns (for example, seeing God's plan unfold through hardship).[81] However, these narratives also assert that personal experience is a source of knowledge for both the rhetor and the audience. We see this in Alsup's story, which cultivates analogical imagination. In another example, Trillia Newbell places her life experience alongside biblical exegesis. In an interview on the *Christianity Today* podcast *The Calling*, she links the two:

> **Host:** I wonder if you've thought through, like, "What do people gain from reading about my life?"
>
> **Newbell:** Well, the scriptures say, "Comfort with the comfort you received from Christ," right? So what comfort have I received, I'm going to share in order to–

> **Host:** A very specific kind of comfort.
>
> **Newbell:** Yeah, incredibly specific. So it would be hard for me to say, "Oh yes, comfort from the comfort you received." I could easily say, "Okay, I'm just going to share scripture, exegetical writing, yeah I could do that." Or, I can also share personal, "Okay, this is actually how the Lord has been faithful, how I've seen Him work." And "This is what the scriptures say about that." So I like both. I think both are good and important, and each played their own role.[82]

Conservative evangelicals belong to a tradition shaped by "the conviction that belief in the inerrant truth of the Bible [is] more than a doctrine." For these believers, the Bible is "the clarifying lens necessary to rightly perceive reality, a biblical 'world and life view.'"[83] Orthodox evangelicals do not deny this belief, but—like Newbell's reflection—a generous orthodoxy makes space to appreciate spiritual, theological, and relational knowledge from experience.

Personal Narratives Question Inerrancy and Certainty

Personal narratives provide an avenue for critique and model alternatives to proof-texting and simplistic "answer manual" conceptions of the Bible. Writing from the authority of experience, rather than the certainty of literal interpretation or complete submission to mainstream teaching, they develop a type of spiritual discourse suited to their community. Through this avenue, they reach readers who have been similarly affected or alienated by fundamentalist discourse. In *Humble Roots*, Hannah Anderson points out that evangelicals fall into habits of "proof-texting, confusing principle and application, and relying on apologetics to produce faith."[84] Generous orthodoxy requires a different set of skills: thoughtful deliberation, rhetorical listening,[85] and a self-reflexive approach to one's faith. Orthodox evangelical writers express hope that these qualities can translate into productive and mutually respectful debate. Anderson explicitly advocates for an epistemological humility that clarifies "the limits of our mental categories and our ability to process ideas."[86] She explains, "Not only does humility teach us that knowledge comes from outside us, it also reminds us that we cannot perfectly categorize and process the knowledge that we do have," and contrasts this humility with modernist thinking that "rejects divine revelation and centers knowledge in the human mind."[87] If modernism fails to account for "a God whose 'ways are past finding out,'"[88] personal narratives can step in to recount and reflect on glimpses of those superhuman ways.

Alsup doesn't use the phrase "epistemological humility" but, like Anderson, she calls audiences to examine the positions from which they read. After explaining how she learned to critique evangelical attitudes toward gender (in *Is the Bible Good for Women?*), she prompts readers, "Let's examine any personal baggage we might bring to this study," and "It is helpful to acknowledge your preconceptions as you start this study."[89] Notably, she calls the book a "study," which positions her personal narrative in a supporting role. However, her own perspective models critical self-reflection and a process of forming knowledge from experience—significantly, experience gained outside the church.

Personal narratives align with orthodoxy, but that does not mean evangelicals universally recognize their value. When Jonna Petry relates spiritual abuse by Driscoll, she tries to preempt objections that she is speaking from a personal grudge and trying to ruin a good man's career. Alsup has written about fellow evangelicals being "blindsided" when she shares her experience with divorce. Her story runs counter to a version of the commonplace of God's providence that says, "Surely, if I obey God, I won't have these types of struggles in my life. Surely, if I make the right decisions in youth group and Christian college, my children will turn out right, and I'll have a happy marriage until 'death doth us part.'"[90] Conservative pastor and writer Denny Burk levels another critique of personal narrative. He says of writers like Du Mez, Byrd, and Barr, "They believe they'll win the day by appealing not to Bible or to reason but to emotion and experience." He calls "a strategy of normalization then acceptance" the same strategy "always" used to make theological error appealing.[91] Burk's critique seems driven by his antipathy to the egalitarian argument that he believes Barr, Du Mez, Byrd, and others are making (though Barr and Byrd never claim that label). If their appeals to emotion and experience served to defend submission and complementarianism, would he call the strategy illegitimate? I do not give much weight to Burk's bad-faith argument, but I include it here as an example of the resistance that personal narratives meet from some evangelical factions.

Personal Narratives Expand Biblical Manhood and Womanhood

Generous orthodoxy has implications for evangelical debates about gender. Orthodox writers portray a religious subculture that is in conflict over gender roles even as it insists that traditional readings of the Bible paint a clear picture of God's design for gender. In *Is the Bible Good for Women?* Wendy Alsup describes this conflation of conservatism and orthodoxy: "Much of God's vision for image-bearing womanhood is wrapped up in the single word *helper*. For many years, even as an earnest Christian girl hoping to grow up to be a faithful Christian woman, I secretly chafed at this concept. The word *help* didn't inspire me. It felt condescending. An image of a 1950s female secretary and her sexist, chain-smoking male boss came to mind."[92] Orthodox writers recount experiences in their own lives to clarify and nuance terms like "helper," "submission," or "God's vision for image-bearing womanhood." For some, this means distinguishing biblical teaching from cultural norms; for others, it means explaining how a pattern of male headship and female submission is not oppressive or demeaning.

These conversations about women's roles in the church and family tap into long debates about gender and authority, with high stakes. Complementarianism or appeals to biblical manhood and womanhood do more than guide family relationships and church hierarchy. Many evangelicals equate a person's stance on gender with their biblical worldview—or their concessions to destructive secularizing influences. The rise and ongoing influence of feminism is one cause for conservative evangelical defensiveness. Complementarianism emerged as an official defense of traditional gender roles during the women's movements of the 1970s. That philosophy can take on extreme expressions. In *Recovering Biblical Manhood and Womanhood: A Response to Evangelical Feminism*, John Piper and Wayne Grudem claim that any women in a position of authority "would invariably violate the essential femininity and masculinity (i.e. the essential nature) of both the woman in authority and the man in subordination."[93] Karen Swallow Prior might point out that these gender roles have roots in Victorian culture, not the Bible.

Aside from formal leadership like pastors and theologians, evangelicals do not necessarily use the terms *complementarian* and *egalitarian* to describe their values and experiences. Through multiple avenues, including written and spoken personal narratives across a range of platforms, these teachings on biblical gender roles reach believers who may not be cognizant of the theology undergirding a term like *complementarian*, its most extreme expressions, or the history of this debate. I noticed this dynamic in a conversation with my sister. She belongs to a Southern Baptist church (her pastor was elected SBC president in 2018) and holds fairly orthodox views (though not conservative ones). Despite belonging to a church at the heart of mainstream conservative evangelicalism, and even volunteering as premarriage counselor to engaged couples, she wasn't familiar with the terms *complementarian* and *egalitarian*. I offer this anecdote to illustrate the diffuse role that theological terms play in evangelical culture. Complementarianism and egalitarianism evolve from theological terms to more generalized principles that underpin debates about gender. As Ingersoll explains, "While elites formulate (and fight over) conservative Christian gender ideology, members of the subculture mold it and shape it depending on their own circumstances."[94] This gap between elites and members offers space for creativity and hope.

Orthodox evangelical women don't aim to overturn the notion that the Bible holds insight about gender. However, a generous orthodoxy leads to readings of the Bible that steer clear of the commonplaces of authority and combat that cause damage within evangelical churches. Wendy Alsup offers one such reading in a series of articles for the site *Modern Reformation*:

> I would like to argue that the warrior mentality is not the Biblical paradigm for Christian manhood, or womanhood for that matter.
>
> After the implosion of Mars Hill Church and a divorce I didn't want, I moved from Seattle, Washington to my grandparents' farm in South Carolina. My elderly father still shares crops with the farmer who rents our land. For the last six years of my life, rocking on my screened porch overlooking the fields, recovering from both my divorce and the cancer diagnosis that followed two years later, I have been detoxing from the poor discipleship around sex and gender I received at Mars Hill and the warrior mentality for Christians, particularly Christian men, of my upbringing. The fog has cleared in my brain, and the true model for Christian manhood and womanhood has become as clear in my head as it actually is in Scripture. I stare at it every day.
>
> Land. Seed. Work. Harvest.
>
> The model for Christian manhood isn't a warrior. It's a farmer. Once you see it in Scripture, you'll never unsee it. I wonder sometimes how I missed it myself for so long. *The LORD God took the man and placed him in the garden of Eden to work it and watch over it.* (Gen. 2:15)[95]

Alsup finds an alternative to the "warrior mentality" by attending even more closely to the Bible. Her generous, orthodox model could contribute to remolding evangelical masculinity among those whose allegiance is to that text and have begun to separate orthodox from conservative.

Conclusion: Teaching a Generously Orthodox Evangelical Rhetoric

In their individual writing and group deliberation, evangelicals worry over the nature and uses of rhetoric and public debate. North American culture in the twentieth and twenty-first centuries shows us many examples of evangelicals engaging in combative or authoritarian rhetoric, and many of the rhetoric scholars who take up the subject of evangelicals focus on these tendencies (like Crowley). However, in paying attention to the spectrum of evangelical teachers and writers, I repeatedly noticed their deep concern with the types of arguments evangelicals use and the consequences of their argumentative strategies. Some find hope in teaching their readers to engage texts and arguments critically.

As part of this discussion, Karen Swallow Prior advocates for evangelicals to learn to read rhetorically. From her vantage point as an English professor, she tries to teach her audience how to approach a book or article: "To read well is not to scour books for lessons on what to think. Rather, to read well is to be formed in how to think. Reading well adds to our life—not in the way a tool from the hardware store adds to our life, for a tool does us no good once lost or broken, but in the way a friendship adds to our life, altering us forever."[96] Other writers immersed in conservative evangelical culture have insight into the problematic rhetoric of public and private conversations in that community. In *Humble Roots*, Hannah Anderson teaches her readers to be critical of unethical argumentation that manipulates an audience by appealing solely to emotions:

> In *Rhetoric*, his treatise on effective persuasion, Aristotle points to the power of emotion and recommends "awakening emotion (*pathos*) in the audience so as to induce them to make the judgment desired." For Aristotle, *pathos* should be combined with *ethos* (appeal to morality) and *logos* (appeal to the mind). Working together, these elements engage the whole person; they honor the mind, the emotions, and the moral context in which we find ourselves. But, quite frankly, such robust and ethical argumentation is a lot of work. It's much easier to take shortcuts. It's much easier to simply manipulate people's emotions. Because human beings so readily act on their emotions, all you have to do is stimulate a certain emotional response, and you can lead them wherever you want them to go. That is why politicians stir up fear and greed to convince you to vote for them . . . and it is why celebrity preachers appeal to guilt and self-righteousness to solicit money.[97]

Anderson goes on to argue that "we manipulate each other in our churches, friendships, and families" because such rhetoric is easier than robust and ethical argumentation.[98] The manipulation she describes is by no means exclusive to churches, as this passage allows, and she places a preacher's "appeal to guilt and self-righteousness" in tawdry secular company. This short primer on rhetorical appeals—in both the vernacular rhetoric of lay members and the institutional rhetoric of leaders—seeks to form a more ethical and nuanced evangelical rhetoric.

Orthodox evangelical women offer rich material for feminist rhetoric scholars because they exercise rhetorical power within communities that unambiguously support hierarchy and explicitly limit women's speech. Of course, evangelicalism includes a range of positions on questions of leadership and public speech. Women who disagree with conservative theology can move to more liberal congregations; many do so because of troubling misogyny and silence or hideously insufficient responses to abuse. But evangelical women also remain in their conservative communities and seek reform based in a combination of anger and orthodox belief. From 2008 to 2018, several women opened themselves to public controversy to show where male leadership deflects responsibility and to call conservative institutions to reform.

3
Storytelling as Verbal Hospitality

In her first memoir, *Evolving in Monkey Town: How a Girl Who Knew All the Answers Learned to Ask the Questions*, Rachel Held Evans recalls how an evangelical upbringing taught her to craft and analyze arguments: "The Christian community sat perpetually on the witness stand, always ready for a fight, always ready to defend itself against the world, always ready to give an answer."[1] After college, she discovered that these rhetorical skills left her poorly equipped to respond to the concerns of real people. She realized, "People didn't argue with me about the problem of evil; they argued about why Christians aren't doing more to alleviate human suffering, support the poor, and oppose violence and war."[2] In her four bestselling memoirs, Evans describes the rhetoric she learned growing up in the church and critiques evangelical rhetorics of certainty and combat. Her personal narratives, in print and in years of blog posts, testify that these discourses drive evangelicals, particularly young believers, away from the church. She also testifies to how inadequately churches respond to genuine questions and to intellectual journeys that do not resolve with acceptable conclusions. Evans herself experienced years of faith crises and pursued theological study that ultimately dissolved her evangelical convictions. After making a public split from evangelicalism in 2015,[3] she continued to write as a former insider who understood white evangelical subculture. As a knowledgeable outsider, she gained clear insight into the movement's fault lines and blind spots.

This chapter begins by introducing Evans, her ex-evangelical ethos, and her distinct role in twenty-first-century evangelical culture. I first show how Evans situates personal narrative as a contrast to evangelical apologetics, "the art and science of explaining and defending the truth claims of Christian theism."[4] Evans recognizes the limits of such argumentation and instead explores vernacular religious creativity: "The conscious or unconscious process of negotiating beliefs that believers enact in order to make sense of their faith in relation to their social, political, cultural, discursive, and institutional contexts."[5] I conclude by delineating how Evans' memoirs model an approach to interpreting the Bible through the lenses of genre and justice, and how she teaches a form of biblical literacy that replaces the grand narratives of culture wars and objective truth.

Studying Rachel Held Evans reveals an evangelical culture deeply invested in rhetoric that is rooted in the fundamentalist-modernist controversy. Orthodox evangelical women detach conservative culture and politics from orthodox belief; progressives translate or reframe feminism and antiracism for an evangelical audience. Evans engages in a parallel, yet distinct project. She shows how that rhetoric is inhospitable to young evangelicals, creates evangelical strategies of argument that do not effectively communicate with Americans beyond the movement, and even leads some believers to deconstruct their faith. Evans uses her stories to direct readers' attention to a wide and varied evangelical landscape. The liberatory rhetoric and reading practices that she models offer hospitality to an audience on the periphery of the church and to millennials in the process of leaving the church.

"The Most Polarizing Woman in Evangelicalism"

This project of critiquing evangelical rhetoric made Rachel Held Evans, in the words of a 2015 *Washington Post* article, the most polarizing woman in evangelicalism.[6] By then she had become a prolific author of memoirs, as well as personal narratives in blogs, podcasts, and essays beginning in 2007. Her first book-length memoir, *Evolving in Monkey Town*, recounts her childhood in conservative southern evangelical culture and her early embrace of evangelical theology and rhetoric. *A Year of Biblical Womanhood: How a Liberated Woman Found Herself Sitting on Her Roof,*

Covering Her Head, and Calling Her Husband "Master" records her study of gender in the Bible and evangelical culture. *Searching for Sunday: Loving, Leaving, and Finding the Church* describes a period of painful spiritual growth and exit from evangelicalism. Evans' fourth book, *Inspired: Slaying Giants, Walking on Water, and Loving the Bible Again* weaves narratives of her own study with retellings of biblical passages that spotlight genre. Across these four books, and in blogs and social media, Evans asks readers to confront rhetoric that is destructive and gender roles that are more cultural than biblical.

Evans grew up in a church saturated with the culture wars of the 1980s and 1990s. In *Evolving* she writes, "I learned how to effectively blame everything from crime rates to suicide rates on the removal of prayer from public schools," and recalls, "I cried for hours when I learned that my paternal grandfather, a lifelong Democrat, supported Bill Clinton in 1996; I was under the impression this meant Grandpa would go to hell."[7] Evans became a prominent and controversial figure through her personal narratives that declared subversive stances on sexuality, women's leadership, and hell and salvation. Evans nonetheless remained conservative in ways that kept her relevant to evangelicals. Her memoirs affirm that humans are fundamentally in need of redemption. She details her pursuit of a deeper faith and fuller understanding of the Christian God. She does not entirely reject evangelicalism in her personal narratives, which convey the importance of her faith. They do bear out her conviction that evangelical theology and culture need to be self-critical about their political and patriarchal foundations. These facts keep her in conversation and community with evangelicals and support her ethos as a doubter who is nevertheless worth hearing. However, responses to Evans' writing reflect the radicalism of her reliance on personal narrative as a rhetorical practice. Even though many women gain access to this form of public expression, those who validate experience as a source of knowledge—both spiritual and intellectual—come under attack for transgressing traditional authority.

Rachel Held Evans deserves her own chapter in this book. Whereas the other chapters in *"I Grew Up in the Church"* trace the ways like-minded writers unite around shared goals, this one studies ex-evangelicals by focusing primarily on Rachel Held Evans. Her sustained use of personal narrative exemplifies how the form works rhetorically in evangelical discourse and her body of writing consistently probes the central concerns of this book: gender roles, biblical interpretation, the rhetoric that marks doctrinal and cultural boundaries, and storytelling as a productive and invitational practice. Finally, readers, leaders, and observers of religious culture in the United States hailed Evans as a representative ex-evangelical who held a mirror up to evangelical rhetoric. Hers was a knowledgeable outsider perspective that mainstream—and, significantly, male—leaders read and engaged in dialogue.

When Evans died in 2019 at age thirty-seven (from an allergic reaction to antibiotics during treatment for the flu), secular and Christian publications eulogized her influence on the evangelical movement. In a *Slate* article, Ruth Graham describes Evans' niche:

> High-profile female writers and speakers in American evangelicalism have traditionally focused on spiritual questions and shied away from controversy and confrontation. But Evans often used her platform to challenge male pastors and leaders. Over the years, she sparred about theology, culture, and politics with prominent Christian men including Russell Moore, John Piper, Rod Dreher, and Mark Driscoll.[8]

Graham describes Evans' public voice as simultaneously "forceful and winsome."[9] In the *Washington Post,* Katelyn Beaty celebrated "her ability to minister to millions through her blogging and best-selling books."[10] Evans created a distinctive voice through her blog, beginning in 2007. Beaty writes, "When the Christian blogosphere was mostly pastors' musings on one hand and women's devotional 'encouragement' on the other, Rachel wrote confidently that her mind was made to know God."[11] Beaty, Graham, and others recall her work as generative. In *Christianity Today*, pastor and writer Ed Stetzer wrote, "Rachel Held Evans stirred the evangelical pot in ways that were uncomfortable and distressing," and recalls, "She pointed out my logical fallacies and forced me to defend my assumptions."[12] After her death, such remembrances crystallized her place as a writer and speaker who renovated evangelical rhetoric.

An Ecological Ethos

In "Seeking Adequate Rhetorical Witnesses for Life Writing," Amy Robillard calls rhetoricians to expand our understanding of personal narrative beyond "the reductive phrase 'personal experience as evidence.'"[13] With Robillard's call in mind, I argue that Rachel Held Evans uses personal narrative in multiple ways, including to enact a feminist conception of ethos. Two conversations in feminist rhetorical studies help to explain how she built this writerly voice. First, her ethos is situated in experience and perspective, rather than in prestige or credentials. She unpacks the problems in white evangelicalism through her own account of first learning its persuasive strategies and then finding herself a target of that rhetoric. Feminist literary critic Susan Gubar proposes that memoir is rhetorically effective because it locates knowledge in situated perspectives:

> When embedded in anecdotal particularity, insights about gender and about race, ethnicity, class, age, sexuality, and nation seem to arise with more tonality and flexibility, a resonant timbre and honesty, with less reductive generalizing, than they do when cramped under the theoretical rubrics usually used to engage them. Feminist scholars have much to gain by exploring the techniques of the memoir.[14]

Evans gained a platform through her stories of churches alienating young evangelicals. These stories—her own, and those of other young Christians—give "resonant timbre" and "anecdotal particularity" to accounts of the decline of white Christian America. By "telling a story rather than arguing a legal case,"[15] Evans recasts this trend as a failure of church communities rather than impersonal, inevitable demographic forces.

While Evans doesn't hold the formal education of a theologian or the authority of a preacher, leaders call on her to explain the exodus of young adults from the church. Evans builds what Stenberg and Hogg call "rhetorical sway": "Rhetorical impact demonstrated through creating or connecting to cultural flashpoints that forward or respond to gendered issues."[16] She acknowledges that she can't "speak exhaustively about the social and historical currents that shape American religious life."[17] However, she can tell her own story, "which studies suggest is an increasingly common one":

> I can talk about growing up evangelical, about doubting everything I believed about God, about loving, leaving, and longing for church, about searching for it and finding it in unexpected places. And I can share the stories of my friends and readers, people young and old whose comments, letters, and e-mails read like postcards from their own spiritual journey, dispatches from America's post-Christian frontier.[18]

As this passage indicates, she takes seriously the stories of young Christians she meets and uses her platform to bring attention to voices and experiences other than her own.

Second, Evans builds an ethos that is ecological. By ecological, I mean she locates herself and her story in a "landscape of being with others."[19] Evans situates her story in a landscape of common evangelical and ex-evangelical experiences—the churches she attended, the biblical worldview courses she took, the books she read, and the youth group games she played. Feminist rhetoricians show that an ecological notion of ethos grounds authority in the knowledge conferred by a writer's location and the complex set of relations that inform their subjectivity.[20] That location and set of relations also conveys responsibility. Rather than use memoir to position herself as a "solitary individual, crafting [her] character to firm up reputation and persuasive power,"[21] Evans scrutinizes her place among other evangelicals. As Robillard notes, "Story shapes and directs our attention in ways [rhetoricians] have not fully accounted for."[22] I contend that Evans uses her stories to direct readers' attention to a wide and varied evangelical landscape.

One way she does this is by including other voices—as she calls them, the "dispatches" from the frontier of post-Christian America—to trace how her experience with evangelicalism is like and unlike those of her friends and readers. This ecological ethos gives her memoirs persuasive power and effects changes beyond the scope of her writing. Evans used her blog to introduce and amplify queer Christians and women of color that evangelical culture often marginalizes or explicitly silences. In 2013, she introduced Austin Channing Brown—who described herself as a blogger and counselor—and directed readers to Brown's blog and Twitter.[23] Readers who identify with Rachel's story would also encounter her "Follow Friday" blog posts highlighting transgender Christian writers or radically inclusive congregations. Evans invites readers to see the landscape of the evangelical movement as expansive—"a story bigger than ourselves, bigger than our culture, bigger than our imaginations."[24]

Studying Evans' writing shows how situated and ecological notions of authority and voice give memoir rhetorical power and explains why they meet friction within her community. This feminist rhetorical scholarship finds an unexpected parallel in evangelical debates about authority. Anglican priest Tish Harrison Warren raises questions about training and accountability in an article for *Christianity Today*:

> Where do bloggers and speakers like Hatmaker derive their authority to speak and teach? And who holds them accountable for their teaching? What kinds of theological training and ecclesial credentialing are necessary for Christian teachers and leaders? What interpretive body and tradition do these bloggers speak out of? Who decides what is true Christian orthodoxy?[25]

Warren's exigence for these questions is Jen Hatmaker's support for same-sex marriage (which I discuss in chapter 4). But both Hatmaker and Evans navigate an evangelicalism that "extols individualism but ensnares every individual in a web of clashing authorities,"[26] and build readers who listen to and respect them because they identify with their narratives, not because these writers hold any institutional authority. In this community with uncertain authority structures but clear battle lines, especially around gender, building an ethos on situated knowledge and ecological storytelling exposes Evans to criticism.

Evans takes on weighty problems, but she is funny. She admits that she was "the only teenager on the planet who enjoyed guilt-based purity lessons more than the adults giving them."[27] After leaving the church, she compares evangelicalism to "the boyfriend you broke up with two years ago but whose Facebook page you still check compulsively."[28] Her humor leavens heavy topics, disarms resistant audiences, and welcomes readers to her evangelical landscape. Along with offering an antidote to reductive forms of argument, memoir can be an antidote to abstract or self-serious religious discourse. Personal narratives can display those qualities, to be sure. But by wryly finding humor in her own actions, Evans locates herself among the worst of sinners and distinguishes theology from human subjectivity.

Apologetics and the End of White Christian America

As Evans recounts learning to read, form arguments, and debate nonbelievers, she speaks to an evangelical preoccupation with rhetoric. Her ecological, situated ethos stands in contrast to combative, winner-take-all evangelical rhetorics, particularly arguments to defend and spread the faith. Communication scholars Timothy M. Muehlhoff and Richard Langer argue that evangelicalism promotes a "culture war rhetoric" that trains people "to interpret mere disagreement as personal attack."[29] Seeing congregations shrink has heightened evangelical anxiety about communicating their beliefs to nonbelievers in "the world" and persuading members who are thinking of leaving the church. In a *Christianity Today* interview, Os Guinness says, "The Christian consensus has collapsed, and much of the rise of the so-called religious Nones is really the falling away of people who were only loosely attached to a church tradition. So there is a grand moment of clarification, and among the many things we need to clarify is our ability to communicate."[30] Nevertheless, as James Beitler III shows in *Seasoned Speech*, evangelicals rarely study the rhetorical tradition or reflect on the rhetorical practices of their churches. When they do study persuasion, that discussion is likely to be narrowly focused on apologetics.[31]

The practice of apologetics shapes evangelical rhetoric throughout the church. As my rhetorical history of the movement explains, apologetics appeals to rational argument and aims to marshal objective evidence for Christian truth claims. Theologians like Jerry Root see apologetics as valuable "to help seekers and doubters to get over the intellectual barriers keeping them from embracing faith in Christ" or for believers to "gain confidence and assurance for [their] own faith."[32] Advocates present apologetics as historical, high-minded, and unoffensive, but critics of the practice argue that it "ignores complexity in favor of easy answers, functionally assumes an outdated epistemology, or turns even the smallest disagreements into hostile conflicts."[33] Christians like Rachel Held Evans describe even more damaging effects for evangelical culture. Evans argues that combative discourse and insistence on compelling evidence drives evangelicals away from the church. She sees the decline of white Christian America—and the reasons for that decline—as a kairotic moment to illustrate the many problems with evangelical rhetorics of certainty, combat, and conversion.

A Rhetorical Education in the Church

Rachel Held Evans grew up immersed in evangelical theology and a church culture still reckoning with the fundamentalist-modernist controversy of the 1920s. When Rachel was thirteen, the Held family moved to Dayton, Tennessee. Her first memoir *Evolving in Monkey Town* takes its name from Dayton, the location of the 1925 Scopes trial. The famous trial publicized a debate about teaching evolution in public schools and furthered the split between fundamentalist and modernist schools of biblical interpretation. Evans' father taught theology at Bryan College in Dayton; Evans attended the conservative college (named for anti-evolution crusader and Scopes prosecutor William Jennings Bryan). Decades later, evangelicals continued to use evolution as a dividing line. In *Searching for Sunday* Evans recalls a professor telling the Bryan student body, "You can believe the Bible or you can believe in evolution, but you can't believe both. You have to choose."[34] By denying the fact of evolution, evangelicals created a conflict between faith and science—and between faith and reason more broadly. Evans writes:

> That recurring *choice*—between faith and science, Christianity and feminism, the Bible and historical criticism, doctrine and compassion—kept tripping me up like roots on a forest trail. I wanted to believe, of course, but I wanted to believe with my intellectual integrity and intuition intact, with both my head and heart fully engaged. The more I was asked to *choose*, the more fragmented and frayed my faith became, the more it stretched the gossamer of belief that held my world view together.[35]

Evans is not alone. A Barna Group study of young evangelicals from 2007 to 2011 found that antagonism toward science and evolution contributed to millennials leaving the church in their late teens.[36] Evans locates her story amid the "apologetics movement of the 1970s, '80s, and '90s." She was shaped by "the necessity to more effectively engage modernism and avoid embarrassments like the Scopes trial" and a "cultural withdrawal toward hard rationalism, systematic theology, and political action."[37] In this landscape, she learned an approach to studying and discussing faith that was based in certainty, the construction of a biblical worldview, and combative engagement with nonbelievers.

Churches taught Evans and other young Christians "to always be ready with an answer in defense of their faith."[38] She paraphrases the often-quoted New Testament verse 1 Peter 3:15—"but in your hearts sanctify Christ as Lord. Always be ready to make your defense to anyone who demands from you an accounting for the hope that is in you"—in several places throughout her first memoir, *Evolving in Monkey Town*. Evangelical appeals to objective truth and ready answers depend on and celebrate literal readings of the Bible. Evans and her peers "grew up with a fervent devotion to the inerrancy of the Bible and learned that whatever the questions might be, an answer could be found within its pages."[39] In *Evolving*, Evans documents her increasing discomfort using the Bible this way and the limitations of literal readings. Evans recounts one conversation with her college friend Sarah when she unburdened her doubts about evangelical teaching:

> "We just assume that little kids and mentally disabled people go to heaven," I said. "The Bible doesn't come right out and say that. So why can't we believe that people without the gospel go to heaven? What's the difference? Why won't anyone give me a straight answer on this?"
>
> Poor Sarah looked stricken, and I realized I may have pushed a little too hard.
>
> "Why don't you ask your dad?" she asked tentatively.[40]

Here, Evans portrays a moment when she understood that biblical authority and traditional male authority are intertwined. Moreover, she learned how it felt to push too hard on "an absolute difference between the saved and the unsaved."[41] By questioning this evangelical commonplace and its implications, she threatened the community and her place in it. In Sarah's response, Evans (and her readers) hear echoes of the patriarchal assumption that young evangelicals should resolve their questions about the Bible under the guidance of theologians and pastors.

As Evans traces her rhetorical education, she probes the idea of adherence to a biblical worldview that Bryan promoted. She defines worldview as "a comprehensive approach to life," including the disciplines of science, history, economics, art, psychology, politics, and literature, "in which we looked at the world wearing Christian glasses."[42] That appeal to the Bible as an all-encompassing authority facilitated arguments in which "verses were lifted from the Bible to support political positions like gun rights, strong national defense, capital punishment, and limited intervention in the free market."[43] Evans contends that insistence on the Bible as clear proof for personal and political questions (and, simultaneously, churches' failures to provide "straight answers" on the thorniest of those questions) stunts believers' growth. Parents, teachers, and theologians provided her and her peers with biblical answers "before we ever had time to really wrestle with the questions."[44] Learning to poke holes in the arguments of unbelievers equipped her to find contradictions in the answers she had learned.

Evans reached a faith crisis when she realized she was no longer asking questions about faith and salvation rhetorically or in preparation for imaginary debates, but instead as a doubter deconstructing her own faith. While biblical worldview promised clarity, this education fueled her deconstruction. "I'd gotten so good at critiquing all the fallacies of opposing worldviews, at searching for truth through objective analysis," she recalls, "that it was only a matter of time before I turned the same skeptical eye upon my own faith."[45] She discovered a second, even more damaging consequence of her training in apologetics: rationalism and ready answers distort Christian morality. Evans explains, "Not once after graduating from Bryan was I asked to make a case for the scientific feasibility of miracles, but often I was asked why Christians aren't more like Jesus."[46] Evangelical rhetoric frames faith in terms of rationality and objective truth, mistakenly believing that these are the grounds on which nonbelievers can be reached. Apologetics is not only damaging; it misses the point of faith. As Evans writes, "You can't get too far into the Gospels without noticing that Jesus made a pretty lousy apologist."[47]

In the experiences Evans narrates, evangelicals prepare answers and study worldviews in order to enter rhetorical combat. During the apologetics movement, she recalls, "Defending America from the perceived takeover of secular humanism became the purpose of the modern church."[48] Many welcome contentious debates in which they can take aim at the beliefs and reasons of their opponents. They might point to the Apostle Paul's instruction to "put on the full armor of God" in Ephesians 6. Even as children, they might encounter this rhetoric through "sword drills." Named for Paul's reference to scripture as the "sword of truth," this practice of "competitive Bible-verse finding"[49] at Sunday school and summer camps trained "young soldiers" in the basic layout of the Bible. Evans saw that many evangelicals never grew out of these sword drills. Instead, they "learned to adapt the overall technique to more adult circumstances, like theological debates, political positions, or confrontations with other Christians."[50] During her life in the church, Evans held both the offensive and defensive positions in these conflicts. In her later memoir *Searching for Sunday*, she quips, "Fun fact: more Christians were martyred by one another in the decades after the Reformation than were martyred by the Roman Empire."[51] Having seen both sides, she argues that these battles rarely advance the work Jesus modeled.

Evangelicalism trained members like Evans to take a combative posture toward non-Christians too. She and her classmates at Bryan "knew what atheists and humanists and Buddhists believed before we actually met any atheists or humanists or Buddhists, and we knew how to effectively discredit their worldviews before ever encountering them on our own."[52] At her first job after college, Evans encountered a colleague who called out this combative posture. "Sam the Feminist" remarked, "Most Christians I know are only interested in winning arguments, converts, and elections." Evans recalls how her training failed her in that moment:

> I should have been ready with an answer, but I wasn't. The truth was, I thought Sam was right. Somewhere along the way, the gospel had gotten buried under a massive pile of extras: political positions, lifestyle requirements, and unspoken rules that for whatever reason came with the Christian territory. Sometimes Jesus himself seemed buried beneath the rubble.
>
> "I know what you mean," I said. "I'm sorry that the church doesn't look more like Jesus."

> "Oh, honey, it's not your fault," Sam said. "It's probably just because it's run by men."[53]

Here, Evans invites readers to join her in laughing at the "cleavage between 'us' and 'them'" that "motivates contemporary conservative rhetoric."[54] She softens her critique with "somewhere along the way" and "for whatever reason," though she seems to know the reason. By voicing the problem through Sam the Feminist, she shows evangelicals that their carefully curated culture makes them irrelevant to the wider world. Sam the Feminist has heard their arguments and reasons, but she's just not interested.

In *Evolving*, Evans describes her family life and early faith in loving terms that contrast with the inflexible political discourse she absorbed. Her father, a theologian, was "gentle, playful, and kind." Her mother, a homemaker, was determined to avoid legalism, had a "private disdain for potlucks and church business meetings," and "got a little fidgety whenever the pastor discussed wives submitting to their husbands."[55] Evans writes of her early teenage years:

> I prayed incessantly, casting all the insecurities of adolescence at the feet of my heavenly Father, who loved me better than any boy ever could and who looked past my braces and bangs to see his beautiful, unblemished child. The Bible read like poetry to me, each word and verse ripe with spiritual sustenance. It fed me, and I swallowed without asking questions or entertaining doubts or choking on the bones.[56]

The contrast between this deeply personal, tender faith and politically charged evangelical subculture is significant for establishing Evans as not merely a critic. She experienced faith as a positive force in her own life and learned from her mother's example that believers live with complicated relationships to their churches.

Evolving in Monkey Town portrays the consequences of rhetoric that carries the weight of theology. Most significantly, that rhetoric harms and alienates many evangelicals. Evans critiques discourses of certainty, worldview, and combat by narrating their damaging effects in her own life and in the institutions she has known. She turns to personal narrative not to build a theological case against evangelical beliefs, but rather to show the effects that doctrine and rhetoric have on intellectually curious young evangelicals, and, through them, on the entire church body.

Gender

As her faith in literal readings and rational arguments unraveled, Evans questioned "biblical womanhood." She recalls the way apologetics summer camp taught this anti-feminist ideology:

> On the day we discussed gender roles, the speaker explained that the Bible serves as the single authority regarding matters of church, state, and home. Women should therefore take their cues from Scripture, as God's Word contains everything we need to know about gender identity. Feminism was decried as an abomination and blamed for societal ills such as divorce, consumer debt, and unruly children. At the mention of Hillary Clinton, the room erupted with groans and snickers from the audience. The speaker said that when it comes to dating, the Bible includes some clear guidelines. . . . For men, this means assuming the role of leader in the relationship. For women, it means stepping back to allow men to take the lead.[57]

These statements about gender demonstrate how evangelicals spin biblical texts into arguments about politics, economics, and culture. Where scripture omits detail about dating and housework, evangelicals extrapolate from principles to deliver specific guidance. Writing in 2010, Evans distinguishes between her younger self, who felt that "sexuality and ambition were liabilities in [her] relationship with men and with God," and her conviction as an adult that "womanhood, like the Bible, is far too lovely and mysterious and transcendent to systematize or explain."[58]

In *A Year of Biblical Womanhood*, her second memoir, Evans documents her project of living "in pursuit of *true* biblical womanhood."[59] During 2010 and 2011, she set out to learn how women worldwide understood and applied biblical passages. Each month she observed a different virtue—gentleness, domesticity, obedience, valor, beauty, modesty, purity, fertility, submission, justice, silence, and grace—and emulated models in the Bible. Each chapter chronicles the to-do list, research, and personal reflection of one month. For example, during month one, Evans worked to "cultivate a gentle and quiet spirit, even during football games (1 Peter 3:3–4)" by refraining from gossip and swearing, practicing contemplative prayer, and taking an etiquette lesson.[60] She also began yearlong practices: covering her head during prayer, deferring to her husband, and devoting herself to housework.

Evans shows how evangelicals like the Council on Biblical Manhood and Womanhood (CBMW) impose biblical authority onto cultural norms when they uphold "biblical womanhood" as a contrast to feminism and secular culture. Evans opens *A Year* by rejecting "biblical womanhood" as a political, selective reading of scripture. Pairing *biblical* with loaded words like *womanhood* or *politics* creates "the impression that God has definitive opinions about such things," Evans argues. She continues, "Despite insistent claims that we don't 'pick and choose' what parts of the Bible we take seriously, using the word *biblical* prescriptively like this almost always involves selectivity." She points out that it is technically biblical for a woman to be forced to marry her rapist, cover her head in church, or be one of multiple wives.[61] In this opening to *A Year*, Evans introduces her three primary critiques: the fact that "biblical womanhood" involves selectivity but condemns selectivity in others, the fact that it claims clarity and accessibility, and the fact that it treats Western politics and social norms as divine teachings while denouncing feminism as sinful human culture.

This experiment illustrates insidious constraints on women's speech, where "biblical womanhood" becomes a blunt weapon in the conflicts between different factions of the evangelical movement. In the chapter on gentleness, Evans observes that 1 Peter 3:3–4 "serves as a handy deterrent for Christian girls whose pesky questions in Sunday school or enthusiasm for the kickball field made their mamas worry."[62] She quotes readers who wrote in with their own experiences to confirm that admonitions to have "a gentle and quiet spirit" serve to silence opinionated women and bar them from leadership. Evangelicals misunderstand this text—which, Evans points out, was written with the specific audience of the Christians of Asia Minor in mind—when they give it a universal relevance rather than recognize its rhetorical context.

While her experiment and her self-regulation seem trivial (a "swear jar" for gossiping, complaining, nagging, exaggerating, or snark) the memoir narrates discoveries that counter evangelical teaching on speech. Reading beyond the "gentle and quiet spirit," Evans notes other passages in the books of Proverbs, 1 Timothy, and Numbers that name the real and damaging effects of contentious or malicious speech. Similarly, contemplative prayer helps her reframe gentleness. Practicing *lectio divina*, the monastic practice of slow reading, meditation, and prayer, brought her a powerful experience: "As I prayed, it felt as though my feet were extending through the ground, growing into long, winding roots, while my torso stretched like a trunk, my arms and fingers extending like branches. With every prayer and every silence, the image of a great tree returned to me again and again until I found myself sitting up straighter, breathing in deeper, and looking up." She adds, "What they forgot to tell us in Sunday school is that the 'gentle and quiet spirit' Peter wrote about is not, in fact, an exclusively feminine virtue, but is elevated throughout the New Testament as a trait expected of *all* Christians."[63]

A Year continues to analyze biblical womanhood through experience. Each month, Evans experiments with tasks that are useful but not mandated, like sewing. She also finds unexpected value in qualities and traits she previously thought were only worthy goals for women "who didn't care about theology or politics or changing the world."[64] For example, Evans reframes gentleness as a manifestation of integrity and self-control. Working her way through *Martha Stewart's Cooking School* leads her to realize that God "inhabits and transcends our daily vocations."[65] She discovers layers of meaning outside the biblical/secular dichotomy. Through this project, Evans calls evangelicals to see that selective, ahistorical interpretive practices constrain women's identities. During her month of studying motherhood, she reflects:

> I understand that many pastors elevate motherhood in order to counter the ways contemporary culture often dismisses the value of moms. This is a noble goal indeed, and the Church should be a place where moms are affirmed, celebrated, honored, and revered. But the teaching that motherhood is a woman's highest calling can be painful and isolating for women who remain unmarried or childless.[66]

At the time of writing, Evans was childfree with "a growing collection of fears regarding motherhood."[67] This passage is emblematic of Evans' critique: she acknowledges the evangelical desire to oppose worldly culture, offers a charitable reading of how a value or practice might nurture community and growth, but then holds up a way that value or practice actually excludes many women. Framing this study as an exploration for her own clarity and personal growth, she avoids mirroring troubling evangelical rhetoric of certainty.

A Year also names the recurring violence against women in the Bible. "Those who seek to glorify biblical womanhood" forget accounts of violence; some minimize rape, violence, and slavery as parts of a divine plan. Evans and a friend hold a ceremony to memorialize the Old Testament women "exploited, neglected, ravaged, and crushed at the hand of patriarchy":[68]

> Kristine read the story of the concubine from Judges 19 who was thrown to a mob by her husband, gang-raped, killed, and dismembered. I lit a tiny tea candle, and together we said, "We remember the unnamed concubine."
>
> Next we honored Hagar, whose banishment from the house of Abraham nearly cost her life. I read her story from Genesis 21 and a poem by Tamam Kahn titled "No Less than the Prophets, Hagar speaks." For Hagar, we set aside a damask votive, which we lit before saying together, "We remember Hagar."[69]

The ceremony represents an antidote to evangelical practices—literal interpretation, winning debates rather than exploring difficult questions—that minimize the dark stories. Evans critiques this erasure but her commemoration is even more powerful. She names and sits with the violence that the Bible records. Her ritual writes these dark stories and victims' dignity back into the evangelical landscape.

A Year of Biblical Womanhood crystallizes Evans' ethos as a writer who holds the Bible in high regard but thinks critically about evangelical mandates. Her experience of studying the Bible and living out its teachings for women leads her to conclude, "As much as we may long for the simplicity of a single definition of 'biblical womanhood' there is no one right way to be a woman, no mold into which we must each cram ourselves—not if Deborah, Ruth, Rachel, Tamar, Vashti, Esther, Priscilla, Mary Magdalene, and Tabitha have anything to say about it."[70] The memoir ultimately embraces biblical texts and argues that they are more affirming of diverse personalities, readings, and experiences than evangelical rhetoric typically allows.

Controversy

Rachel Held Evans was a subject of simmering controversy when she blogged and spoke frankly about the rhetoric and culture of the evangelical movement in North America. Along with naming the problems with "literal" interpretation, Evans confronted leaders, culture, and theology. Her blog called out theologian John Piper for proposing traditional gender roles as a solution for sexual harassment and abuse.[71] She chided "super-hip" megachurches for excluding many worshippers[72] and reproached Christian retailers for sanitizing the Christian music and book industries "while its best artists look elsewhere for publication."[73] Furthermore, her open wrestling with the ideological constructs of biblical inerrancy and "biblical womanhood" made Evans vulnerable to allegations that she did not regard scripture as the authoritative, inspired word of God.

These criticisms coalesced in controversy over *A Year of Biblical Womanhood*. To my mind, Evans arrives at conclusions that are compatible with orthodoxy. "The Bible does not present us with a single model for womanhood, and the notion that it contains a one-size-fits-all formula for how to be a woman of faith is a myth," she determines.[74] Evans explains that all readers are selective: "We all go to the text looking for something, and we all have a tendency to find it."[75] Reviews illuminate that Evans became a lightning rod, not for any claim about the Bible, but because of the type of public questioning she represented. In a review published on John Piper's *Desiring God* website, Trillia Newbell critiques the memoir:

> As I read the book, it became increasingly clear to me of one theme: God's word was on trial. It was the court of Rachel Held Evans. She was the prosecution, judge, and jury. The verdict was out. And with authority and confidence, she would have the final word on womanhood. Evans makes it clear that although she holds the Bible in high esteem as a historical document, she would warn us to be careful in attempting to use it as a guide for living out the Christian faith.[76]

I think Newbell's review misreads Evans' purpose and claims, but it also signals the strategies by which evangelicals dismiss arguments. Individuals are not to speak on their own authority or place too much confidence in their own judgments, particularly on questions about the Bible. Newbell concludes her review: "At its root this book questions the validity of the Bible. And denying the inerrancy and sufficiency of Scripture is a denial that will ultimately erode the gospel of our Savior."[77] Following the logic of orthodox interpretations, Newbell conflates the inerrancy of scripture with its authority, and then with the entire Christian message.

Kathy Keller, wife and occasional coauthor of megachurch pastor Tim Keller, likewise places questions of authority at the center of her critique. She first criticizes Evans for reading the Bible without following established rules of interpretation. More egregiously, Evans derives authority from sources outside the Bible. Keller argues, "If you say, 'Parts of the Bible express love, and other parts express power interests,' you've clearly gotten your standard and definition of love from outside the Bible—specifically, from contemporary sensibilities—and these are your ultimate authority and norm."[78] Keller goes on to say, "*You have become what you claim to despise; you have imposed your own agenda on Scripture in order to advance your own goals.*"[79] For Keller and Newbell, and the evangelical subgroups they influence, narratives or reflections on the Bible become suspect if they regard experience as a valid source of knowledge. This antipathy intensifies when a writer like Evans narrates tension between experience and scripture or objects to evangelical rhetoric. For many evangelicals, a woman's personal experience conveys insights but not authority.

In a blog post responding to Keller, Evans sets aside her self-deprecating tone and narrative rhetoric to flex her biblical literacy:

> *What is less clear to me* is why complementarians like Keller insist that 1 Timothy 2:12 is a part of biblical womanhood, but Acts 2 is not; why the presence of twelve male disciples implies restrictions on female leadership, but the presence of the apostle Junia is inconsequential; why the Greco-Roman household codes represent God's ideal familial structure for husbands and wives, but not for slaves and masters; why the apostle Paul's instructions to Timothy about Ephesian women teaching in the church are universally applicable, but his instructions to Corinthian women regarding head coverings are culturally conditioned (even though Paul uses the same line of argumentation—appealing [to] the creation narrative—to support both); why the poetry of Proverbs 31 is often applied prescriptively and other poetry is not; why Abraham, Isaac, and Jacob represent the supremecy [*sic*] of male leadership while Deborah and Huldah and Miriam are mere exceptions to the rule; why "wives submit to your husbands" carries more weight than "submit one to another"; why the laws of the Old Testament are treated as irrelevant in one moment, but important enough to display in public courthouses and schools the next; why a feminist reading of the text represents a capitulation to culture but a reading that turns an ancient Near Eastern text into an apologetic for the post-Industrial Revolution nuclear

> family is not; why the curse of Genesis 3 has the final word on gender relationships rather than the new creation that began at the resurrection.[80]

This forceful passage shows the skills Evans learned in the church and at Bryan College—she can assemble verses to support her argument that the complementarians who claim they submit to God's word in fact depend on "picking and choosing" and personal lenses as much as the egalitarians they denigrate. But rather than winning on conservative evangelicals' terms, Evans sets out to explain how "biblical" operates in evangelical conversations about gender: "By its nature, it implies clarity, simplicity, and finality. By its nature, it is immune to questions."[81] When Evans displays her mastery of biblical messages about gender, her catalog of examples undermines any claims to clarity, simplicity, and finality.

"Her Life Was Her Greatest Apologetic"

Though Evans is fluent in apologetics and biblical hermeneutics, she contends that the certainty evangelicals claim is a rhetorical tool or tactic rather than a biblical principle or a necessary foundation of faith. She turns to personal narrative as a rhetorical practice that underscores the subjectivity in biblical interpretation and application. Furthermore, she defends that subjectivity by showing that her own relationship with the Bible is both rooted and flexible, reverent and rigorous.

In *Evolving in Monkey Town*, Evans writes that "battles over biblical inerrancy" are where "the weapons of mass destruction surface."[82] She finds herself a target of those weapons in *A Year of Biblical Womanhood* and ensuing controversy. In her third memoir, *Searching for Sunday*, Evans laments the pain this rhetoric inflicts on queer evangelicals. In one scene of the memoir, she quotes a conservative pastor who spoke at a Gay Christian Network conference. He describes himself as an "antigay apologist":

> I knew every argument, every Bible verse, every angle, and every position. I could win a debate with just about anyone and I confess I yelled down more than a few "heretics" in my time. I was

> absolutely certain that what I was saying was true and I assumed I'd defend that truth to death. But then I met a young lesbian woman who, over a period of many years, slowly changed my mind. She is a person of great faith and grace, and her life was her greatest apologetic.[83]

Speaking to the conference audience, the pastor repents of his "misguided apologetics" and his later "silent complicity." He then recounts a car ride when he shared this evolution with his son, and his son responded, "Dad, I'm gay."[84] The scene reads as a tidy parable about evangelical homophobia, and it is. It also presents readers with a parable about apologetics. Rhetoric and interpretation that aim at certainty and winning arguments have devastating consequences, particularly for marginalized groups. By setting story in contrast to apologetics, Evans offers her audience "not personal experience as evidence but personal experience as starting point."[85] Encountering the lives of others—through relationships and storytelling—is a starting point to personal growth and more ethical expressions of faith.

In *Searching for Sunday*, Rachel Held Evans traces the ways evangelical belief and identity inform one another. She recalls her own teenage experience: "I knew exactly who I was: the church girl, the girl who always had a place in her youth group family, the girl on fire for God. I'm not sure I can ever calculate the value of that community, the sense of belonging and of being loved."[86] She then turns to the stories of fellow evangelicals to show that her rosy experience was far from universal. One such story comes from her friend Andrew:

> "What sort of church did you grow up in?" I asked.
>
> In response, Andrew pulled out his smartphone, scrolled through his pictures for a moment, found what he was looking for, and then handed his phone to me. On the cracked screen was a picture of the editorial page of a church newsletter. As I zoomed in closer, I could see the article was about same-sex relationships, which the author described as sickening. To the left of

> the headline, a silver-haired man in a suit and tie looked back at me with eyes that looked familiar.
>
> "That's my dad," Andrew said. "He's a pastor, and he published this right after I came out."
>
> My heart sank. For every teenager like me who knew only love and acceptance growing up in church, there were teenagers like Andrew who felt like strangers in the pews, strangers even in their own homes.[87]

Evangelical opposition to same-sex marriage spurred Evans' own decision to leave her church and, later, evangelicalism as a whole. *Searching* recounts the Bible-based cruelty that she witnessed in her Tennessee church in 2006 when the state debated a marriage protection amendment. Evans situates her own loss of faith in a place and era marked by this conflation of faith and politics.

Evangelical rhetoric of certainty resurfaces as Evans shares her concerns with her community. Her friends and professors diagnosed her crisis of faith "as a deliberate act of rebellion" and as rumors circulated, she "found [herself] on the prayer lists of churches [she] didn't even attend."[88] They imagined that apologetics could reverse her apostasy; Evans remarks, "I still have about a dozen gifted copies of *The Case for Christ* stored in my attic."[89] *Evolving* shows how apologetics left her unprepared to navigate thorny questions or differences in worldview; *Searching* continues this critique by arguing that an emphasis on combat and ready answers is wholly inadequate for engaging human complexity and diversity. When biblical evidence and rational argument are the grounds of debate, evangelical communities disregard doubt that is genuine and generative. Or, in the cases of queer Christians, certainty and combat perpetuate violence.

As Evans deconstructs her beliefs and role in evangelical communities, she introduces readers to a landscape of questioners and ex-evangelicals. That is, her own experience is not just evidence supporting her critique—it serves as a starting point for ethical engagements with diverse lives and perspectives. The larger impacts of her personal narrative are the verbal hospitality she extends to readers and the ecological ethos she creates by situating her own platform amidst fellow questioners:

> It is perhaps no coincidence that I discovered blogging around the same time [I stopped going to church], and along with it, a whole community of people from across the world who smiled back at me from the tiny avatars in the comment section and bestowed upon me, like gifts wrapped in delicate paper, two very powerful words: *me too*. Turns out I wasn't the only one struggling with doubt. I wasn't the only one questioning my church's position on homosexuality and gender roles and a whole host of other issues. I wasn't the only one who felt lonely on Sunday mornings.[90]

Using "me too" before the phrase came to be associated with activism against sexual assault, Evans introduces readers to an online community replacing the churches bound up in culture wars and damaging rhetoric. In my research on "narrative archives"—collections of stories that represent multiple voices addressing a problem or topic—I find that "collections that encompass multitudes of voices give evidence of active and growing movements."[91] For Evans, individual and collective storytelling indicates the numbers of readers who experienced alienation within their churches. From their comments on her blog, she "came to see just how much tension and misunderstanding can exist between the churched and the unchurched, particularly when we are unfamiliar with one another's stories."[92] Yet as in feminist communities, individual and collective storytelling offers a path to reckoning with past failures and building new communities.

As I analyze personal narratives by evangelical women, I remind myself that these texts change evangelical culture by reaching actual readers. That is, they work not only in abstract and collective ways, but in private, individual reading experiences. Memorials to Rachel Held Evans after she died celebrated the concrete change she brought about in readers' lives. Her personal narratives, I argue, are skilled responses to the problems of evangelical culture and rhetoric. However, as Katelyn Beaty writes, "Hers were not theoretical musings but deeply lived questions, doubts, and insights on faith that she knew in her bones."[93] Her readers could commune with fellow travelers. Evans' memoirs and online essays made visible the experience of being Christian, questioning, or ex-evangelical, so her readers "grew less alone, less afraid, in their own lives of faith."[94]

Other ex-evangelical writers join Evans in exploring the implications of evangelical rhetoric and culture for marginalized groups. In *Rescuing Jesus*, journalist Deborah Jian Lee portrays the pervasive racism in evangelical culture. While the book is primarily a journalistic study, Lee draws on her own story to make visible Asian American evangelicals, "whose experiences are frequently unseen and unheard."[95] As a teenager she attended a nondenominational, Chinese immigrant church and became a true believer. Like Evans, Lee first encountered church as life-giving. For her, church was a respite from "habitual drive-by racial slurs" that made her believe she was "worthless."[96] After this early experience, the culture wars and racial animus in mainstream white evangelical spaces surprised her. Lee describes the environment among evangelicals at her college:

> Minority students assimilated to white theology, which focused on personal piety and conversion; white worship styles, including contemporary Christian rock (think syrupy ballads set to rhythmic guitars and drums); and white evangelical culture, which bought into the capitalistic framework of conferences, merchandising, books, T-shirts, and trendy bracelets. InterVarsity sermons and Bible studies ignored traditions such as black theology and liberation theology, both of which had sprung out of the belief that the gospel calls Christians to dismantle oppressive social structures.[97]

As a leader in InterVarsity, a college ministry organization, Lee tried to address these issues by inviting speakers who could further discussions about race and social justice. White counterparts viewed her insights as trivial; some perceived her concerns as steering the group away from the core gospel. Others maintained that

InterVarsity had no problems related to race. "Nobody was hostile, but they were dismissive," Lee writes.[98]

Lee ultimately left evangelicalism because she encountered a consistent unwillingness to genuinely engage diversity of thought, experience, and identity. She describes her attempts to "change this subculture from within" as "naïve."[99] When she initiated study of the history of racism in the church, friends asked "why [she] needed to talk about race so much, or questioned whether [her] racial identity had become more important than [her] identity as a Christian." Fellow InterVarsity members responded to her liberal views on gender and sexuality by asking, "Are you even a Christian anymore?"[100] Like Evans, Lee portrays her deconversion as a long process driven by the rigidity of other believers. While evangelicals are aware of the data on American church demographics, Lee's story demonstrates exactly how much this decline has to do with willful ignorance and racial resentment of white evangelical communities.

Lee and Evans are discouraging to read at times. Both show how evangelical rhetoric minimizes social justice activism and bolsters theology that centers white, straight, male perspectives. Even as they employ the testimonial rhetoric that evangelicals prize, these writers struggle to persuade mainstream churches and organizations to approach diversity of beliefs and backgrounds with humility. And evangelical women of color fight a print industry that promotes white authors and a marketplace that rewards white perspectives. Lee and Evans find greater success, and perhaps more long-term influence on the future direction of evangelicalism, by writing for a younger generation. Both cite numbers of young evangelicals leaving their churches, and both recount their own lives to give this data resonance. For young readers in precarious relationships to their faith communities, Lee and Evans offer narratives that might replace the rhetoric of certainty and combat with the invitational rhetoric of personal story.

Evans writes a deconversion memoir, not a secularization memoir. Faith remains an organizing principle in her life and *Searching* traces her work to build a new spiritual home. She never fully succeeds, and the memoir concludes with an expansive vision that decenters church:

> God surprises us by showing up in ordinary things: in bread, in wine, in water, in words, in sickness, in healing, in death, in a manger of hay, in a mother's womb, in an empty tomb. Church isn't some community you join or some place you arrive. Church is what happens when someone taps you on the shoulder and whispers in your ear, *Pay attention, this is holy ground; God is here.*[101]

Teaching Biblical Literacy

Reading *Searching for Sunday* through a lens of feminist rhetoric, we see Evans discover that "the personal may be political, but the difficulties for women that feel personal are actually systemic."[102] The censures leveled against her are tendrils of pervasive evangelical rhetoric that marginalize all who are not straight, white, male adherents to orthodoxy. In her final book, *Inspired: Slaying Giants, Walking on Water, and Loving the Bible Again*, Evans proposes a systemic answer. To replace close analysis of individual verses, she models holistic readings of poetry or narratives; in place of apologetics, she teaches her readers critical imagination. She proposes reading practices that center genre and power structures to begin correcting hierarchies and oppression in evangelical culture.

Evans opens *Inspired* by revisiting her education in an evangelical worldview, which met her questions with minimization, justifications, and suspicion:

> The harder my fellow Christians worked to minimize my objections, the more pronounced these objections became. Beneath all the elaborate justifications for Israel's ethnic cleansing, all the strange theories for where Cain got his wife and how Judas managed to die in two different ways ("he hung himself and *then* fell headlong onto the ground") I sensed a deep insecurity. There was a move-along-nothing-to-see-here quality to their arguments that only reinforced my suspicion that maybe the Bible wasn't magic after all, and maybe, deep down, they

> knew it. Instead of bolstering my confidence in the Bible, its most strident defenders inadvertently weakened it.[103]

This retelling foregrounds evangelical rhetoric about the Bible—not the Bible itself—as a stumbling block. Writing as an ex-evangelical now at peace outside that community, Evans sees her experience as an exigence for teaching new reading practices. *Inspired* teaches rhetoric not in the sense of "formal instruction in writing or speaking" or "classical rhetoric," but in line with the definition Gold and Hobbs offer: "education designed to promote rhetorical competence, be it writing, speaking, reading, listening."[104] Evans continues a feminist tradition of informal rhetorical education. Feminist rhetoricians like Shirley Wilson Logan, Jane Donawerth, and Kristen Garrison have uncovered nontraditional sites where women educated themselves and others in rhetorical tactics and practices.[105] Evans envisions memoir as a tool to teach liberatory reading practices like analysis of genre, reflection on power, and critical imagination.

Genre

Evans suggests that evangelical rhetoric of the Bible, particularly its deployment as a weapon in political debates, is based in misidentification of genre:

> If the Bible of my childhood functioned as a storybook and the Bible of my adolescence as a handbook, then the Bible of my young adulthood functioned as an answer book, or position paper, useful because it was *right*. The Bible, I learned, was the reason why Christians voted for Republicans, rejected evolution, and opposed same-sex marriage. It was the reason I could never, as a woman, be a pastor, the reason I should always, as a woman, mind my neckline.[106]

Evans names three genres here: storybook, handbook, and answer book. As Carolyn Miller's foundational essay explains, genres have less to do with "the substance or the form of discourse" than with "the action it is used to accomplish."[107] Reading the Bible as handbook or answer book leads believers to fixate on its reliability and accuracy, the qualities that make the text a foundation for politics, family life, and personal morality. Instead, *Inspired* brings the narrative nature of the Bible into focus: the book of Job is retold as a screenplay, the story of Jesus walking on water is retold as a modern-day choose-your-own adventure story from the point of view of an apostle in the crowded boat. Between these "creative retellings of familiar Bible stories," Evans explores biblical genres like "War Stories" and "Resistance Stories" and offers reflections from her life that invite readers "to consider how their stories intersect with those of the Bible."[108] Through these genre explorations, she hopes to show readers new ways "to participate in the actions of a [faith] community."[109]

In "The Letter," Evans imagines a young and poor woman named Aelia who hears Paul's letter to the Colossians read aloud in a home church (*ekklesia*) in first-century Laodicea. In this narrative, the hostess reads the letter aloud, including Paul's instructions, "Wives submit yourselves to your husbands," "Husbands love your wives," and "Masters provide your slaves with what is right and fair, because you know that you also have a master in heaven."[110] Aelia notices as listeners recognize the familiar Roman household codes, murmur at the strange mention of love, and "erupt" at the "subversive" suggestion that enslavers have a master themselves. After the reading, women discuss the letter over a meal, and Aelia reflects that the ekklesia revealed "insight, wisdom, and leadership in her mother-in-law once obscured by lowly status and rural accent."[111] This imagined scene underscores that Paul's writings were letters—read aloud, crafted for a distinct audience and purpose, and understood through discussion and debate where women participated as emboldened members of the community.

Inspired prompts readers of the Bible to consider rhetorical situations and authorial decisions. Evans asks evangelicals to acknowledge that "the authors of Scripture, like the authors of any other work" wrote with agendas and "wrote for a specific audience for a specific religious, social, and political context, and thus made creative decisions based on that audience and context."[112] For readers who maintain that God is the author, Evans points out that God chose to speak in languages and forms that humans would understand. Such a rhetorical reading does not devalue the Bible. As Evans asserts, it leads her to a deeper relationship with God and greater love for the text. Uncertainty only diminishes the Bible for those who use it to win arguments, converts, and elections.

Power

For Evans, reading the Bible as an answer book fostered a damaging complicity in conservative politics. Those selective readings mean that "in many states, you can still get fired from your job for simply being gay, but you can be a serial womanizer who brags about grabbing married women 'by the pussy' and still get elected president."[113] *Inspired* reflects her anger with readings that justify violence and hierarchy:

> The more time I spent seeking clarity from Scripture, the more problems I uncovered. For example, why did my church appeal to Paul's letter to Timothy to oppose women preaching from the pulpit, but ignore his instructions to the Corinthians regarding women covering their heads (1 Timothy 2:12; 1 Corinthians 11:6)? How could we insist the Bible is morally superior to every other religious text when the book of Deuteronomy calls for stoning rebellious children, committing genocide against enemies, and enslaving women captured in war (Deuteronomy 20:14–17; 21:18–21)?[114]

Evangelical groups like the CBMW claim to see a clear pattern for human relationships laid out in scripture. Evans undermines those claims, since "with Christ, hierarchical relationships are exposed for the sham that they are, as the last are made first, the first are made last, the poor are blessed, the meek inherit the earth, and the God of the universe takes the form of a slave."[115] Retellings like "The Letter" unpack the context for biblical passages about gender and marriage; they also imagine the meanings those texts might have held for the original, multiple marginalized listeners rather than contemporary white evangelicals.

In print and online, Evans asks readers to recognize their interpretive frameworks. In *Inspired*, she explicitly links interpretive frameworks to readers' positions in structures of power. Evans reflects on ways her race and class limited her ability to interpret and apply the Bible:

> I grew up in a world where every pastor I knew was white and male, every theologian I admired came from Western cultures, every Bible study I attended was held in sprawling suburban homes. Rarely did I hear the words of Scripture spoken in an accent other than my own, and when it came time to color the faces of Moses, Mary, and Jesus in my coloring books, I reached for "peach." As a result, I failed not only to see important patterns of oppression and liberation in the Bible, but also in the world around me. I remained complicit in systems of injustice that hurt my neighbors of color, and those with disabilities, and those living in the developing world because I hadn't learned to center their stories, to see things from their point of view.[116]

Personal narrative gave Evans a platform as an evangelical (now ex-evangelical) voice, and in *Inspired* she acknowledges that her limited experience meant she should seek out the theological insights of non-white and non-Western women. During a 2019 interview on *The Bible for Normal People* podcast, she quips, "Being a white dude at a Baptist seminary is actually also a social location."[117]

Evans also makes a case for understanding the Bible—both its stories and the interpretive practices that Christians learn—in relation to antiracist activism. For *Inspired*, she reads from authors like Wilda Gafney (*Womanist Midrash*), Delores S. Williams (*Sisters in the Wilderness*), James Cone (*God of the Oppressed*), and Nyasha Junior (*An Introduction to Womanist Biblical Interpretation*) instead of white dudes at Baptist seminaries. They inform her rereading of Hagar—the only person in the Bible to name God—as an origin story for "the millions of black and brown people whose names the world has forgotten but whose God never failed to see."[118] "Resistance Stories" begins with Bree Newsome removing the Confederate flag from the South Carolina capitol. Evans describes the Old

Testament book of Esther as "a resistance story" that reminds readers "a misogynistic king running a dangerously dysfunctional superpower is nothing new, and nothing God can't handle."[119]

Critical Imagination

Inspired models an uncertainty that is neither shaky nor weak. Questions about violence and misogyny did not lead Evans away from the Bible, but rather into it. She writes, "I decided to face the Bible's war stories head on, mind and heart fully engaged, willing to risk the loss of faith if that's where the search led."[120] *Inspired* builds on the "serious but not literal" interpretation of the Bible that Christians like Marcus Borg have theorized. Evans proposes a stance toward the Bible that regards that text as "mythic, yet real; true, yet more than true."[121] She sees the logic in treating the Bible as "an entirely human construction, responsible for more vice than virtue."[122] This "true, yet more than true" interpretation Evans teaches looks quite a bit like *critical imagination*, the feminist methodology that Jacqueline Jones Royster describes in *Traces of a Stream* and discusses further, with Gesa Kirsch, in *Feminist Rhetorical Practices.* Critical imagination begins with gathering evidence and then thinking "between, above, around, and beyond this evidence" in order to "look beyond typically anointed assumptions in the field in anticipation of the possibility of seeing something not previously noticed or considered."[123] This methodology finds an echo in Wilda Gafney's *Womanist Midrash*, which Evans cites: "Midrash interprets not only the text before the reader, but also the text behind and beyond the text and the text between the lines of the text."[124] In historical work—or in biblical interpretation—"this process involves interrogating the contexts, conditions, lives, and practices of women who are no longer alive to speak directly on their own behalf."[125]

Evangelicals who ground their faith in certainty or write off Evans as an apostate might reject these reading strategies.[126] Indeed, Evans names her audience: questioning evangelicals who "find themselves navigating the great chasm between Scripture as they learned it and Scripture as what it actually is."[127] As *Searching for Sunday* and demographic research explains, that audience comprises a substantial percentage of evangelicals. For these readers, she unpacks judgments like "biblical" long used to approve, elevate, or silence voices. *Inspired* instead conveys how story and nuance operate in the Bible to create meaning. Evans shows her audience how to savor story and nuance so that "the sacred text becomes a crucial point of contact, a great dining room table, erected by God and set by God's people, where those who hunger for nourishment and companionship can gather together and be filled."[128] But she also challenges them to understand if they "belong to the privileged class of the most powerful global military superpower in the world" they might struggle to "relate to the oppressed minorities who wrote so much of the Bible."[129]

Conclusion: Rhetorical Hospitality

Evans draws on her situated, ecological ethos to expand the role storytelling holds in the evangelical movement and evangelical discourse. As an evangelical, she found that the cramped theological rubrics holding sway in her community, like apologetics and biblical literalism, offered little to help her work through her questions. As a feminist, she maintained that her subjective experience had meaning, including her doubts about the Bible's violence toward women and the church's suffocating emphasis on heterosexual marriage and motherhood. And as a writer, Evans found that the anecdotal particularities of stories, like Sam the Feminist or Andrew the pastor's son, resonate with readers seeking flexibility and honesty. In her memoirs and the reading practices that grow out of her experience, personal narrative serves as more than evidence for her critiques of evangelicalism. Personal narrative illustrates the harms of evangelical rhetoric, models alternatives to that rhetoric, and enacts verbal hospitality. Evans validates a reader's lived experience and subjectivity in place of assertions about objective truth. After her death, fellow evangelicals commemorated the hospitality her work extends to readers left hungry and lonely by evangelical rhetorics of certainty and combat.

Debates over Rachel Held Evans and her writings point to a simmering dispute about the value of personal narratives, especially those by women. Evangelicals value personal accounts—like testimonies and conversion stories—but do not afford them the authority that they afford to supposedly objective analyses of scripture. The orthodox writers I examined in chapter 2 distrust the "fallen" self and call readers to submit to biblical truth. In the controversy over *A Year of Biblical Womanhood* we see how orthodox writers responded to one personal narrative that claims the validity of experiential knowledge. In *Inspired*, Evans describes "the deleterious snare of fundamentalism" that she internalized as a young Christian:

> [Fundamentalism] claims the heart is so corrupted by sin, it simply cannot be trusted to sort right from wrong, good from evil, divine from depraved. Instinct, intuition, conscience, critical thinking—these impulses must be set aside whenever they appear to contradict the biblical text, because the good Christian never questions the "clear teachings of Scripture"; the good Christian listens to God, not her gut.[130]

Where evangelicals holding to a biblical worldview find a dangerous reliance on the subjective self, Evans and her readers find resonance and honesty.

Evans expands the rhetorical possibilities of two evangelical identity scripts: conversion narratives and the "I grew up in the church" trope. Her memoirs recount her "fallenness," moments of realization and repentance, and the work of building a new and redeemed life. However, Evans names inerrancy and winner-take-all argument—her "death grip" on "certain theologies and interpretations of Scripture"—as her sinful error.[131] Her epiphanies come when she confronts thorny texts and alienating consequences of evangelical rhetoric. Finally, her path to a redeemed life leads her away from the commonplaces of white Christian America and toward a willingness to learn from feminism, women of color, and the LGBTQ movement. Evans reenvisions a redemptive narrative arc that welcomes readers' questioning and asks them to reenvision their relationships with religious authorities and with the ideological enemies of the evangelical movement.

4
The "Resisterhood" of Progressive Evangelical Women

Demographic changes and political turmoil among American evangelicals from 2008–2018 revealed diversity within that movement and the presence of dissenters who disrupt evangelical commonplaces. Some, like Jen Hatmaker, already had wide followings but were largely known for writing that did little to challenge mainstream evangelicalism. In this decade, their commentaries on evangelical subculture found an audience as they circulated in social media, blogs, and memoirs. In these personal narratives, progressive voices advance pointed critiques of evangelical ideology. One such activist and writer, Austin Channing Brown, calls attention to the pernicious racism in North American evangelicalism in a 2016 blog post:

> Surely, if we were truly against everything Trump embodies, his campaign would never have gotten off the ground. Instead it appears to be sweeping the nation. And its [*sic*] not because Trump is so charismatic that he has seduced people. Its [*sic*] because Trump is saying out loud what has been nurtured in America (well, for centuries but) especially in the last few years of Obama's presidency.[1]

Brown's reflection points to the racist origins of evangelicalism and poses a question that other pastors, writers, and scholars would echo: How do evangelicals actually translate their beliefs into rhetoric and practice? While orthodox and mainstream voices express their hope for the church to move toward harmony and reconciliation, progressive evangelicals call for a more serious reckoning with the racist and sexist elements of white evangelicalism and the doctrinal foundations that support them.

Those influential progressive writers use vernacular rhetoric based in narratives of personal experience to promote alternatives to the evangelical rhetoric I lay out in chapter 1. Chapter 2 shows that some evangelical women tell their stories to clarify and defend orthodoxy but understand that goal to include calling out the misogyny that betrays Christian belief. Chapter 3 analyzes ex-evangelical narratives and the alienating effects of evangelical rhetoric. This chapter takes up progressive writers who pursue a third goal: they remain within evangelical communities but destabilize mainstream evangelical discourses of gender, race, and biblical authority. I focus on Sarah Bessey, Austin Channing Brown, and Jen Hatmaker, three representative writers who address gender, race, and the politics of personal narrative. Even more importantly, they tackle the difficult work of addressing conflicted or resistant audiences; for example, they criticize the Religious Right to readers immersed in that very culture and ask white readers to understand how white supremacy pervades churches and ministries. They do so while projecting a winsome persona. On Facebook, Jen Hatmaker shared a photo of herself in a camouflage-print trucker hat emblazoned with "resisterhood"—a play on the "resistance" label that liberals claimed during the Trump administration. Each writer builds influence by situating herself firmly within an evangelical ethos and creating community in spaces—and around topics—that traditional thought leaders neglect.

These progressive evangelicals are recent figures in a long line of women rhetors who navigate gendered constraints to stake out positions their conservative religious communities find radical. I begin this chapter with a section outlining their biographies and publications, followed by a section that draws out common threads in the ways this group uses personal narrative. The third section contextualizes them in a tradition of progressive feminist religious rhetoric. This chapter then goes on to examine how they craft subversive arguments about gender roles, their stances on biblical authority, and the ways they accommodate the shifting values and worries of evangelical audiences in North America. I conclude by articulating what I call a "memoir consciousness." Progressive writers make their greatest impact in teaching readers how to adopt an invitational rhetoric and value subjective experience—a needed complement to evangelical rhetoric of recent decades.

Prominent Progressives

Sarah Bessey

In books like *Jesus Feminist*, Bessey confronts evangelical conversations about gender head-on. She describes *Jesus Feminist*, her first memoir, as a book that "engages critically with Scripture and church practices that are often used against full equality and shares how following Jesus made a feminist out of her."[2] In her second book, *Out of Sorts: Making Peace with an Evolving Faith*, she claims a "narrative theology." Bessey explains, "I'm usually just wanting to write what I think and experience about God and the best way I know how to do that is through story-telling."[3] She encourages grassroots storytelling, too. In April 2017, she introduced the hashtag #ThingsOnlyChristianWomenHear, which created a space for women to tell stories of misogyny, abuse, sexism, and rape culture in the church. After graduating from evangelical liberal arts college Oral Roberts University, Bessey and her husband lived in Texas where he worked in church ministry. She now writes from slightly outside the United States evangelical context—she and her family live in her native Western Canada—but draws upon her experiences as a pastor's wife in that culture.

Austin Channing Brown

Brown published her book-length memoir *I'm Still Here: Black Dignity in a World Made for Whiteness* in 2018. This memoir recounted her childhood, her experience as a Black student studying business and social justice at white universities, and her work at the evangelical nonprofit City Door where she organized student service trips in Chicago's Garfield Park neighborhood. In summer 2020, *I'm Still Here* earned another wave of attention for its portrayal of the white, middle-class evangelicalism that contributed to rising racial hostility. That year, the memoir was a *New York Times* bestseller and a choice for Reese Witherspoon's book club, expanding Brown's audience and visibility as a progressive evangelical writer. Before *I'm Still Here*, Brown had written for evangelical publications like *Christianity Today* and *Relevant* magazines and had built a career in evangelical organizations. Brown's writing draws on her experience as a staff member specializing in racial reconciliation at Willow Creek Community Church, a megachurch and hub for evangelical leadership training outside Chicago, and as a Resident Director at Calvin College in Grand Rapids, Michigan.

Jen Hatmaker

Hatmaker is a prolific writer, serial memoirist, and popular speaker. With her then-husband, Brandon Hatmaker, she founded the Austin New Church, a cross-denominational church with a stated commitment to the underserved in Austin, Texas. Readers encounter her life writing in her blog, her social media posts, and in her books, which include *Interrupted: When Jesus Wrecks Your Comfortable Christianity*, *For the Love: Fighting for Grace in a World of Impossible Standards*, and *Of Mess and Moxie*. She invokes women as her audience, writing, "Girls, you make up the brunt of my mission on this planet."[4] Hatmaker's lively self-narration mixes hyperbole, self-deprecation, and conversational references to her five children, college football, and popular culture. Her popularity as a writer led to even greater visibility through talk show appearances, an HGTV home renovation show, speeches at women's conferences, and her *For the Love* podcast.

These three women writers are far from alone as progressives in the evangelical movement. Two other white women in particular, Shauna Niequist and Glennon Doyle, published best-selling memoirs and built platforms that reach both devout and loosely affiliated or culturally evangelical women. Niequist's books *Bittersweet*, *Bread and Wine*, and *Present Over Perfect* recount her experiences as a pastor's wife and staff member at megachurches. Doyle tells her story of parenting, sobriety, marriage, and divorce in her blog *Momastery* and in memoirs *Carry On, Warrior* and *Love Warrior*. In 2017, Doyle came out as a self-described queer evangelical woman and began dating soccer player Abby Wambach (whom she later married). Memoirs by Black women have also called evangelicalism to reckon with persistent racism. These include *Undivided: A Muslim Daughter, Her Christian Mother, Their Path to Peace* by Patricia and Alana Raybon, *Bipolar Faith: A Black Woman's Journey with Depression and Faith* by Monica Coleman, and *Shalom Sistas: Living Wholeheartedly in a Brokenhearted World* by Osheta Moore. Bessey, Brown, and Hatmaker represent a growing number of women articulating a progressive evangelicalism and the rhetorical and doctrinal significance of sharing lived experiences.

Outlining a Progressive Evangelical Rhetoric

Progressive writers navigate the constraints and affordances of evangelical rhetoric to address three issues in particular: gender roles, interpreting and applying the Bible, and social justice. In each of these discussions, progressives distinguish their views from established leaders and envision a church in which practice and doctrine evolve through conversation with secular movements. Their feminist rhetorical practice of personal narrative includes and defends postmodern approaches to truth to remake the orthodox evangelical practices of witnessing and exegesis that alienate many within the church.

Like orthodox writers, these women draw upon the spiritual autobiography tradition, but use the form to engage readers who reject mainstream feminism or liberal theology. As they balance loyalty and critique, progressive evangelicals negotiate identities and affiliations like "feminist," "conservative," and even "evangelical." Knowing that many evangelicals raise their eyebrows at references to feminism, writers qualify their use of the term. In a *Christianity Today* interview, Bessey distances herself from the label and describes *Jesus Feminist* as "less a book about Christian feminism and more about the kingdom of God, and what it means to move with God to rescue and restore and redeem women on a global scale."[5] Knowing that evangelicalism carries associations with bitter culture wars and white supremacist thought, many distinguish their faith from the activism of the Religious Right. In her 2016 book *For the Love*, Hatmaker acknowledges her participation in conflating faith and culture:

> It has taken me forty years to assess the difference between the gospel and the American evangelical version of the gospel. Those were one and the same for ages—no take-backs, no prisoners, no holds barred. I filtered the kingdom through my upper middle-class, white, advantaged, denominational lens, and by golly, I found a way to make most of it fit! (It was a complicated task, but I managed. Please be impressed.)[6]

Their personal narratives do not forward overtly feminist agendas, but they consistently name and undermine patriarchal ideologies. In confessional moments like Hatmaker's account of growing up in a white middle-class church, progressive evangelicals testify to the blind spots and distortions in the theology and rhetoric of the movement.

In Hatmaker's passage, we also see the characteristic "sisterly" style of this group. She names the role race and class play in distorting Christianity but couches her critique in self-deprecating humor. A tradition of testimonies and confessions, placing the writer or speaker among the worst of sinners and then narrating their reform, serves as the antecedent genre for these personal narratives. They adapt this pattern for new purposes. The blindness they describe is not only personal sin but a failure to recognize collective sin and injustice; they are "found" not only by converting and building a relationship with God but by recognizing the failures of white Christian America. Writers who frame their critiques as storytelling adopt a pillar of shared evangelical discourse and a norm of evangelical women's culture. They expand the traditional uses of this form, though, when they engage audiences who are used to rejecting feminism, marriage equality, and movements for racial and economic quality—and are used to citing the Bible as they do so. Narrowing the gulf between feminist and evangelical worldviews, therefore, requires that progressive writers tread carefully as they nuance their positions on biblical authority and reinterpret passages about gender and justice. Some evangelicals express ambivalent or flexible views of traditional gender roles, but biblical inerrancy is a distinguishing tenet of that movement. Fundamentalist or combative forms of argument and persuasion appeal to this certainty but personal narratives model joyful feminism and faith.

A Tradition of Progressive Evangelical Women

Progressive evangelical women offer a socially engaged rhetoric to replace the adversarial discourse common in the evangelical movement during the twentieth and twenty-first centuries. In "The Last Temptation," Michael Gerson describes "the primary evangelical political narrative" in this period as "an angry tale about the aggression of evangelicalism's cultural rivals":[7] namely, social justice, secularization, and sexual revolution. Whereas nineteenth-century evangelicals advocated for abolition, prison reform, and humane treatment of the mentally disabled, twentieth-century evangelicals divided over evolution and literal or historical biblical interpretation. As my history in chapter one discusses, many leaders, including Billy Graham, declined to support civil rights; others opposed antiracism movements. For Gerson, this recent history and public face represent a "fall from a great height." While evangelicals are the largest religious demographic in the country, they regard themselves as "a besieged and disrespected minority." As a result, their public voice is "off-puttingly apocalyptic" and leaders compromise moral values to maximize their access to political power.[8]

As feminist rhetoricians have shown, women were prominent in the nineteenth-century social movements that created this "great height" of North American evangelicalism. Preachers Phoebe Palmer and Frances Willard advocated for antipoverty, temperance, and abolition movements; they gained reputations as celebrated speakers.[9] Contemporary progressives join these long traditions of evangelical women's preaching, faith-based activism, and spiritual autobiography—a tradition that in fact formed the foundation of American Protestantism. Scholars of feminist rhetoric like Bizzell, Shaver, and Donawerth have mapped the relationship between the church, women's social activism, and their rhetorical development. However, this research on sermon rhetoric and struggles for official leadership positions primarily focused on a group of iconoclastic women and their strategies to gain access to the pulpit before the twentieth century. By studying the religious rhetoric of lay writers and more recent contexts, we can see how the progressive evangelicalism of the nineteenth century creates a tradition and precedent for twenty-first-century reformers. In these vernacular forms of writing and speaking, and in these contemporary spaces, a wider group of women exercise rhetorical influence than previous research has shown.

An Evangelical Vision of Feminism

Hatmaker and Bessey speak directly to complementarian mandates and both begin their discussions of gender with observations, memories, and introspection. The debate over complementarianism and egalitarianism provides one reference point for their arguments. However, neither writer feels obligated to fit within—or defend—one camp or the other. Instead, they depart from many evangelical writers in that they do not always feel obligated to support their claims with biblical exegesis. Narrative provides a more appropriate tool to introduce and analyze problems and to bring conversations about marriage and ministry, "the prime points of disagreement between the two schools of thought,"[10] in line with the lives of most women. Jen Hatmaker summarizes her experiences in complementarian church culture:

> Spiritually, I grew up with mixed messages regarding a woman's worth. Church taught that women were great in their place, but that place was pretty narrow. My mothers and grandmothers were incredibly capable and smart. I never understood their small place in the kingdom when they occupied such enormous

> space in my development. Their collective skill set was stunning: they were teachers, entrepreneurs, business-owners, courtroom professionals, realtors, administrators. They led at home and at work, but I didn't see their authority translate to church.[11]

Hatmaker takes care to foreground her evangelical worldview while testifying to these rigid distinctions in roles for women. She treats this complementarian model—which affirms patriarchal gender roles and excludes women from leadership and teaching—as a phenomenon of the past, portrays women's exclusion from formal leadership as a paradox and a waste, and does not step beyond her own observations. Distancing herself from feminist critiques of systemic oppression and injustice, Hatmaker uses evangelical language like "the kingdom" to reframe sexism as an unwise restriction on individual spiritual gifts and calls to serve God.

Bessey aspires to sketch an alternative to debates about complementarianism and egalitarianism that reflects this lived reality. For Bessey, "the unique experiences of humanity" show these "dogmatic labels, while sometimes useful for discussions in books and classes, aren't always the right boundaries for a life or a relationship."[12] She offers her own marriage as an example. The mutuality she and her husband enjoy is "very different than the traditional and stifling language of roles, headship, submission, and soft patriarchy found within many Christian marriage books and seminars."[13] Bessey quotes the questions and judgments that evangelicals raise in conversations about such a marriage:

> *Well, who is in charge here?*
> We are.
> *Yes, but if push comes to shove, who is the leader?*
> We are.
> *But then who is the spiritual head of your home?*
> Only Jesus. Only ever our Jesus.[14]

Her "Jesus Feminism" emphasizes the example of Jesus and the "trajectory of *redemption*" in the Bible.[15] Rather than align with liberal or conservative camps, she contends that "most of us live somewhere in the in-between."[16] Bessey describes that third possibility as rooted in love and in the woman-friendly teachings of Jesus. She writes, "God had a global dream for his daughters and his sons" and contrasts God with male leaders Grudem and Piper when she asserts that dream "is bigger than our narrow interpretations or small box constructions of 'biblical manhood and womanhood' or feminism."[17] She notes that New Testament accounts show him paying attention to figures like Mary, Martha, the woman caught in adultery, and women who approached him seeking healing.[18]

Progressive evangelical women write in—and for—a movement that increasingly recognizes women as equal but largely still limits their opportunities to teach and speak. Prejudice against women's teaching persists in American Protestantism, even in those denominations that do ordain women, and male preachers and evangelical popular culture emphasize traditionally male metaphors and masculine qualities in delivery.[19] One effect of this masculinized evangelical discourse is to reinforce women's exclusion from teaching and leadership. Cope argues that the gendered nature of sermons leaves a "significant gap in evangelical discourse: preaching that appeals to evangelical women."[20] Progressive writers reach national prominence by meeting this need for expanded women's ministries. They address this gap in evangelical discourse and these parameters around acceptable speech by crafting personal narratives. These situate radical teaching and biblical interpretations alongside observations and memories that register as more traditionally feminine in evangelical subculture. When Bessey describes her own marriage and her vision of God's "global dream for his daughters," she does not dive into detailed exegesis of biblical texts pertaining to gender, as feminist theologians like Hardesty have done. Instead, she deploys the invitational rhetoric of storytelling to set readers at ease with the idea of inherent feminism in the teachings of Jesus.

In response to "muscular Christianity," progressive writers highlight the foundational role that women play in the social and spiritual lives of their churches. Austin Channing Brown describes women's work in an exultant passage:

> Black women are the backbone and muscle of every church I've attended. They are prophets speaking a word when it seems God is silent. They are hospitality, welcoming with food and kindness, with a seat at the table, with a place you can call home. We are capable of building community anywhere—not just at church or at work, but also in the "ethnic" hair care section of stores, in elevators, and other random places where we take the opportunity to simply say "I see you."[21]

Black women, she writes, extend God's healing and build community even when church culture constrains their participation and denies their formal leadership. Brown's storytelling and reflection on experience create critical awareness of the ways that women negotiate cultures based on racial and gender inequalities—within and outside the evangelical movement. Her use of "we" invites identification from those who share her experiences. In this passage, and throughout the stories in *I'm Still Here*, Brown effectively offers an "I see you" to readers who have similarly grappled with racism and sexism in evangelical spaces.

But Brown also hopes to reach white readers who have not shared her experiences and convince them of the extent to which evangelical churches marginalize Black women. She introduces *I'm Still Here* as a story "not about condemning white people but about rejecting the assumption—sometimes spoken, sometimes not—that white is right; closer to God, holy, chosen, the epitome of being" and "surviving in a world not made for me."[22] She begins with a childhood anecdote about her unusual name that illustrates her early awareness of Blackness. After a librarian questioned the name Austin on her library card, Brown's mother explained its origins: "We knew that anyone who saw it before meeting you would assume you are a white man. One day you will have to apply for jobs. We just wanted to make sure you could make it to the interview."[23] The name—her grandmother's maiden name—worked "almost too well."[24] Brown explains that she repeatedly sees interviewers blink in surprise when they meet her in person. They glance back over her resume for "clues" and Brown infers the "unspoken question" that grows out of this gap between expectation and reality: "*Since we didn't vet her knowing she is a Black woman, are we sure she'll fit in with our* [white] *culture?*"[25] These experiences reveal the assumptions of evangelical culture, even in progressive circles. Brown goes on to share other early experiences with bias, like a teacher who made a seating chart based on a "stereotype about sassy, disrespectful Black girls."[26] Those stereotypes are neither innocuous nor confined to secular spaces. She spells out the significance for adult readers: "How could I know if beneath other amicable interactions, the stereotypes and biases of those in power were operating against students who looked like me?"[27] Brown later narrates scenarios she encounters in white evangelical workplaces and spells out the implicit messages: "*My body is being scrutinized in ways that others are not subjected to, and the worst is being assumed of me*," or "*I need white approval and interpretation before my idea will be considered good.*"[28] Brown shows readers her exhaustion in these spaces, asking white readers to accept painful identification with the teachers, colleagues, and fellow believers who have devalued her.

Hatmaker, too, came to a progressive stance from life rather than theory. In her book *Of Mess and Moxie*, she recounts the ways that the evangelical emphasis on purity shaped her identity as a young woman:

> Holiness culture meant you were always one careless French kiss away from divine disapproval, because, like I said, why buy the cow when you're giving the milk away under the bleachers? I spent all my spiritual energy trying to stay on God's Good Side, which I managed around twenty-three minutes a day. It was exhausting and scary and impossible. I was petrified of God. I don't remember what I thought of Jesus.[29]

Hatmaker's account of purity culture—a humorous memory, safely in the past—derides this culture but accommodates conservative views of gender. If the church manipulates women, she seems to say, the real loss is their diminished knowledge of Jesus. Her message about capable women in the church likewise does not alienate readers who have strong beliefs in male headship or who see benefits in complementarianism. Hatmaker remains acceptable by addressing gender through playful anecdotes and Bible-based exhortations, rather than direct critiques of patriarchal doctrines. Hatmaker does not explicitly take issue with prohibitions on women's leadership or preaching. She instead points to Acts 10:15—"What God has made clean, you must not call profane"—and Paul's instruction in 2 Timothy 2:15—"Do your best to present yourself to God as one approved by him, a worker who has no need to be ashamed, rightly explaining the word of truth"—as verses giving permission.[30] Hatmaker herself regularly preached from the pulpit of the Austin New Church. However, her caution around the topic suggests her underlying conservatism and unwillingness to confront orthodoxy in her published work at this point in her career. That caution also reflects her audience; women's ordination remains an important debate, but it might not be a pressing concern in the lives of most readers. Platforms for influential teaching exist outside the church and evangelical rhetorical practices increasingly involve reading, sharing, and responding to blogs and memoirs. As progressive women explore these possibilities for rhetorical agency, the male-dominated sermon appears to be losing its power as "the organizing event of evangelical culture."[31]

Evangelical Audiences in the Twenty-First Century

Progressive writers walk a fine line when they critique complementarianism, purity culture, or evangelical assumptions of whiteness. Many evangelical readers resist these messages from progressives or "secular humanists"—the "ideological enemy" of the Christian Right.[32] Even those who do not identify with the politicized Christian Right are often steeped in antipathy to feminism and social justice movements, in large part because conservatives habitually dismiss these as "less guided by the Bible and more influenced by the surrounding culture."[33] At the same time, their cultural and political values do not necessarily align with male leaders. Journalist Anne Helen Petersen describes the feminist leanings of this "new evangelical woman":

> She believes in treating LGBT people with love; she might even believe they should be allowed to be married. She might also admit that single evangelicals sometimes have sex before marriage.
>
> She is black, she is Latina, she is Asian, but mostly she is white—and she is middle-class. In many ways, she resembles an intersectional feminist, even if she does not use the term herself. Her theological posture is one of acceptance, of *belonging*—not of shame and condemnation. And amongst this current generation of Christian women, she is legion.[34]

The evangelicals who flock to progressive writers are dissenting from twenty-first-century evangelical leaders on many points of belief and practice. However, the conservatism in their churches (and, for some, their other communities) shapes their faith, political stances, and discursive norms—and therefore the writers they accept as legitimate teachers and leaders.

These women also belong to a religious culture intertwined with political debates. Petersen's "new evangelical women" do not describe themselves as political, but most hold political positions that emerge from their faith. Petersen observes, "She is also conservative, and identifies as such: she cherishes the bond of marriage; she's pro-life; she is anti-pornography."[35] Ex-evangelical Deborah Jian Lee describes the sway of conservative leaders who mobilized against women's movements and "conditioned" evangelicals "to reject feminism." She describes conservatives' strategy: "By branding feminism as antifamily, conservatives very effectively defanged the evangelical feminist movement over the past decades. In fact, much of today's popular evangelical feminist dialogue steers clear of truly radical proclamations."[36] Progressive writers navigate this entrenched anti-feminism in faith communities, readers' ambivalence towards politics, and terms like *feminist* or *privilege* that act as terministic screens dividing biblical worldviews from secular thought.

In past decades, writers proposed feminist interpretations and applications of the Bible, but these "defanged" voices now have little influence among white evangelicals. Evangelical feminism of the 1960s and 1970s advocated for women's vocations in the church and theorized new ways to interpret scripture.[37] The Evangelical Women's Caucus, founded in 1974, sought to advance feminist biblical interpretation and women's leadership. However, these scholars and activists struggled to gain popular acceptance. As progressives "floundered" in persuading believers, conservatives condemned feminism and successfully "enlisted evangelical women on the right side of the culture wars."[38] Evangelical women's memoirs renew the work of discerning cultural norms from God-given truths about gender roles. They take up many of the goals and concerns of the evangelical feminist movement using the feminist rhetorical practice of life writing to reach new audiences.

Writing from experience in the evangelical movement and their positions as mothers and pastors' wives, Bessey and Hatmaker destabilize ingrained, uncritical antipathies to feminism. When Hatmaker celebrates the "courage and resolve" with which "mothers and grandmothers moved the needle forward for women," she describes a non combative feminism appealing to readers who say they aren't political.[39] In a similar vein, Bessey insists, "I call myself a Jesus feminist because to me, the qualifier means I am a feminist precisely *because* of my life-long commitment to Jesus and his Way."[40] She speaks to desires for a woman-friendly Christianity and a Jesus-friendly feminism. When Bessey declares, "Most of what has passed for a description of feminism is fearmongering misinformation," she undermines the branding that alienates many women from the term.[41]

The stakes are high for writers who break from orthodox doctrines like traditional marriage, complementarianism, or prioritizing gospel evangelism over social justice. Still, progressive writers find persuasive power in addressing a growing audience of women with roots in conservatism and openness to progressive notions of race and gender. Their lowest common denominator feminism, perhaps shaped by a postfeminist view that previous generations fought all the important battles, will strike some readers as tepid. Their focus on individual women carving out spaces for leadership does little to change institutional policies of exclusion. They make concessions and express loyalty to conservative evangelicalism, which might dismay (or irritate) some scholars. However, they earn success and prominence in reaching devout women who are frustrated with overt misogyny in the church, the bigoted reluctance to engage racial injustice, and the tight relationship between evangelicalism and politics. They merit attention from rhetoricians for these reasons as well. By collapsing the distance between secular feminism and evangelical Christianity, progressive rhetors prepare their audiences to receive insights from feminist conversations outside the church and to resist control of women's bodies and beliefs.

Controversy

Jen Hatmaker has experienced the consequences of announcing a stance that contradicts mainstream evangelical thought. In an October 2016 interview with Jonathan Merritt, Hatmaker declared, "Any two adults have the right to choose who they want to love. And they should be afforded the same legal protections as any of us." She went on to add, "'The church hasn't treated the LGBT community like family. We have to do better." When Merritt asked, "If an LGBT friend of yours got married, would you attend that wedding?" and "Do you think an LGBT relationship can be holy?" she said yes to both, unequivocally.[42] Hatmaker did not walk back or qualify these statements. Instead, she later defended her position on Facebook, writing: "We wrestled with and through Scripture, not around it. Our view of the Word is still very high, as is it for the hundreds of thousands of faithful believers who believe likewise."[43] She also shared an explanation posted by Brandon, which begins, "We realized that while we had heard sermons listing homosexuality as a clear sin, and we had read all the verses referenced, that we had personally neglected to do the hard work of faithfully studying the scriptures."[44] He describes their season of prayer and study in a 1654-word post. Significantly for evangelical audiences, he centers the Bible in that explanation:

> For more than a year we studied every version of every verse in the Bible that appeared to discuss "homosexuality". We studied the Greek. We studied the Hebrew. We read every commentary we could find related specifically to the related passages.
>
> As we would for any topic seeking truth, we did our best to look at each verse with fresh eyes. We applied all the rules to faithfully and ethically interpret scripture: We considered the type of literature, the context in which each was written, what other scriptures say about it giving clues to God's intent, and viewed each through the lens of the Gospel.
>
> The historical view is that scripture is clear on homosexuality. What we found is that it's not as simple as traditionally taught.[45]

Brandon Hatmaker goes on to explain that based on this prayer and study they determined "we don't believe a committed life-long monogamous same-sex marriage violates anything seen in scripture about God's hopes for the marriage relationship."[46] Their positions on sexuality and same-sex marriage are products of close study of the Bible and attention to the ways that text contradicts accepted evangelical positions.

Much as the Mark Driscoll controversy asked orthodox evangelicals to grapple with their tacit acceptance of misogyny and abuse of power, Hatmaker's declarations forced evangelicals to grapple with the tacit parameters around women's leadership. She had described herself as "low-grade Christian famous"[47] before the interview with Merritt, but afterward received widespread attention in secular and evangelical media. Lifeway Christian Stores, a chain associated with the Southern Baptist Convention, pulled Hatmaker's books. Churches cancelled invitations for her to speak at their gatherings, and prominent evangelicals denounced her stance as apostasy.[48] Writer Rosaria Butterfield also rejected Hatmaker's statement, though less caustically:

> I hear Jen's words—words meant to encourage, not discourage, to build up, not tear down, to defend the marginalized, not broker unearned power—and a thin trickle of sweat creeps down my back. . . . I learned through conversion that when something feels right and good and real and necessary—but stands against God's Word—this reveals the particular way Adam's sin marks my life. Our sin natures deceive us. Sin's deception isn't just "out there"; it's also deep in the caverns of our hearts.[49]

Hatmaker's teaching from the pulpit never elicited this kind of outcry or criticism—maybe evangelicals react harshly to public statements but can allow unorthodox actions if they remain under the radar. The anger following her statement also revealed that evangelicals of the time used this single doctrinal question as a litmus test for leadership.

Following these denunciations, Hatmaker reflected in a blog post that she had grown painfully aware of the "evangelical machine"[50] that enforces adherence to orthodoxy. Merritt points out that Hatmaker's determination to "not just stick around, but actually call out the institutional machine that has become remarkably efficient at pulverizing its uncompliant members" compounded the controversy.[51] In April 2017, Tish Harrison Warren published "Who's in Charge of the Christian Blogosphere?" an article that continued the debate. Warren distinguishes "winsome, relatable writing, good storytelling, and compelling life experiences" from "theological teaching, presuppositions, or argument,"[52] implying that the former brings large audiences, but the latter confers authority. For Warren, Hatmaker's statement raises questions about the legitimacy of lay writers. She asks, "Where do bloggers and speakers like Hatmaker derive their authority to speak and teach? And who holds them accountable for their teaching?" If any woman who tells compelling stories can gain a platform, Warren asks, "Who decides what is true Christian orthodoxy? And how do we as listeners decide whom to trust as a Christian leader and teacher?"[53] These last questions indicate that Hatmaker's position on same-sex marriage poses a threat to the evangelical community because she contradicts traditional beliefs, but even more so because she steps outside established sources of authority located in ordination and church oversight.

Hatmaker's blog post "My Saddest Good Friday in Memory" describes her disappointment after the insults, rejection, and threats from friends and teachers. She connects her personal controversy to the election, which left evangelicals "staring at each other, trying our damnedest to figure out how we understand the gospel so differently," and left the community "maligned, mocked, dragged, and dissected publicly."[54] However, her disappointment proved fruitful. In *Rhetorical Feminism and This Thing Called Hope*, Cheryl Glenn conceptualizes disappointment anew "as a judgment, an action, and inquiry that leads directly to hope."[55] Hatmaker takes a similar stance: "New life is always possible evidently, well past the moment it makes sense to still hope for it."[56] Hatmaker's role in the evangelical mainstream had depended on her orthodox positions, but rejecting those gave her an entry point into overdue conversations and an expanded sphere of influence. A profile in *Politico* describes her continued success and influence a year after her interview: "At a time when the white evangelical share of the American electorate is on the decline, Hatmaker is out with a best-selling book, a top-rated podcast and a speaking tour that's selling out."[57] I see Hatmaker taking this controversy as a moment to reshape her ethos as a leader so that it is rooted, not in expertise or correct belief, but instead in her disappointment, action, and hope.

Taking the Bible Seriously

Progressive writers address gender with rhetorical strategies that engage changes in evangelical culture, particularly in the forms of discourse it considers authoritative. Hatmaker waves aside formal argumentation from scholarly Bible interpretations: "Talking heads dissecting apologetics stopped inspiring me a few years ago."[58] She and the other writers I study in this chapter treat personal experience, including the experience of reading and meditating on scripture, as a source of authority. They insist on connections between secular feminism and biblical teachings;

they invite readers to set aside official theology, authorities, and interpretive strategies. As Hatmaker's controversy shows, these writers are not immune from the hierarchies and patriarchal constraints that characterize evangelicalism in explicit and implicit ways. They largely shape their messages to not overtly reject established leaders or political orthodoxy like opposition to abortion. They are conservative in this regard, and particularly in the books they bring out with evangelical publishers. However, the Hatmaker controversy shows that online media creates opportunities for outspoken opposition to doctrine and politics, a change in the "rhetorical ecology that regulates who speaks, who remains silent, who listens, and who acts responsively."[59] Although their calls for change are limited when they muffle criticisms of hierarchy and oppression in order to remain acceptable to conservative readers, they shift the grounds of the conversation about gender and insist on including new voices.

As Molly Worthen explains, the debate over women in the church is "at root, an argument about the Bible's authority."[60] Ringer, Cope, Worthen, and other scholars point out that evangelical beliefs "vary widely across the theological and political spectrum," but an emphasis on scriptural authority—which many take to mean factual inerrancy—lies at the center of most statements of belief.[61] Complementarianism appeals to evangelicals because it offers a countercultural alternative to secular feminism; it also appeals to their belief in straightforward, unchanging biblical truth.[62] Evangelical writers who address gender must therefore grapple with the biblical hermeneutics that establish complementarianism and other doctrines. In this section, I analyze their stances toward the Bible and toward conventions of evangelical discourse that revolve around close reading and interpretation.

Sarah Bessey contends with centuries of discussion centering on the Bible to elaborate on her "Jesus Feminism." In her second memoir, *Out of Sorts*, she reflects on her process of grappling with the "clobber verses" in the Apostle Paul's letters that conservative

Christians cite to limit women's roles: "As I was writing my first book, *Jesus Feminist*, a strange transformation took place in me: I began to love Paul. Really, truly love him as a brother, precisely *because* I was writing about life on the other side of the gender debates, advocating for the full equality of women." She explains this shift in her reading:

> But as I worked my way through the passages of Scripture that I used to hate, I began to see Paul more clearly, to understand Scripture even better. I began to see his wisdom, his subversion, his heart. When I looked at his full ministry—how he praised and esteemed women in leadership in the church, how he turned household codes within a patriarchal society on their heads, how he used feminine metaphors, how he subverted the systems, how he passionately defended equality—the verses that used to clobber me began to embrace me.
>
> The truth broke through. I wasn't fighting *against* Paul—I was fighting *with* him. I read Paul's words in Scripture and I began to realize I had not known him, his world, his context, his brilliance.[63]

In choosing personal narrative—here, narrating her intellectual and spiritual journey—Bessey rejects the evangelical practice of building arguments by close-reading passages and using traditional interpretations of texts to refute counterarguments. Bessey alludes to exegeses by feminist theologians, but instead of laying out a series of interpretations she lays out her process of coming to a new relationship with the text. This approach to the Bible also informs her discussion of gender in *Jesus Feminist*. She explains, "My purpose here on earth isn't to win arguments or perform hermeneutical gymnastics to impress the wealthiest 2 percent of the world. I don't think God is glorified by tightly crafted arguments wielded as weaponry."[64] Bessey offers alternative meaning-making practices. She asserts that *Out of Sorts* "isn't an argument to make or a point to take," but rather a process of "sorting out a life" and "making sense of the stories and the moments and the intersections."[65] For Bessey, examining the self leads to the "sacred ground or scary ground" of deep belief.[66]

Out of Sorts reflects on this experience of revisiting biblical teachings and assessing dominant reading practices. Bessey recalls, "I used to elevate the Bible to being a fourth member of the Trinity" and was attracted to systematic theology with charts, graphs, "easy-to-decode secrets," answers, and clarity.[67] Arguments and exegeses that ask readers to suppress critical thinking under the rubrics of authority and inerrancy "use the Bible as a conversation stopper, not as a starting point."[68] Even as they share how they revisited received interpretations, evangelical writers express a high regard for scripture. Bessey locates her feminism in Bible study, writing, "After years of reading the Gospels and the full canon of Scripture, here is, very simply, what I learned about Jesus and the ladies: he loves us."[69] She explains that Jesus transgressed hierarchies and customs of public address when he spoke to women:

> During his time on earth Jesus subverted the social norms dictating how a rabbi spoke to women, to the rich, the powerful, the housewife, the mother-in-law, the despised, the prostitute, the adulteress, the mentally ill and demon possessed, the poor. He spoke to women directly, instead of through their male-headship standards and contrary to the order of the day (and even of some religious sects today).
>
> No, it was just him, incarnation of three-in-one on one. Women were not excluded or exempted from the community of God. Women stood before God on their own soul's feet, and he called us, gathered us, as his own.[70]

Bessey aims not to resist biblical authority, but to demonstrate the complexity of the text and faith-based ways of knowing. Performing their knowledge of the Bible and evangelical doctrine, she and other like-minded writers reproduce the values of that community of practice. This is orthodox behavior, but it enables unorthodox readings.

Hatmaker and Bessey exhort readers to step into leadership and teaching roles, using "powerful, concrete, and absolute language" that "arouses pathos" in place of argumentation.[71] "Don't wait for permission: we've already been given it," Hatmaker writes. She continues, quoting the Apostle Paul:

> Lead, sister. You have authority to use your home as a sanctuary, your hands as tools of healing, your voice as an instrument of hope, your gifts as channels of incredible power. "If your gift is prophesying, then prophesy in accordance with your faith; if it is serving, then serve; if it is teaching, then teach; if it is to encourage, then give encouragement; if it is giving, then give generously; if it is to lead, do it diligently; if it is to show mercy, do it cheerfully" (Rom. 12:6–8).[72]

Hatmaker invokes authority, the very language of the evangelical debate about gender roles. Without speaking directly to prohibitions on preaching and ordination, she insists that women have authority for a range of vital roles. Hatmaker does support this claim by quoting scripture, but not the often-cited verses in 1 Timothy, Titus 2, and Ephesians 5 around which evangelical discussions of gender typically revolve. She replaces these passages with passages from Romans 12:6–8, Acts 10:15, and 2 Timothy 2:15, which speak of believers in gender-neutral terms. By citing them, Hatmaker enacts an expansive view of biblical teaching and an inclusive, joyful approach to women's work. For her, church imposes narrow roles that neither lived experience nor the Bible clearly justify. When she invites women to lead and take active roles, she exhorts them to embrace that call in scripture, not to smash the patriarchy.

Anne Helen Petersen names familiarity with secular culture as one of the hallmarks of contemporary "Xvangelical" women and a departure from male-led evangelical traditions. This trait includes not only fluency in popular culture but also interest in philosophies like feminism and participation in phenomena like the memoir boom of the past three decades.[73] Hatmaker takes up postmodernism as another cultural change that evangelicals should understand and embrace. In *For the Love*, she paraphrases the postmodern "mantra" as "I don't have all the answers and neither do you."[74] Hatmaker acknowledges that this summary is reductive, but her mantra casts postmodernism as resistance to human authority rather than denial of biblical truth. She cites her own education that qualifies her to translate postmodernism for the modernists:

> Postmoderns experience God differently than most of us did at their age. I learned apologetics and practiced defending my faith (*I have all the answers and so can you*). They hunger for community and justice, humility and anticonsumerism. They don't like slick. They don't trust a leader without a limp. Since they question everything, they require safe spiritual environments where struggles are welcomed and discussed (*I don't have all the answers and neither do you*). They must be allowed to wrestle without being shamed, or they'll default to their open-armed peers and we will lose them.
>
> We cannot shrug this off because this is the next generation of the church.[75]

In Hatmaker's formulation, a postmodern worldview threatens neither the church nor the Bible. She identifies herself—and the readers who comprise her "us"—with an evangelical rhetoric that values declarations of certainty and defenses of its practices and positions.

When Hatmaker entertains postmodernism and advocates for wrestling with questions, she offers readers a vision of faith that is not based on certainty—an idea that is radical within evangelicalism. In *The Sin of Certainty*, Pete Enns calls certainty "a major, almost universal preoccupation" among evangelicals and describes sermons that "explain what is there [in the Bible text] so you can know what is right and what is wrong to believe."[76] Hatmaker explains that this drive toward certainty and the ways evangelicals deploy biblical truths appeals to a part of her too: "Give me a rule any day. Give me a clear 'in' and 'out' because boundaries make me feel safe. If I can clearly mark the borders, then I am assured of my insider status—the position I feel compelled to defend, the one thing I can be sure of. I want to stand before God having gotten it right."[77] She links evangelical desire for certainty to a penchant for exclusion, placing herself among the Christian insiders most guilty of this sin. The postmodern stance she describes instead values open-ended discussion and defines spiritual growth as deeper exploration rather than greater knowledge.

Writing from a posture of shared concern for young evangelicals, Hatmaker and Bessey pry open resistance to postmodern thought and envision a church that places less value on certainty. Hatmaker reflects on constricting evangelical hermeneutics without denouncing those interpretive methodologies. She casts postmodern questioning postures and reading practices as productive for the church, even essential for its ongoing relevance. Furthermore, she places her defense of postmodernism in a chapter that is ostensibly about parenting, not about critiques of evangelical ideology. Bessey sets aside apologetics when she avows that watertight arguments do not glorify God and asserts, "The purpose of the Bible is to equip us to be sent out into the world, to proclaim the Kingdom of God, to lift up our eyes and see each other and see God at work—and then, to participate fully in that life."[78] Even in her subversive call not to read the Bible literally, she reveres its teachings: "I am challenged and changed in ways I never was when I took every word literally—now that I take them so seriously."[79] Hatmaker, too, creates space for a rhetoric of the Bible not based in certainty or literal readings. She claims that questioning and subjectivity provides a welcome balance to the excesses of evangelical rhetoric and a path to deep engagement with the Bible.

Austin Channing Brown's story makes a case that debating inerrancy and performing close readings limits Christians' understandings of scripture. She describes an alternative to evangelical rhetoric based in biblical hermeneutics. Early in her childhood, her experience of church had revolved around Friday chapel at her school, with "[white] Christian contemporary songs, a passage read from our [white] illustrated Bibles, a [white] speaker sharing some sort of testimony, and finally accepting [white] Jesus as our Savior."[80] Brown experiences no connection to God or the community in these sedate services that centered spiritual, disembodied experiences of the gospel. Later, at a Black evangelical church:

> I fell in love with the soaring voices and the songs that moved us to tears and then chased the blues away. I fell in love with peppermint-dealing church mothers and hymn-singing deacons. I fell in love with fiery preaching that moved so deep, it would undergird you and push you to your feet in praise. I fell in love with a Jesus who saw the poor and sick and hurting, a Jesus who had bigger plans for me than keeping me a virgin, a Jesus who loved and reveled in our Blackness.[81]

Brown never contests the value and authority of the Bible, but she invites readers to envision a church that seeks connection with and application to the material world, rather than merely correct interpretations of the text.

As a guest on the podcast *The Bible for Normal People*, Brown further explains that this contrast between the two styles of service reflects both style and theology. Distinctions between faith and justice don't exist in the rhetoric of Black churches, she argues. In the sermons she heard, "Jesus sounded like a Black person, dealing with familiar hardships of life—injustice, broken relationships, the pain of being called names."[82] She experienced spiritual transformation in services that taught her "Jesus cared about my soul, but he also cared about the woman who didn't have transportation or couldn't pay the light or water bill."[83] As the rhetorical history in chapter 1 traces, many white Christians insist on a tension between preaching the gospel and responding to injustice; between personal and collective sins; and between spiritual salvation and the material world. Brown rejects those disembodied readings, showing her readers how her spiritual growth was intertwined with embodied experiences.

Bessey, Brown, and Hatmaker offer their readers stories about study and discovery, positioning themselves not as preachers, but fellow worshippers and readers of scripture—an invitational ethos. Framing these insights as God's work, they speak the language of evangelicalism to question received knowledge. In this way, they enact "humble dogma," Ringer's term for "beliefs that allow for and even prompt reflection into one's own beliefs, research into unfamiliar topics, or exploration of various sides of a debate."[84]

They question reading practices and accepted interpretations, while upholding the authority—but not necessarily the inerrancy—of the Bible. In rhetorical study, evangelical women's rhetorics are usually subsumed under conservative doctrines and rhetoric that revolves around politics and culture wars. Studying these personal narratives instead, we see the critiques taking place within the evangelical movement that propel new knowledge.

A Memoir Consciousness

The personal narratives of progressive evangelical women contrast with other forms of religious discourse, like prophetic rhetoric and sermons. While progressive evangelical figures like Jim Wallis use prophetic rhetoric to trigger a crisis and subsequent change, the progressive writers I study here recount and reveal private experience to cultivate reflective practices among their audiences. The examples I consider in this chapter show that, by framing their insights as acts of testimony and witnessing, a progressive writer can craft effective messages from within an ethos as a woman of faith.

Bessey, Brown, and Hatmaker claim authority and model faith-based questioning of rigid gender roles and literal readings of the Bible. They also model forms of feminism and evangelicalism that pointedly avoid the combative models of dialogue that drive toward winning arguments. While Brown articulates her anger, she situates it within her identity as a member of the evangelical movement: "I continue to be drawn toward the collective participation of seeking good, even when that means critiquing the institution I love for its commitment to whiteness."[85] This final section focuses on the "memoir consciousness" that I observe in evangelical writers. Bessey, Brown, and Hatmaker all craft stories of their experiences with an acute awareness of the significance of personal narrative and its potential to influence the evangelical movement.

Bessey recounts a particularly emotional moment in her early life. In her blog post "I Am Damaged Goods," she narrates a scene from her youth in the church:

> I was nineteen years old and crazy in love with Jesus when that preacher told an auditorium I was "damaged goods" because of my sexual past. He was making every effort to encourage this crowd of young adults to "stay pure for marriage." He was passionate, yes, well-intentioned, and he was a good speaker, very convincing indeed.
>
> And he stood up there and shamed me, over and over and over again.
>
> Oh, he didn't call me up to the front and name me. But he stood up there and talked about me with such *disgust*, like I couldn't be in that real-life crowd of young people worshipping in that church. I felt spotlighted and singled out amongst the holy, surely my red face announced my guilt to every one.
>
> He passed around a cup of water and asked us all to spit into it. Some boys horked and honked their worst into that cup while everyone laughed. Then he held up that cup of cloudy saliva from the crowd and asked, "Who wants to drink this?!"
>
> And every one in the crowd made barfing noises, *no way, gross*!
>
> "This is what you are like if you have sex before marriage," he said seriously, "you are asking your future husband or wife to drink this cup."[86]

Bessey concludes with reassurances to her younger self and to her readers: "So, you had sex before you were married. *It's okay.* Really. It's okay." She goes on to say, "Your husband won't hold it against you, he's not that weak and ego-driven," and concludes: "*It's likely you would make different choices, if you knew then what you know now, but, darling, don't make it more than it is, and don't make it less than it is.* Let it be true, and don't let anyone silence you or the redeeming work of Christ out of shame."[87] Readers exposed to purity culture will recognize the scenario she describes. Bessey's exhortative self-talk models ways readers might respond to guilt and assumptions about male ego and female worth.

Bessey repeatedly addresses her blog and book readers as "luv" and "darling," evoking intimacy and sustaining a sense of conversation in her writing. In this, she follows female rhetors who historically responded to constraints on speech or writing by taking conversation as a model for their rhetorical work.[88] Conversation continues to be useful for women who address audiences conditioned to reject their teaching or preaching. Echoing or adapting oral conversation in their writing situates Bessey as a friend who leads "from nonthreatening gentleness and warmth rather than direct authority" or political conviction.[89] The parameters of their feminine style—a personal, anecdotal, inductive style that identifies with the audience and treats the audience as peers—are based in domestic experiences like hospitality and fellowship between believers.

In *I'm Still Here*, Austin Channing Brown calls readers' attention to the ways writing and speaking from experience can demand personal and collective change. She reflects on her own purpose for writing the memoir: "I am trying to clarify what it's like to exist in a Black body in an organization that doesn't understand it is not only Christian but also white."[90] Her stories illustrate and explain this statement. They bear out her claim that "white people who expect me to be white have not yet realized that their cultural way of being is not in fact the result of goodness, rightness, of God's blessing. Pushing back, resisting the lie, is hella work."[91] Brown's writing clarifies and indicts; she also exhorts readers to "embody a community eager to name whiteness, celebrate Blackness, and, in a world still governed by systems of racial oppression, begin to see that there's another way."[92] In her account of working with the Christian nonprofit Open Door Chicago, she reflects that giving testimony during mission trips offered white students in her program a way to "face their own racism."[93] Brown uses storytelling to challenge her audience, a weightier experience than a simple celebration of growing in one's faith or clarifying one's beliefs.

Brown also speaks from her experience to call out the power imbalances in evangelical practices of confession and testimony. In spaces for dialogue and truth-telling, she sees white people reveal racism from their own lives in order to seek forgiveness and "the easy comfort of having spoken the confession."[94] Moreover, transformation requires an audience willing to listen rhetorically.

Brown summarizes what her experience in this culture has shown her:

> I am convinced that one of the reasons white churches favor dialogue is that the parameters of dialogue can be easily manipulated to benefit whiteness. Tone policing takes priority over listening to the pain inflicted on people of color. People of color are told they should be nicer, kinder, more gracious, less angry in their delivery, or that white people's needs, feelings, and thoughts should be given equal weight. But we cannot negotiate our way to reconciliation. White people need to listen, to pause so that people of color can clearly articulate both the disappointment they've endured and what it would take for reparations to be made. Too often, dialogue functions as a stall tactic, allowing white people to believe they've done something heroic when the real work is yet to be done.[95]

Brown's reflection shows how personal narrative participates in the evangelical rhetorical ecology. Sharing stories can contain reconciliation so that it only reflects the goals, values, and blind spots of white evangelicals. In the world of evangelical ministry, racism and sexism constrain her ability to narrate the emotional experiences that give storytelling persuasive power. She explains, "Because I am a Black person, my anger is considered dangerous, explosive, and unwarranted. Because I am a woman, my anger supposedly reveals an emotional problem or gets dismissed as a temporary state that will go away once I choose to be rational." Personal narrative finds meaning in experience, but Christians dismiss anger "as a character flaw, showing just how far I have turned from Jesus."[96] She calls on white readers to pause their stories and arguments, to receive her anger and accounts of Black femininity, and to hear her claim that overt racism and assumptions of whiteness form the foundations of many evangelical churches.

Bessey, Brown, and Hatmaker work within constraints, but these concessions do not necessarily compromise their messages. They successfully model conversations about faith and orthodoxy that revolve around story rather than certainty. Hatmaker educates readers in rhetorical practices that center self-narration and the personal investments that underpin difficult conversations. She offers her readers phrases to facilitate story-based exchanges: "Tell me how your thoughts progressed in this" and "I appreciate your experience with this. I'm listening."[97] She frames productive disagreement as an act of love, asserting, "Love refuses to deny or dismantle another person's perspective simply because I don't share it."[98] Bessey, likewise, declares her faith in the rhetorical and spiritual power of self-narrative. "Most of our theology is formed by autobiography," she writes in *Out of Sorts*.[99] Brown asks readers to recognize the ways evangelical patterns of testimony and storytelling silence Black women and deflect necessary conversations about race. Personal narrative—with elements of testimony, exhortation, and conversation—is not merely accessible and appropriate for women. Bessey, Brown, and Hatmaker maintain that these practices serve readers, create new knowledge, and follow the teachings of Jesus, rather than fostering the "outrage, offense, and polarization"[100] they see in evangelical and American culture.

Conclusion

Progressive writers successfully modulate their messages about gender, biblical authority, and evangelical identity for a conservative community that is evolving. In some ways, that evolution is slow; in the 2016, 2018, and 2020 elections, white evangelical women remained a reliably conservative voting demographic.[101] Still, research consistently finds that younger Christians are dissatisfied with the beliefs and climates of their churches. In surveys conducted by Barna Group researchers between 2007 and 2011, 23 percent of 18- to 29-year-old Christians agreed that "Christians demonize everything outside of the church."[102] This age group also expressed frustration at not being able "to ask my most pressing life questions in church" (36 percent) and reported "significant intellectual doubts about my faith" (23 percent). In 2013, Barna surveys found that "substantial majorities of Millennials who don't go to church say they see Christians as judgmental (87%), hypocritical

(85%), anti-homosexual (91%) and insensitive to others (70%)."[103] In their writing, Bessey, Brown, and Hatmaker mirror these beliefs and respond by using their platforms to reject the politics, cultural norms, and biblical teachings of conservative evangelicalism. Their storytelling creates a space for such conversations and envisions an evangelical discourse based in "curiosity, cooperation, discovery, and learning rather than persuasion, competition, fear, and conflict."[104] Hatmaker's list mirrors Glenn's descriptions of "new ways of being rhetorical": being accessible, invitational, inclusionary, networked, silent, thoughtful, resistant, and active.[105] Progressive evangelical writers take "a leap of faith beyond the evidence" and write with hope for material change in their world.[106]

In many ways, I fit the demographic these writers address. When I attended an evangelical church, I worked through many of the questions and frustrations they name. Rather than remain at odds with the church, or with myself, I followed the examples of Rachel Held Evans and Deborah Jian Lee and found other communities in which to practice my faith. If I had read Bessey during that time, I might have recognized the progressive current in evangelical thought and rhetoric. I find these writers to be important subjects for rhetoric scholarship because of their work to propose new directions for the evangelical movement and their success invoking an audience of readers who join them in this project.

Studying these contemporary applications of feminist and religious rhetorics illuminates the complexities of evangelicalism, the relationships between conservatives and progressives, and the critiques emerging within the movement—a long called-for investigation.[107] This body of evangelical writing illuminates a part of the community that is in productive conflict with male preaching and leadership. They also counter orthodox women writers who ultimately do uphold dominant patriarchal norms like male leadership, whether openly or tacitly. Progressives simultaneously engage the evangelical church, its critics, and the theory and activism of secular culture. Through this work, they revitalize a feminist evangelical rhetorical tradition that predates twentieth-century culture wars.

The writers I take up in this chapter accommodate readers who have been steeped in conservative rhetoric and recognize that this audience might be searching for new a way to reconcile evangelical faith with the good work they see in secular movements. As Crowley and Gerson describe, and as we saw in the first three chapters, some evangelicals employ combative and apocalyptic rhetoric that puts them fundamentally at odds with secular culture. Bessey, Brown, and Hatmaker differ from these other twentieth-century and contemporary figures in their specific doctrinal and political positions, in abstract beliefs, and in their approaches to debate. Their print and online writings model the open-ended dialogue that their readers, particularly younger evangelicals, seek. By remaining in conversation and community with their more orthodox counterparts, but exhorting readers to reexamine orthodox positions on gender, race, and biblical interpretation, they participate in renovating evangelical rhetoric to be a space where these readers can remain.

5 The Rhetorical Leadership of Contemporary *Evangélicas*

Evangelical women like Alsup, Anderson, Newbell, Prior, Evans, Hatmaker, Brown, and Bessey use personal narrative to build identity and community, with reverberations through American religious and political discourse. They bring distinctive, varying strategies to pursuing their goals. Orthodox evangelical women recount personal experiences to bolster and explain historic doctrine, model evangelical identity and worldview formation, and distinguish orthodoxy from conservatism. Women who have left evangelicalism write as knowledgeable outsiders with insight into the destructive nature of evangelical rhetoric. Progressive writers use personal narrative to chip away at evangelical antipathy toward social justice and feminism and show how orthodox interpretations fail women. Evangelical communities on the whole respect and value personal witness to faith journeys and God's work in believers' lives. These narratives can change minds, motives, and worlds, but they can also inspire backlash.

This final chapter closes several lines of inquiry I have followed through my earlier chapters and turns to a fourth distinct, vocal group of rhetors: women with leadership roles in evangelical institutions. The examples I study are also Latinas and were relatively early in leadership careers at the time they wrote. Leadership is a concern for every woman who claims a public voice in a movement that has traditionally affirmed male authority. However, women who hold positions of authority and influence in churches, nonprofits, and universities address this issue head-on. While writers like Karen Swallow Prior or Rachel Held Evans enact rhetorical leadership in their personal narratives, their accounts reflect perspectives from their private lives. In contrast, personal narratives by women who are leading evangelical organizations help rhetoricians understand the "unique challenges and opportunities for women worker-rhetors," particularly the unique challenges women navigate in religious spaces.[1] In this chapter, I focus on three figures who navigated not only opposition to women's leadership but also antipathy to non-white voices and bodies. Natalia Kohn, Noemi Vega Quiñones, and Kristy Garza Robinson detail the obstacles they overcame as Latina leaders in their book *Hermanas: Deepening Our Identity and Growing Our Influence*, published in January 2019. To encourage women who might likewise feel a call to lead, and to address racism and sexism in the church, *Hermanas* both models and advocates for an expanded role for women in the evangelical movement.[2]

Perhaps more than any other personal narratives I study in *"I Grew Up in the Church"* these stories aim to teach other women. Kohn, Vega Quiñones, and Robinson begin *Hermanas* with a welcome to readers:

> We invite you into our lives, our stories, and the stories of other Latina women who've gone ahead of us and are currently walking beside us. We also welcome you to the primary storytellers, our ancient mentors who lived long before us and will continue to live long after us. These twelve women in the Bible have become dear friends to each of us as they've helped mentor and form us through the years.[3]

This invitation describes their approach to "growing influence" in the movement: sharing personal narratives to mentor and counsel other women. The authors frame storytelling as a dialogue among past, present, and future rhetors—a practice that helps storytellers and listeners alike "live out their gender and their faith in relation to others."[4] Beginning with this welcome, *Hermanas* uses multi-voiced, relational, and embodied self-representation to decenter white readers and theologies from this conversation. As the authors tell their own stories and interpret biblical texts, they call readers "to ask questions, to begin new conversations, to be challenged by past and present women, and to experience growth in your faith and your Latina voice."[5] They guide readers to becoming effective leaders, and, in that process, enact a rhetorical leadership that challenges individualist and racist ideologies among evangelicals.

Hermanas presents personal narratives that combine cultural rhetoric, rhetorical leadership, and situated reading practices, concepts that I explore in this chapter. I begin with an introduction to these writers, an explanation of the structure of the book, and a brief discussion of the theories that guide my reading. I then turn to analyzing the book, published at the very end of the decade of evangelical decline. I first unpack the authors' communal style of personal narrative rooted in a dialogic, activist *testimonio* tradition along with the Protestant tradition of individual testimonies. I then show that this practice amplifies Latina leadership in a religious culture steeped in sexism and white supremacy. Third, I analyze how *Hermanas* tries to shift the worldview or *manera de ser* that discourages women from bold speech and action. Finally, I argue that the book theorizes a Bible-based view of systemic oppression that diverges from evangelical rhetorics of individual sin and salvation. For example, when Noemi Vega Quiñones retells the story of Jesus healing a woman with chronic bleeding, she interprets the miracle as "both physical *and* social, both systemic *and* personal."[6] Readings like these, which ground social justice arguments in orthodox Christian faith, demonstrate how *evangélica* rhetorical leadership can influence the evangelical movement.

Parachurch Leadership

Noemi Vega Quiñones lived in Mexico until moving to the United States with her family at age five. *Hermanas* recounts that experience caught between two cultures and the ways in which religion formed that experience. She met Kohn and Robinson through their positions at InterVarsity Christian Fellowship, an evangelical organization dedicated to college campus Christianity, for which Quiñones serves as the South Texas area director. Prior to writing *Hermanas*, she taught at Fresno Pacific University Biblical

Seminary, where she earned an M.A. in Theology. She specialized in Latino religious epistemologies, which would help her write her contributions to *Hermanas*.

Natalia Kohn (Rivera) was born in Argentina and raised in the United States as a biracial Latina. When she contributed to *Hermanas*, her first foray into publishing, she was the special projects coordinator for InterVarsity's LaFe ministry (its Latino college fellowship) and campus staff. Kohn is on staff at the Pasadena International House of Prayer, a religious meeting place in the charismatic Christian tradition, where she leads missions to the Middle East.

Kristy Garza Robinson is a third-generation Mexican American from South Texas. Her leadership work in the evangelical movement includes working in InterVarsity's LaFe ministry and Destino, a branch of Cru (Campus Crusade for Christ International) that was created to reach Latino students. Robinson is also the cofounder of 58, a nonprofit that seeks to combat social injustices that continue to affront the church. She is a speaker who has given talks at Cru conventions and the IF Gathering, an annual conference for Christian women.

By studying *Hermanas*, I turn to rhetorical leadership outside of preaching and even outside the church setting, an arena of leadership that studies of evangelical women often overlook. All three writers are leaders in *parachurch* organizations (InterVarsity, Cru, 58, the IF Gathering). These nonchurch entities are significant players in the evangelical movement. Bowler defines these organizations:

> A parachurch is a ministerial organization with evangelistic aims (which might include relief and justice work), but is not primarily defined by liturgical functions. It does not typically serve communion, baptize believers, or keep membership as its primary goals. It has a high degree of specialization (women's ministry, college ministry, etc.). Examples include Focus on the Family and InterVarsity Christian Fellowship.[7]

Parachurches represent an alternative path to leadership for women who don't have access to—or don't feel called to—traditional leadership roles in churches. This can take place in high-profile "megaministry" like national conferences that attract thousands of women, but evangelical women also seek out leadership that is local and personal. In these spaces women direct budgets, hire staff, develop curricula, create policies, and plan advocacy strategies for legal and social change—the practical work of leadership.

Parachurches might be a more accessible path to leadership, but that path is not a lesser or easier one. Examples like Focus on the Family and InterVarsity, national organizations that reach evangelicals through local chapters and a range of media channels, show that these organizations often reach larger and wider audiences than individual churches would be able to reach. They address underserved groups that evangelical churches and preachers overlook when they cater to white, male, middle-class (and often conservative) audiences. However, women's leadership meets challenges here too. As we saw in personal narratives by Bessey, Brown, and Hatmaker, churches and preaching are not the only arenas where women encounter opposition to their authority. In *Hermanas* we see how the authors navigate pushback in spaces like seminary classes and university campus groups, and how these parachurch spaces can be sites for women to renovate evangelical debates and rhetoric.[8]

Conceptualizing A Resource for Christian Latina Leaders

In the prologue to *Hermanas*, Kohn recalls that in 2015 she began to dream of a resource to develop Latina voices in the church. She had noted the "paucity in resources for Christian Latina leaders" and envisioned a book that would carry on the conversation that theologian Orlando Crespo began in his 2005 *Being Latino in Christ*. She reached out to friends who might be interested in creating such a resource and Vega Quiñones and Robinson responded to her invitation. The three set out "to coauthor a book where multiple voices would be shown," including the voices of women in the Bible.[9]

Each writer contributes four chapters distributed across the book's two parts, "Identity and Intimacy" and "Influence and Impact."[10] Their chapters convey the writers' distinct voices and experiences, and then layer those personal narratives with textual interpretations to read the stories of twelve biblical "mentors" for insight into Latina leadership (see table). Some chapters recount well-known figures like Ruth and Esther, subjects of entire Old Testament books. Others look at women like Tabitha, a first-century church leader, whose story takes up comparatively little space in the Bible and in evangelical imaginations.

Authors, Chapter Titles, Topics, and Biblical Texts in *Hermanas*

Author	Chapters in Section 1: Identity & Intimacy	Chapters in Section 2: Influence & Impact
Kristy Garza Robinson	Ch. 1, "Esther: Who Am I? A Mestiza for God's Mission"	Ch. 8, "Ruth: Crossing Borders and the *Hesed* of God"
	Ch. 5, "Mary of Bethany: A Vulnerable Leader Choosing Intimacy" (Luke 10, John 11)	Ch. 11, "Deborah: A Warrior Woman Fighting for Her *Gente*" (Judges 4)
Natalia Kohn	Ch. 2, "The Shulamite Woman: Amada, First and Foremost" (Song of Solomon)	Ch. 7, "The Canaanite Woman: Breakthrough at the Margins" (Matthew 15)
	Ch. 4, "Hannah: Forsaken to Faithful" (1 Samuel)	Ch. 10, "Lydia: Women and Men in Gospel Partnership" (Acts 16)
Noemi Vega Quiñones	Ch. 3, "The Bleeding Woman: Mija Leadership" (Matthew 9, Mark 5, Luke 8)	Ch. 9, "Tabitha: Misión Integral y En Conjunto" (Acts 9)
	Ch. 6, "Rahab: *Atrevida*, Allied, and Faithful Liberator" (Joshua 2, 6)	Ch. 12, "Mary: The Word Within" (Luke 1)

Though Kohn, Vega Quiñones, and Robinson name Latina readers as their primary audience, the book also responds to a largely white evangelicalism. Memoirists like Austin Channing Brown, historians like Jemar Tisby, and sociologists like Robert P. Jones have all shown that rhetoric and theology emphasizing literal interpretations and individual faith are tools white evangelicals use to resist reckoning with collective sins of racism and injustice. Within that context, Kohn, Vega Quiñones, and Robinson see their work as valuable for members of their wider evangelical community. White women might "want to hear stories and also wrestle with their faith and their cultural identities" and men might "pick up the book" and engage with the writers and with biblical women.[11] Writing to these multiple audiences, *Hermanas* illustrates how the authors—and biblical mentors—experience both constraints and empowerment from their cultural and religious contexts.

The authors' multicultural experiences equip them to reach these varying audiences. Kohn grew up with a father from Argentina "who only [spoke] Spanish" and an "Americanized Armenian mother."[12] Vega Quiñones describes herself as "a daughter of hard-working immigrant parents" and a "once-undocumented child."[13] Robinson calls herself "a third generation Mexican American" who spent her life in South Texas "geographically and emotionally straddling the border of the United States and Mexico, finding [her] home and feeling displaced in both countries and cultures."[14] The authors recount experiences in these family spaces and in evangelical spaces like Campus Crusade and InterVarsity, college ministries where all three worked. Their stories also espouse the Bible-centered, activist faith that evangelicals prioritize in their belief and rhetoric. However, they also draw from *evangélica* discourse that contrasts with, and even contradicts, white evangelical rhetoric.

Culture, Narrative, and Rhetorical Leadership

Personal narratives gain rhetorical power from the cultural contexts in which they emerge, and from the mutual influences that they (personal narratives and culture) exert upon one another.

Each chapter of *"I Grew Up in the Church"* responds to Robillard's call to consider how "personal experience is more than evidence and it is more than personal"[15] and ask what other goals life narratives might pursue and what influence they might have. This chapter answers that question by reading *Hermanas* through a lens of cultural rhetorics. The text is immersed in white evangelical culture and Latina or *evangélica* culture, two important currents within the evangelical movement. The book demonstrates how personal narratives take shape from cultural context, especially by tapping into cultural notions of self-representation and traditions like religious practices. To tell their stories and illuminate biblical texts, Kohn, Vega Quiñones, and Robinson draw upon vectors of cultural rhetoric like "systems, beliefs, relationships to the past, practices of meaning-making, and practices of carrying culture forward to future generations"[16] in evangelical and Latina cultures. Personal narrative, in fact, is one of these practices of meaning-making and carrying culture forward. As I have begun to show, it is also a space for analyzing systems, articulating and questioning beliefs, and examining relationships to the past.

I'd like to explain the language I use in discussing this text. While some writers and scholars use the gender inclusive *Latinx* or *Latine*, the three authors of *Hermanas* use *Latina* when they refer to themselves and to their families, colleagues, and readers. They include an "intentional reminder that it [the term *Latina*] is limited and must include African, Asian, and indigenous descendants" and give readers freedom "to identify with the term or not."[17] I follow their lead and use *Latina* when I describe, quote, or analyze the book's content. Kohn, Vega Quiñones, and Robinson also use *evangélica* to describe themselves and their communities. The term looks like a cognate for *evangelical*, but it does not denote political identity like *evangelical*; instead *evangélica* is a broader term that names those who see themselves as preaching *el evangelio*, the gospel.[18] In Sandra Maria Van Opstal's words, "This isn't merely a translation of the word into Spanish, it is a different expression of faith."[19] It also marks a contrast with white evangelicalism; as Van Opstal writes of her community, "Some might say 'We're not evangelical, *somos evangelicos.*'"[20] In *Hermanas*, the choice of *evangélica* embraces a broad definition of evangelicals, with an activist and outward focus but not conservative political commitments.

In their parachurch leadership and in writing *Hermanas*, Kohn, Vega Quiñones, and Robinson exert *rhetorical leadership.*[21] By this I mean their "ability to control the meaning or interpretation people give to events" and their work of "maneuver[ing] within and expand[ing] the opportunities of symbolic engagement and public influence."[22] In addition to the rhetoric that allows women to attain and hold leadership positions, I'm interested in identifying the ways rhetoric comprises their leadership and teasing out the ways their rhetoric has influence beyond the specific leadership role they occupy. Even beyond their explicit leadership roles, Kohn, Vega Quiñones, and Robinson "shape [their] community by defining and reinterpreting meanings"[23] and defining public language like *atrevida*. In *Hermanas*, they recount the rhetorical leadership they do in addition to the material leadership involved in their parachurch jobs, including speaking into local debates and publicly advocating for women. As *Hermanas* encourages women to pursue leadership roles, the book itself enacts rhetorical influence by maneuvering within the personal narrative genre and expanding opportunities for women to craft narratives about their lives.

Testimony and *Testimonio*

Kohn, Vega Quiñones, and Robinson recount scenes from their family lives, personal growth, and leadership, noting the resonance between these experiences and biblical stories. For example, Robinson opens her chapter on the Old Testament leader Deborah by recalling a moment from her seminary education when a professor affirmed that women could be leaders in evangelical churches. She watched male students, current or aspiring leaders in ministry, "swarm" the professor with their concerns and questions:

> Their biggest pushback was about the verses in 1 Timothy that state women should learn in submission and silence. They eagerly peppered him with questions and verses like these. It was glaringly obvious to me, though, that there were no women in this circle hovering around my professor. I remember thinking, *Do they not realize they aren't arguing about an issue but about my very existence here? Do they not understand what it feels like to be the object of a debate? This is not a theological conflict over a particular stance—this is personal to me. It involves the body I inhabit.*[24]

This scene captures central themes of *Hermanas*. Robinson portrays the resistance to women's leadership that these men confirm for one another and justify with the Bible. She begins with a scene of abstract debate over the text and then shifts focus to her embodied experience as a Latina Christian—another source of knowledge. This event in a seminary class underscores the ways evangelical institutions shape beliefs and practices when they argue about issues rather than witnessing lived experiences. I elaborate on those themes in following sections. Here, though, I explain how recollections like this one deploy cultural rhetorical practices of testimony and *testimonio*, two "meaningful theoretical frames from inside the [evangelical and Latinx] culture[s] in which they are situating their work."[25]

Testimony

Hermanas joins an evangelical tradition of testimony—what English professor Alan Jacobs calls "thinking narratively about individual lives."[26] Jacobs lays out how narrative has been a vital Christian practice from Augustine's fourth-century work *Confessions* to the present.[27] Contemporary Christians are "obliged" to "make their own lives into stories"[28] in a culture that calls on them to talk about their conversions and their growing faith. Verses like the Apostle Peter's admonition "always be ready to make your defense to anyone who demands from you an accounting for the hope that is in you"[29] can be interpreted as an impetus to apologetics arguments but can also be read as a call to share the experiences that brought them that hope. In fact, as Rachel Held Evans, Jen Hatmaker, and the other subjects of this book have argued, that storytelling can be a more productive and faithful "defense" than apologetics. Sometimes, though, these accounts of faith are merely self-absorbed or sentimental. Jacobs observes: "The triviality, even fatuousness, of many current ways of talking about 'our stories' has led many thoughtful Christians to abandon the traditions of personal narrative or testimony as tokens of misbegotten 'individualism.'"[30] In place of spiritually rich retrospection, we see "the proliferation of bland, solipsistic personal 'stories'" when self-narration is "removed from the webs of communal life."[31] Jacobs does not argue for abandoning the practice. Instead, he argues that twenty-first-century Christians need to enrich the practice of testimony by learning to tell "better and more responsible and more coherent personal stories"[32] that counsel their listeners and readers.

One way to do so is with analogical imagination, a tool that Kohn, Vega Quiñones, and Robinson deploy in their blend of personal narrative and textual exegesis. Jacobs defines analogical imagination as "the discovery of how different lives in different times and places belong nonetheless to the same genre."[33] I introduced this idea in chapter 2—analogical imagination is the ability to "see that when Mother Teresa of Calcutta speaks to the graduating students at Harvard she is doing something very like what Paul did when he spoke in the Areopagus of Athens."[34] This analogical imagination appears in *Hermanas* as the authors tease out parallels among ancient texts, personal experience of faith, and Latina communities in the United States. For Jacobs, cultivating this analogical imagination helps communities recognize a variety of genres as stories worth telling. Christians are likely familiar with the formulaic and sometimes not dramatic conversion story but they can come to "a stronger, deeper consciousness of the many life genres of the Christian faith."[35] These can include "testimonies of imitation and vocation"—stories of following Christ's teaching and living in the way God has called them to. Kohn, Vega Quiñones, and Robinson seem to agree. Their collection finds analogies between their lives and the accounts of biblical women, thereby expanding the "approved stories"[36] of contemporary United States evangelicalism to make space for diverse and complex experiences.

The chapter on the woman with chronic bleeding counsels readers to see themselves as women whose stories are worth telling because Jesus has called them to share the truths of their lives. In "*Mija* Leadership," Noemi Vega Quiñones retells the story from Matthew 9, Mark 5, and Luke 8. The woman in this story is unnamed, but "she is championed for her faith and called *Mija* (*mi hija*, my daughter) by Jesus."[37] The gospel accounts say she had been bleeding for twelve years, and Vega Quiñones conjectures that "her condition was probably a continual period of nonstop bleeding since the day she started menstruating" and would have made her life "socially insufferable."[38] Rather than approach Jesus directly, she touches his hem as he passes in the street. That contact heals her, but Jesus stops and insists on knowing who touched his clothes. When she steps forward to explain her need and her miraculous healing, he recognizes her faith and calls her "my daughter." Vega Quiñones interprets this encounter as a moment when Jesus invites *Mija* "to tell her story, to use her voice, and publicly receive her complete restoration."[39]

In her retelling, Vega Quiñones finds analogies to Latina experience and elaborates those analogies by thinking narratively about her own life. "Latinas in the United States may identify with the bleeding woman as overlooked, nameless, invisible, and in the margins," she writes.[40] The analogy is not only in her social location but in the invitation to receive healing and tell their stories. Latina readers can emulate the woman's courage and find power in their identities as "mijas and hermanas in the kingdom of God."[41] Like *Mija*, they can influence later generations by telling the truths about their lives and stories of their encounters with Jesus. Vega Quiñones then recounts her "own story of personal Mija transformation." After years of insecurity in her body and doubts about her leadership abilities, seeing "how Jesus interacted with women" healed her and offered "the leadership guide [she] had been seeking."[42] Stories like these in *Hermanas* continue a tradition of "autobiographical genres"—like conversion stories or Puritan spiritual journals—that "plot the graph of God's work in our lives."[43] Here and throughout the book, Kohn, Vega Quiñones, and Robinson use analogical imagination to expand those familiar genres with the complex stories of women in ancient texts.

Testimonio

Hermanas collects individual personal narratives, which we have seen is a common evangelical rhetorical and spiritual practice. However, the book expands this tradition by explicitly situating the authors' lives in their cultural and political contexts. The concept of *testimonio*, which names a "technique for the constitution of a subject that has undergone trauma or been marginalized and silenced by being placed in a 'border' condition between official or hegemonic discourses,"[44] more fully explains this rhetorical work. To paraphrase Casie Cobos et al., *testimonios* (re)historicize and (re)inscribe bodies and knowledges of Latina women who have been overlooked by the Western and white evangelical rhetorical tradition that values Protestant individualist genres of testimony.[45] Further, as Delgado Bernal, Burciaga, and Flores Carmona explain, "*Testimonio* differs from oral history or autobiography in that it involves the participant in a critical reflection of their personal experience within particular sociopolitical realities."[46] In *Hermanas*, that critical reflection, rehistoricization, and reinscription take place through individual stories, dialogues among stories, and biblical exegesis focused on lives in the margins. This critical reflection has rhetorical and political implications: "It engages the reader to understand and establish a sense of solidarity as a first step toward social change."[47]

Vega Quiñones uses *testimonio* as a framework to read and expound lessons about identity in the story of the woman with chronic bleeding. She reads trauma, silencing, and marginalization in the woman's fear as she approached Jesus in the crowd:

> She wanted to remain in the margins, in anonymity of her condition. Maybe that was her full identity—one forever hidden in

> the margins. Maybe she was embarrassed or maybe she was too focused on being healed to think of anything else. Maybe she didn't think she was worthy of approaching Jesus *cara a cara*, face to face. Maybe years of being treated as a nobody made her think she was a nobody. But Jesus wants her to be seen. And heard. Jesus helped her see the truth of who she really was.[48]

This retelling amplifies the bleeding woman's marginal position and finds a "perseverant attitude about life" in her resolve to seek healing.[49] Neither point—the woman's marginal position nor her perseverance—is apparent on the surface of the text, but analogical imagination uncovers those facets of the story. Couching her reading in "maybe," Vega Quiñones explores *Mija*'s interiority to bring immediacy and directness to the story and refocus readers on the woman's sociopolitical realities. She uses analogical imagination to reconstitute the bleeding woman's subjectivity, but rather than examine a biblical figure to uncover meaning in contemporary lives, she draws on contemporary experiences of marginalization, silencing, and trauma to uncover the deep meaning in the text.

The *Mija* chapter shows how *testimonio* can self-consciously craft a text collaboratively and locate knowledge in experience. A rhetor's individual subjectivity is an important feature, but the genre "challenges objectivity by situating the individual in communion with a collective experience marked by marginalization, oppression, or resistance."[50] This quality is salient in the ways Kohn, Vega Quiñones, and Robinson position themselves as coauthors, craft their stories in relation to biblical women, and invite readers to see themselves in the text. Vega Quiñones closes her discussion with a section titled "From Mija's Story to Your Story." She asks readers to speak back to her story and the biblical text: "What is your suffering? What truth do you have to tell?"[51] She exhorts them, "Repeat this truth to yourself for a season until you know in your bones that this is true: You are Mija, in whom the Lord delights."[52] The invitations to feel solidarity with Vega Quiñones and the New Testament woman, to speak back to the text, and to read *Mija*'s suffering and healing as a call to share their own truths all reimagine the Protestant testimony as a collective project.

Hermanas layers the practices of testimony and *testimonio*, emerging from and engaging both white evangelical culture and the cultures of Latina readers. The story of the woman with chronic bleeding, and the stories of Esther and Rahab that I study in the next two sections, call Latinas to cultivate a deep sense of their God-given dignity and conviction in the value of their stories. Kohn, Vega Quiñones, and Robinson invite readers to sit at the table and listen as they tell of individual encounters with evangelical culture and with God, meditate on contemporary applications of biblical texts, and name the material conditions of their lives. They also invite these far-flung *hermanas* to join in this practice of personal witness. Crafting and sharing personal narratives can be a profound and weighty practice. As theologian Elizabeth Conde-Frazier writes, "Some Latinas have come from places where their wish was for death, but the strength of the God of life gave them the power to face another day. They testify of this experience to others who need that same strength."[53] Telling, retelling, and reading these stories communally seeks to build that solidarity and strength.

"*Bienvenidos a la mesa, hermanas*!" Latina Perspectives and Leadership

Kohn, Vega Quiñones, and Robinson write from a perspective that evangelicals rarely hear and rarely recognize as a spiritual authority. Women of color inhabit multiply marginalized positions in twenty-first-century evangelicalism and work within a movement that actively tries to silence them. This present social reality has historical roots. In *White Too Long*, Robert P. Jones reviews "the historical record of lived Christianity in America," which "reveals that Christian theology and institutions have been the central cultural tent pole holding up the very idea of white supremacy."[54] Historians like Thomas Kidd and Mark Noll show that white evangelicals cited the Bible to defend legal and social inequality. Jerry Falwell opposed the civil rights movement by claiming that such political activity was a distraction from their mission of preaching the gospel. These stances are not just part of evangelical history. Many Christians were passive onlookers to these debates, and many continue to be silent "regarding concerns of people of color."[55] Anthea Butler is more direct in *White Evangelical Racism*. Butler writes, "The set of evangelicals who believed in and continue to believe in the inferiority of people of color are complicit in supporting structures of oppression that are antithetical to the gospel they claim to believe in."[56] These evangelical discourses of race and gender give books like *Hermanas* rhetorical force and urgency.[57]

Robinson interprets the Old Testament story of Esther as relevant to this context because it calls Latina women to claim identity and leadership "in the midst of unjust realities."[58] Robinson describes Esther's context: as a Hebrew woman, she belonged to "an ethnic minority community displaced and dispersed all over the provinces of King Xerxes of Persia."[59] Esther became a concubine of Xerxes and later became queen while hiding her Hebrew ethnicity.[60] As Robinson paraphrases the story, she elaborates on Esther's bicultural identity and imagines how Esther's experience of moving between dominant and minority cultures might offer a model of leadership to Latina readers:

> Initially, [Esther's cousin] Mordecai told Esther to keep her ethnicity a secret from others, which leads one to believe Esther was able to assimilate well into Persian culture. She was a *mestiza*, a bicultural woman holding onto two cultural worlds. She fit in with the dominant culture of the time, and the Lord granted her favor in a situation that was challenging and oppressive in many ways.[61]

Robinson's language here is incongruous with the ancient Middle Eastern context, though not inaccurate. Words and phrases like "assimilate," "*mestiza*," and "oppressive" do not appear in the original text, but they reframe that Old Testament story to have clear parallels with contemporary injustices and readers' "ethnic identity journey[s]."[62] That journey is one toward service and leadership. Esther learned to "use her power for the sake of her people." She grew from "a young bride who hid her Jewish identity" to "a leader who offered God all of who she was for his purposes in the world."[63] Robinson uses analogical imagination to connect Esther's story to her own experience of assimilation:

> To my Latino family, my fair complexion and lack of fluency in the language of my roots made me an outsider. Whenever I went to Mexico to visit relatives, I was known as a foreigner who didn't belong. Yet back in America I knew I didn't fit in either, even if on the surface I appeared to be at home among the dominant culture of the United States. While both spaces felt comfortable to me and both were part of me, neither felt like home. It can be challenging to live in this liminal space, but like Esther I found it opened doors for me, as well.[64]

Robinson took a job leading college ministry for Latino students and saw her ministry grow "from 10 to 150 people in just three years." At the same time, anti-immigrant legislation, racist rhetoric, and hateful behavior on her campus made work and life difficult for her community. "As a light-skinned Latina," she writes, "I had a choice to make." She could remain "a timid voice" and tolerate the rhetoric and behavior or use her reputation and influence to "proclaim that we as Latinos are people made in God's image."[65]

Both Esther and Robinson found themselves in kairotic moments, in both the rhetorical sense of the word (generally meaning timing, opportunity, or due measure) and the spiritual sense of "God's time."[66] When the government official Haman plotted to exterminate the Jews in Persia, Mordecai encouraged Esther, "And who knows but that you have come to your royal position for such a time as this."[67] Esther reveals her Hebrew identity to Xerxes, risking her own life, and asks him to prevent the genocide. Xerxes does so, and Robinson interprets this conclusion to mean that God opened "doors" of favor for Esther "for the purpose of rescuing his people."[68] Robinson had recognized a moment in her own life when violent, anti-immigrant rhetoric meant "it was no longer an option to hide behind my light complexion."[69] While her story doesn't have the decisive, heroic outcome of Esther's, she responded to God's call to "leverage whatever power [she] had to advocate for change."[70] She chose to be "a vocal advocate for [her] Latino community," particularly undocumented Latino students, acknowledging that her risk and struggle "paled in comparison" to theirs.[71]

Kohn, Vega Quiñones, and Robinson are generous in sharing their experiences, but they are clear that the white evangelical landscape makes personal narrative risky for women of color. Even though testifying to spiritual growth and God's work in believers' lives is a common and valued practice in both white evangelical and *evangélica* communities, Kohn, Vega Quiñones, and Robinson all describe obstacles to speaking. In her reading of the woman who seeks healing from Jesus, Vega Quiñones observes, "Sometimes, we shy away from telling the whole truth because of what others may say or because we are afraid to expose powers and principalities at work in our barrios."[72] In her chapter on Esther, Robinson recalls times in her early life when she "stored [her] cultural narratives away in the past." "Such stories were beautiful and meaningful," Robinson reflects, "yet they were narratives no one around me would understand or consider normal. I just wanted to be normal."[73] In other words, they lack adequate witnesses who will pay attention, listen without judging, and respond ethically.

Further, not all women know how to use their stories rhetorically. In their cowritten introduction, Kohn, Vega Quiñones, and Robinson write, "We seek to be women who learn from one another and who learn to share our stories with each other."[74] Obstacles to speaking, or the idea that storytelling is a learned skill rather than an organic one, are consistent with the cultural practice of *testimonio*. The central rhetorical trope of *testimonio* is the "speaker who narrates his or her story under the duress of the social order's threat of abjection, invisibility, or death" and "who is the direct, personal witness of a collective traumatic condition or event."[75] For *Mija*, telling one's story allows the world to see private suffering. In Esther's narrative, telling one's story makes the speaker vulnerable to violence. *Hermanas* warns readers that learning to testify to their experiences requires care. Their accounts of invisibility, violence, or silencing cut against the grain of a white evangelicalism that denies or minimizes racism and sexism and opposes women's leadership. Women risk alienation from their faith communities for describing these realities.

In their stories, Kohn, Vega Quiñones, and Robinson reflect on their roles as Latina leaders in evangelical organizations. They tell of being doubted, discouraged, and denied the authority afforded to their male counterparts. They also tell stories of witnessing pain and injustice in the culture around them but seeing little response from white evangelicals, or confronting limits on their speech when they wish to address social justice issues. In all these cases, though, they contend that personal narrative can be transformative for the tellers and for other women, even across time. Robinson invites readers to speak back to the text and reflect on how their identity might be "a gift for [God's] greater purposes." She asks, "Who will be the multicultural Latinas that God will continue to raise up 'for such a time as this' in each coming generation?" Her exegesis of Esther's story, and the analogy she finds in her own story, encourage Latina women by telling them they have been positioned to play a role "in the unfinished narrative of God's unfolding kingdom."[76] For Latina Christians, claiming that influence is a risk worth taking.

Shaping an Evangelical *Manera de Ser*

Kohn, Vega Quiñones, and Robinson bring visibility to sexism and racism in evangelical spaces to present evidence of those social realities and to shift readers' worldviews. Not only do they teach women to value their stories and to see analogies in the Bible, they teach women to read the Bible as concerned with practical and emotional realities of their lives, not just doctrine. I have alluded to the ways *Hermanas* teaches audiences to read the Bible—the chapters on *Mija*, Rahab, and Esther model dialogical engagement and analogical imagination—and I expand on that theme here. *Hermanas* teaches readers to find liberation in the Bible by highlighting the material realities of daily life, emotion, and an intimate and challenging relationship with God, all central to a vision of Latina leadership.

Teaching readers to read and interpret the Bible is of course a minefield and exposes the authors to accusations of rejecting the authority or inerrancy of God's word. But Latina theologians hold that the Bible is not a neutral book. It aided in the conquest of Latin America and the Caribbean as "the colonizer used the text and his interpretation of the text to control the colonized."[77] It has also been used to control women, as we have seen across many examples in personal narratives. Even knowing this history, Conde-Frazier argues that biblical texts "facilitate a dialogue of intimacy between God and the reader in which Scripture itself models the possibility for God and the woman to enter into a conversation that allows her to challenge God as much as God challenges her."[78] Advancing their vision—a reading practice that replaces control and literalism with intimacy and conversation—is another risk worth taking.

To elaborate on this intimate and challenging engagement with the Bible, *Hermanas* calls on the concept of *manera de ser* from Latina theology. As Loida I. Martell-Otero explains in the foundational book on this subject, *Latina Evangélicas*, Latina theology (the study of God) emerges from the daily realities of women's lives. Their theology, therefore, is not only intellectual reflection on the Bible or church practice. Latina theology articulates "a given praxis, a reflection on *una manera de ser* ('a way of life') in a community that struggles daily with issues of survival within a context of economic injustice and multilayered discrimination."[79] As Robinson's internal protest, "*This is not a theological conflict over a particular stance—this is personal to me. It involves the body I inhabit*,"[80] and other instances in *Hermanas* show, that experience is an embodied one. Latina *evangélica* theology reflects a "cultural matrix" in which women from Latin American or Latin-Caribbean backgrounds living in the continental United States share "experiences of bilingualism, multiculturalism, popular religious faith, marginality, poverty, colonialization, migration, and cultural alienation."[81]

Conde-Frazier calls it "the experience of crying out, the struggle, and the resistance that come from *lo cotidiano*, everyday life."[82] Like Cherrie Moraga's "theory in the flesh," Kohn, Vega Quiñones, and Robinson develop their knowledge of God from "the physical realities of our lives—our skin color, the land or concrete we grew up on, our sexual longings—all fuse to create a politic born out of necessity."[83] In this theology based in struggle and way of life, Christianity is contextual rather than doctrinal.

Rather than asking readers to set aside their subjective and emotional experiences and privilege literal or objective truth in the Bible, *Hermanas* teaches them "how to feel" as they read. Faith Kurtyka articulates the concept of "learning how to feel" in her study of conversion narratives, where she argues that these stories do not document sudden, 180-degree changes, but rather progressions of socially constructed emotions.[84] Conversion narratives show how people "move through various subjectivities, re-consider opinions and systems of belief, and articulate their emotional journeys as they join new communities."[85] Testimonies and *testimonios*, likewise, document how the rhetors arrived at new ways of feeling about the teaching and leadership of women and prompt similar journeys in readers. Emotion and affective experiences also add to the significance of reading the Bible. This view of the Bible diverges from conservative evangelicalism by holding that "Scripture is important, not because of some a priori argument of infallibility, but rather because it speaks to actual life realities facing the Latina community in the spaces of the everyday."[86] That is, the Bible serves not to support an argument or direct a person's actions, but to connect "the God of the Scriptures with the reader in a communicative moment of intimacy."[87]

Hermanas teaches readers how to feel by highlighting the emotion lying below the surface of stories and encouraging them to approach reading as an intimate, affective encounter. In her chapter on the Song of Solomon, Kohn invites readers to "allow these verses to wash over you, like a waterfall bringing refreshment to your ear and reviving your soul."[88] She centers feelings, not authority or literal truth, when she writes "this ancient and magnificent song holds truths of how Jesus feels about you. You have stolen his heart. . . . You are his *amada*, his beloved."[89] Similarly, in her later chapter on the Old Testament figure Hannah, who prayed desperately for a child and gave birth to the prophet Samuel, Kohn proposes that emotion is at the root of both faith and public influence. "When we feel safe to express ourselves," she writes, "we are generally passionate, expressive, and free with our emotions."[90] She describes Latina women as people who "use their emotions to connect to others" and know "how to celebrate and how to mourn"—a gift to their communities.[91] By entering into Hannah's world to see her "raw pain" and how she interacts with God,[92] readers learn to "value and 'stay with'" the negative emotions that are part of Christian faith.[93]

The chapter on Rahab is one place where the authors try to reshape the emotions that evangelicals bring to their participation in faith communities, particularly toward women's leadership in those communities. Titled "*Atrevida*, Allied, and Faithful Liberator," this section of the book reclaims the word *atrevida* to cultivate appreciation and admiration for women who are "audacious, insolent, bold."[94] As a girl, Noemi Vega Quiñones heard *atrevida* as a rebuke when she was outgoing or bold, like when she spoke to children on the playground who she didn't know, or when she invited her entire second grade class to her birthday party. Vega Quiñones explains that the term reinscribes prohibitions against women's leadership or public teaching: "When a girl exhibits leadership characteristics and assertiveness, she may be labeled una atrevida."[95] After internalizing the rebuke, "*No seas atrevida, Noemi*," she had to learn to feel pride, not shame, about her bold *manera de ser*, her way of being. As an adult in Christian seminary or church, she at first tried to conform to the meek and quiet femininity valued in those spaces. However, experience and stories like Rahab led her to lean into a leadership style she calls "an atrevida for the Lord."[96] Vega Quiñones reads Rahab as both a victim and hero during the Israelite conquest of Canaan (as told in the Old Testament book of

Joshua). She worked as a prostitute in Jericho and encountered two Israelite spies who entered the city. In return for protecting them, she secured a pledge that the Israelites would spare her family in the impending attack. Rahab declared her faith in the God of Israel, left Jericho, and joined the Israelites after the conquest. Vega Quiñones interprets that story as teaching that "God at times calls us to take courageous steps of faith that require tapping into the deep part of us that *is* bold and willing to take risks."[97] Rahab, like Latinas in the United States, "learned to survive in places that were not designed for [her] survival."[98] The New Testament names her as an ancestor of Jesus and a person of notable faith, suggesting that she became active in Israelite society.[99]

Vega Quiñones finds ambiguities in Rahab's story that hold lessons for Latina leadership. She muses, "We don't know the full spectrum of Rahab's personality, and I think that is a very good thing for us as we think about our own leadership development"; and she emboldens readers, saying, "The Lord can partner with you just as you are, just the way you are wired."[100] Rahab's story also leaves her national loyalty ambiguous, but readers can imagine her range of feelings: "She might have been upset that she had to abandon Jericho and flee to the Israelite camp, or she may have felt joyful that she could start a new life with her immediate loved ones."[101] Latina Christians in the contemporary United States can see in Rahab's story a call to be "informed about the political life, health, and impact of [their] communities" but, at the same time, ground their leadership in being "allied to the Lord."[102] Here, dialogic engagement and analogical imagination are powerful strategies to build knowledge from a reader's *manera de ser*. Kohn, Vega Quiñones, and Robinson invite women to see the everyday truths of the lives in the text and give them "prompts" that teach them how to respond to what they read. This dialogic engagement can also create a new *manera de ser*, a new way of being, based on the bone-deep knowledge that "leadership in partnership with God is liberating, freeing, and empowering."[103] Even the tradition of analogical imagination is a practice of speaking to and with a biblical text, rethinking old, destructive ways of being—or feeling—and claiming new, liberating ways.

Hermanas makes clear that Latinas are the book's main audience. In these first three strategies, the writers enact that priority. Reading as a white woman from a Christian background, I understood and learned from the writers' theological points, but I saw my identity and perspective decentered. I felt this most acutely in their readings of Esther and Rahab (and in their attention to Tabitha, a character I had never really noticed). These interpretations also made me aware of the blind spots in the ways I learned to read Bible stories. I had never read Rahab as part of the lineage of Jesus, and I had never read Esther as a girl navigating a multicultural identity. I had never noticed that both were women moving between cultures, and no pastor had ever pointed that out. More commonly, the church held them up as decontextualized examples of women who obeyed God's calls to individual heroic actions. I have often heard women encouraged that God called them to specific work "for such as time as this," but without any recognition of Esther's specific multicultural context. *Hermanas* challenges the assumptions of men and white women and highlights the ways that the mainstream reading practices of U.S. evangelicals are based in assumptions of whiteness.

Confronting Individualism in White Evangelical Belief and Practice

Hermanas extends these discussions of identity to calls for change. The book asks readers to reflect on systemic racism and sexism, a message that presents friction for readers steeped in individualist assumptions about the Bible and their own lives—and perhaps also steeped in reflexive hostility to discussions of privilege. In chapters on *Mija*, Rahab, Tabitha, and Deborah (an Israelite leader), the authors name the oppression and marginalization that Latinas face, including in the contemporary evangelical church. These chapters examine the stories of women who are stark exceptions to a quiet and subordinate model of biblical womanhood. Their examples instead model bold leadership against injustice and their stories are starting points for analyzing power and privilege in Christian terms.

Hermanas shows readers how to think about women's lives within systems of power, approaching this issue through biblical study before turning to political analysis. Reflecting on the woman with chronic bleeding and the neglect and separation she must have felt, Vega Quiñones offers a modern analogy. She writes, "Systemically, barrios are the neglected neighborhoods, separated by race, in our cities known for high crime rates, high pregnancy rates, high dropout rates, low educational attainment, and underfunded schools. When people think of *el barrio* they seldom think of the people who dwell there that are created in the *imago Dei* (the image of God)."[104] Later, she concludes Rahab's chapter and the "Identity" section by reading Rahab as a leader who disrupts systems:

> Her leadership is not only for her advancement, but also for the advancement of her family and her immediate community. She initiates the oath with the men, asking for her personal physical salvation, as well as advocating for her family's physical salvation. Systemically, Rahab's presence as a foreigner in the Israelite community disrupts the attempt to be an ethnically pure community.[105]

Vega Quiñones interprets Rahab as disruptive to traditional gender roles and ethnic purity, and to notions of salvation that are only spiritual and ignore physical safety. She also applies Rahab's story as a lesson about Latina bodies that disrupt predominantly white institutions. She writes, "Latina bodies are a visual indication that certain structures are still unjust, racist, and exclude whole communities."[106] The analogy to Rahab suggests that their disruptive nature is in fact a quality that can bring about necessary and life-saving changes.

These readings of systemic injustice and systemic healing support calls for women's leadership in evangelical and *evangélica* cultures. Kristy Garza Robinson describes how experience in a male-dominated seminary led her to Deborah, a leader and "a key person in the narrative of God."[107] Whereas other stories show unconventional leadership, Deborah held an official position at the head of Israelite society. Robinson summarizes her historical context from the book of Judges. After twenty years, when Israel had been oppressed by the Canaanite army, "God responded [to their oppression] with Deborah, a prophetess and the first woman judge."[108] She led by receiving revelations from God and urging the Israelite commander Barak to fight back against the Canaanite army. Robinson summarizes the role Deborah played:

> She directed [Israelite commander] Barak when to go out to do battle, assuring him that God had promised the victory despite what it may have felt like or looked like in the moment. She marched out with him, and there was a slaughter of all their enemies, including the leader himself being killed by a woman named Jael, hence fulfilling Deborah's prophecy: the victory would fall to a woman.[109]

When Robinson's evangelical colleagues ignored her contributions, she found reassurance in seeing that God gave Deborah authority in her patriarchal culture and knowing that Deborah's work is recorded in a Bible "overwhelmingly tilted toward the stories about and by men."[110] She quotes Deborah's song about the victory, which inspired Robinson to advocate for her own voice "while also elevating the voices of other women."[111] In Robinson's reading, evangelicals might see Deborah as an example when faith and obedience require a woman to transgress gender hierarchies. Her language in critiquing patriarchy is careful—for example, saying the Bible is "tilted" toward men—but a starting point.

Kohn, Vega Quiñones, and Robinson link systems and structures of power with identities and faith communities, readings that contradict the evangelical hermeneutics that emphasize individual sin and salvation. Robert P. Jones explains the individual view of faith that dominates white evangelicalism:

> In the personal Jesus paradigm, Jesus did not die for a cause or for humankind writ large but for each individual person. Responding positively to this invitation, entering into this relationship, is an intimate decision that must be made freely by each person as an accountable act of the will. . . . There's nothing in this conceptual model to provide a toehold for thinking about the way institutions or culture shape, promote, or limit human decisions or well-being.[112]

This mindset has also led some prominent white evangelicals to ignore poverty and violence, which they see as distractions from the essential mission of preaching the gospel. That posture appears in the twentieth century and in evangelical discourse at the time. In 2018, John MacArthur and a dozen other male leaders published "The Statement on Social Justice & the Gospel" online. The statement (which affirms complementarianism and declares, "We reject 'gay Christian' as a legitimate biblical category") states "We . . . deny that one's ethnicity establishes any necessary connection to any particular sin" and "We emphatically deny that lectures on social issues (or activism aimed at reshaping the wider culture) are as vital to the life and health of the church as the preaching of the gospel and the exposition of Scripture."[113] When Kohn, Vega Quiñones, and Robinson lay out biblical insights about systems, identities, and communities, they are rejecting an evangelical hermeneutic with historical and theological roots and prominent contemporary advocates.

Tabitha's story illustrates an alternative to the false division between justice work and the gospel. She participated in *misión integral*, which Vega Quiñones defines as "holistic mission that was deeply Jesus and deeply justice."[114] Vega Quiñones draws a parallel between this term (with origins in South American liberation theology) and Tabitha's reputation in the book of Acts "as a woman who was 'always doing good and helping the poor.'"[115] Specifically, Tabitha made clothes for the poor in her city of Joppa. Far from diverging from the gospel, Tabitha "took seriously Jesus' message to love the poor and care for their needs (Matthew 5, Luke 4, Isaiah 58)."[116] The text says that Tabitha's whole community mourned when she died. When the Apostle Peter raised her back to life, her return represented "personal and systemic revival" because she was "able to continue her ministry to the marginalized."[117] Citing this text, and accounts of Jesus' teachings, Vega Quiñones argues that Christian leadership that cares for people's needs here on earth is part of the essential mission of the church.

When seminaries and evangelical leaders interpret a text narrowly or literally, they ignore the full message of Jesus and the cultural contexts that give stories their full meanings. *Hermanas* contends that the personal Jesus paradigm "results in a truncated gospel," and elevating men over women excludes "key [people] in the narrative of God."[118] Instead, *Hermanas* develops a religious rhetoric that counters individualist readings and decontextualized interpretations of the Bible, both of which have been prevalent in white evangelicalism. For Latina *evangélicas*, the Bible represents a dialectic between oppression and liberation, and in that dialectic Kohn, Vega Quiñones, and Robinson find guidance for their work as leaders.

Conclusion

Kohn, Vega Quiñones, and Robinson build their rhetorical leadership by centering and amplifying Latina voices and experiences within a predominantly white evangelical movement. They hold positions as directors and coordinators in evangelical organizations, where their very presence challenges a legacy of white supremacy. By engaging tenets of the faith like individualism, and the ways those tenets enable oppression, the authors make a case that Latina evangelicals bring vital knowledge to religious communities. They also call readers to contemplate what the Bible and the stories of Latina *evangélicas* say about systemic injustices in the church. In a movement that gives authority to white male voices and theologies, centering women's perspectives and biblical interpretations situated in experience as a minoritized group in the United States is a radical move.

I expect few rhetoricians are familiar with *Hermanas*, but the text opens a window into the ways personal narratives develop from and respond to cultural contexts, as well as the multiple rhetorical goals they can pursue. Despite the patriarchal, white supremacist currents in the churches and organizations where they work, Kohn, Vega Quiñones, and Robinson find that their experiences as Latina women in evangelical spaces empower and call them to write and lead. They unpack biblical models of leadership and enact rhetorical leadership through storytelling that calls on cultural practices of testimony, *testimonio*, and Latina *evangélica* theology. Kohn, Vega Quiñones, and Robinson join other Latina evangelicals who counter individualism and decontextualized readings of the Bible, like pastor Sandra Maria Van Opstal or theologians Loida I. Martell-Otero, Zaida Maldonado Pérez, and Elizabeth Conde-Frazier. A continued discussion of Latina rhetorical leadership in evangelicalism might look to these writers.

For both evangelicals and feminists, "personal narratives have been a productive way to bring dissension and conflict to the activist table."[119] Reading Kohn, Vega Quiñones, and Robinson, we see how their approach to leadership pushes back against the evangelical worldview that marginalizes Latina voices and ignores or denies systemic injustice. *Hermanas* often reads as an encouraging work of woman-to-woman mentorship, but moments of direct critique punctuate their exhortations and call evangelicals to learn from their stories and their interpretations. Both together form the counsel that Jacobs calls for in the modern church.

Conclusion

"No Power of Hell, No Scheme of Man"[1]

Evangelical women's personal narratives of living in, leading in, and sometimes leaving the evangelical movement illustrate the dramatic influences of that environment upon their lives and work. In this way, their accounts call to mind the biblical parable of the sower. The New Testament passages of Matthew 13:1–23, Mark 4:1–20, and Luke 8:4–15 all recount versions of this anecdote from Jesus' ministry:

> That same day Jesus went out of the house and sat beside the sea. Such great crowds gathered around him that he got into a boat and sat there, while the whole crowd stood on the beach. And he told them many things in parables, saying: "Listen! A sower went out to sow. And as he sowed, some seeds fell on the path, and the birds came and ate them up. Other seeds fell on rocky ground, where they did not have much soil, and they sprang up quickly, since they had no depth of soil. But when the sun rose, they were scorched; and since they had no root, they withered away. Other seeds fell among thorns, and the thorns grew up and choked them. Other seeds fell on good soil and brought forth grain, some a hundredfold, some sixty, some thirty."[2]

Jesus goes on to unpack the parable to his listeners:

> "Hear then the parable of the sower. When anyone hears the word of the kingdom and does not understand it, the evil one comes and snatches away what is sown in the heart; this is what was sown on the path. As for what was sown on rocky ground, this is the one who hears the word and immediately receives it with joy; yet such a person has no root, but endures only for a while, and when trouble or persecution arises on account of the word, that person immediately falls away. As for what was sown among thorns, this is the one who hears the word, but the cares

> of the world and the lure of wealth choke the word, and it yields nothing. But as for what was sown on good soil, this is the one who hears the word and understands it, who indeed bears fruit and yields, in one case a hundredfold, in another sixty, and in another thirty."[3]

Pastors like Mark Driscoll can choke out a woman's commitment to the kingdom of God by limiting her role or discouraging curiosity about the difficult passages of the Bible. As Rachel Held Evans attests, congregations might cause nascent beliefs or faith communities to wither by denying the fundamental humanity of those who are not straight white men. In contrast, leaders like Kohn, Vega Quiñones, and Robinson can cultivate faith by encouraging study and participation—by creating good soil. Personal narrative, by attending to both individual experience and broader culture, attests that each of these environments exist within the evangelical movement.

Evangelical women are sowers, too. As the chapters in this book have shown, they are active rhetors who enter into debates about politics, doctrine, culture, and the purpose of religious institutions. Like the seeds in the parable, women's speech and writing about problems in the twentieth-century evangelical movement land among varied audiences. Their personal narratives sometimes fall on deaf ears and other times elicit attention—maybe joy—that quickly dissipates. Those stories might shift discourse only briefly before being drowned out by the combative, dogmatic, entrenched voices in the movement. Women compose and circulate accounts of their lived experiences in an evangelical discourse community that is often thorny, rocky, and arid.

However, we have seen that some personal narratives do land on hospitable soil where they can take root and grow. Evangelical women like Sarah Bessey and Austin Channing Brown write books that become bestsellers; others, like Karen Swallow Prior, work with the most prominent publishers and publications in evangelical media; and writers like Jen Hatmaker attract diverse followings as they narrate parts of their lives on social media. Moreover, research by institutions like PRRI shows that from 2008–2018 evangelicals were receptive to their stories. Political events and the declining numbers and influence of white Christians in America meant that readers were curious about the experiences of women, non-white Christians, and Gen X and millennial writers. These rhetors gained new footholds in evangelical discourse. With their growing influence, they showed readers how to reconsider the commonplaces and practices that had made evangelical rhetoric alienating and damaging to so many in and near the movement.

Studying evangelicalism as a movement asks how its rhetoric spurs or directs public engagement, creates cohesion or division among factions, and reinforces or undermines power structures. By tracing relationships to other movements, like fundamentalism or feminism, this study shows how evangelical rhetoric plays out in the vernacular texts of evangelical women. Print and digital personal narratives shift public evangelical discourse by creating coalitions, voicing critiques, and making space for "new beliefs, identities, and experiences."[4] In some cases, this oppositional discourse can influence the policies of evangelical churches and governing bodies and be a tool for material change.[5] These texts show that personal narrative is a fruitful way for "ordinary" people to participate in public discourse.

As rhetors, evangelical women sow with purpose and care. In personal narratives, orthodox, ex-evangelical, progressive, non-white, and leadership-focused evangelicals craft their rhetorical work for a movement that is varied and turbulent. Gardeners pay attention to which seeds will germinate and thrive in their soil. For example, living in East Tennessee, I know that some plants find our mountain winters too harsh and our growing season too short. I learned that one corner of my garden is in shade by the end of August when the sun follows a path across the sky that is lower than its path in June. Likewise, evangelical women pay attention to the climate and the audiences in the evangelical movement. Like gardeners, they know that a plot of ground can become more fertile over time as old plants die, decay, and become new soil.

My white evangelical background is probably showing in the way I unpack this parable. In that world, I absorbed the practice of connecting a biblical passage to my own life and using it to give meaning to events that are far removed from the original context in which the words were recorded. My interpretation here is probably too tidy. But the parable of the sower is an apt text to sum up how evangelical women are both subjects and agents, how the evangelical movement is both hospitable and hostile, and how writers of personal narratives deploy strategy and knowledge but do not control the impacts their texts might have.

Personal Narrative as the Practice of Hope

For evangelical women, writing and sharing stories from their lives is an exercise in hope. This is the aspect of evangelical women's rhetorical work that I find compelling as I conclude my study of their responses to the 2008–2018 decade of decline. Their faith in divine providence and God's perfect timing, or *kairos*, motivates their work. God, not the writer, ultimately determines whether a text "bears fruit and yields, in one case a hundredfold, in another sixty, and in another thirty."[6] That belief is not discouraging or disempowering. Rather, it emboldens speech and writing in hostile or inhospitable environments.

That hope might embolden self-representation and autobiographical storytelling. In *Writing at the End of the World*, Richard Miller reflects on the rise of technology, the globalized economy, and the violence and disaffection in society and asks, "How—and in what limited ways—might reading and writing be made to matter in the new world that is evolving before our eyes?"[7] He reiterates the question more bluntly: "Why bother with reading and writing when the world is so obviously going to hell?"[8] Miller finds one reason, and an exception to the waning significance of literacy, in the popularity of memoir. Using Mary Karr's 1999 bestseller *The Liar's Club* as an example, Miller argues that "the memoir allows one to plunge into the darkness of the past; it provides the means both for evoking and for making sense of that past; and it can be made to generate a sense of possibility, a sense that a better, brighter future is out there to be secured."[9] Exactly, evangelical women would say. The narratives I have analyzed testify to church abuse, racism, and sexism; they make sense of how those injustices emerge from evangelical doctrine and rhetoric; they imagine new possibilities for evangelical rhetoric and culture.

For evangelical women, the reason to write also lies in faithful obedience and belief in God's ultimate control. A divine call to share their experiences authorizes women like Austin Channing Brown, Jen Hatmaker, Rachel Held Evans, Natalia Kohn, Noemi Vega Quiñones, Kristy Robinson, and others to write against the grain of evangelical rhetoric. It also offers them hope that their work will find audiences and bear fruit even if they do not see that harvest—whether because it happens in private lives or because, like Evans, they die before it can transpire. Women are fully aware of the earthly and human realities of the evangelical movement. They are motivated even more by their belief in transcendent truths and divine power.

Evangelical women, who I position as part of the broader community of feminist rhetoricians, "are buoyed by hope."[10] Their hope proceeds from the conviction that writing and other forms of symbolic action have the power to bring about change—despite all the evidence that many in the movement will resist or dismiss their arguments. In chapter 4 I cited Hatmaker's words, published in a blog post after she was "cancelled" for her views on same-sex marriage: "New life is always possible evidently, well past the moment it makes sense to still hope for it."[11] Entrenched power and persistent racism and sexism mean it makes little sense to call out injustice or advocate for new political commitments. Still, their belief in a divine plan gives them hope that their words will have life.

To be sure, appeals to "God's timing" and divine providence can amount to clichés. In chapter one, my rhetorical history, I explained how the commonplace of divine providence can permit evangelicals to shrug off responsibility for their words and actions.

This type of hope reminds me of the bumper sticker "Let go and let God" or the 2005 Carrie Underwood song "Jesus Take the Wheel." Unlike these passive expressions of faith, the hope I see in evangelical women's writing is active. Like Glenn, who declares, "We can use our feminist rhetorical agency, our rhetorical feminism, to realize our hope,"[12] evangelical and ex-evangelical women find that hope gives them direction and boldness. Rachel Held Evans finds and amplifies marginalized voices on her blog and in her books because she hopes that she can model a more just and hospitable evangelical rhetoric. Kohn, Vega Quiñones, and Robinson interweave their individual stories, their cultural contexts, and their interpretations of biblical texts with the hope that doing so will address a pressing need for mentorship among *evangélicas*. For these rhetors, hope motivates work.

Austin Channing Brown describes a hope that is not only active, but also has endurance. She explains that pain accompanies hope, calling on the evidence from her life as a Black evangelical woman. She writes, "The persistence of racism in America—individual and societal—is altogether overwhelming. It doesn't lay the best fertilizer for hope to grow."[13] In her own life, hope "has died one thousand deaths."[14] She offers examples that lend specificity to this theme: "I hoped that friend would get it, but hope died. I hoped that person would be an ally for life, but hope died. I hoped that my organization really desired change, but hope died. I hoped I'd be treated with the full respect I deserve at my job, but hope died. I hoped that racist policies would change, and just policies would never be reversed, but hope died."[15] Yet she continues to work in evangelical institutions and write from her experiences.

She zooms out, extending her reflections beyond the personal-as-evidence and locating them in the broader landscape of 2018 America:

> I look at the present—police brutality, racial disparities, backlash against being "politically correct," hatred for our first Black president, the gutting of the Voting Rights Act, and the election of a chief executive who stoked the fire of racial animosity to

> win—and I ask myself, *Where is your hope, Austin?* The answer: It is but a shadow.
>
> It is working in the dark, not knowing if anything I do will ever make a difference. It is speaking anyway, writing anyway, loving anyway. It is enduring disappointment and then getting back to work. It is knowing this book may be read only by my Momma, and writing it anyway. It is pushing back, even though my words will never be big enough, powerful enough, weighty enough to change everything. It is knowing that God is God and I am not.[16]

Brown describes a very specific type of hope: the drive to work without tangible encouragement. She demonstrates how rhetoric comes from religious belief. Religious rhetoric often amounts to "rhetoric about religion" or symbolic action that borrows evangelical rhetorical practices, like the confession genre. In Brown, though, we see theology and tenets of belief woven into and empowering rhetorical action. This is an important area of ongoing research: how do belief and theology, which we must analyze as culturally situated, motivate and shape religious rhetoric? The ending to *I'm Still Here* shows how personal narratives rooted in religious experience and faith can resist the formulas often seen in autobiographical speech and writing. This is an account of persisting in vocation, or calling, which is more complex than formulaic testimonies or conversion stories.

Brown offers her experience not only as evidence (of racism, of the seeming futility of resistance) but as a starting point. Her conclusion points to problems that scholars of evangelical rhetoric and of women's personal narratives will want to address. It is worth asking how evangelical women's commitments to a generous orthodoxy, to hospitable rhetoric, to progressive Christianity, and to inclusive leadership might prepare them to respond to the New Right, to white Christian nationalism, and to threats to democracy. That rhetoric might also offer creative ways to build bridges to Christians who deconstruct their faith or grow disillusioned with the church and its anemic responses to trauma and violence.

Evangelical women, too, will run into these questions as they contemplate their role in the movement. After years of limited willingness or ability to discuss politics and racial violence, they will need to ask whether a renovated evangelical rhetoric can address police brutality, racial disparities, and politics that stoke racial animosity. The problems facing evangelicals in the United States are complex. Personal narrative, which looks back to document years of individual and collective struggle and ahead to envision years of individual and collective change, is a rhetorical practice that can hold that complexity.

Epilogue

Evangelical conversations about identity, rhetoric, and justice did not end in 2018. Personal narratives continued to circulate, and controversies continued to flare up, as factions within the movement debated how to engage with each other and with the culture and politics of the United States. Events like the Black Lives Matter protests of 2020 and bestselling books like *Jesus and John Wayne* and *The Making of Biblical Womanhood* further revealed how many tenets of evangelicalism reflect cultural contexts, not timeless biblical truth. And women, including the ones in these chapters, continued to write about their lives. This epilogue turns to those events and texts from the years just after the period *"I Grew Up in the Church"* studies. I ask how they shed light on the rhetorical work of orthodox evangelicals, ex-evangelicals, progressives, and leaders.

Some of those texts featured in my earlier chapters. *Jesus and John Wayne*, a source I used to compile my rhetorical history and analyze Mark Driscoll, came out in 2020. The book and author Kristin Kobes Du Mez received immediate acclaim and attention. *Jesus and John Wayne* analyzes white evangelical culture in the United States after about 1955 to show that

> generations of evangelicals learned to be afraid of communists, feminists, liberals, secular humanists, "the homosexuals," the United Nations, the government, Muslims, and immigrants, and they were primed to respond to those fears by looking to a strong man to rescue them from danger, a man who embodied a God-given, testosterone-driven masculinity.[1]

As a result, the book argues, notions of "biblical manhood" owe more to cultural icons like John Wayne and movies like *Braveheart* than to the teachings of Jesus. In a now widely quoted passage she writes, "In 2016, many observers were stunned at evangelicals' apparent betrayal of their own values," and explains, "In reality, evangelicals did not cast their vote despite their beliefs, but because of them."[2] *Christianity Today* called *Jesus and John Wayne* "paradigm-influencing."[3] The book was a surprise bestseller (and Du Mez gained an even wider audience through podcast interviews), and reviews pointed to its importance for historians and evangelicals alike.[4] *Jesus and John Wayne* became a foundational text for individuals seeking to disentangle Christian faith from toxic elements in evangelical culture and to renovate evangelical views of gender.

One of those seekers, Mike Cosper, drew on *Jesus and John Wayne* for his 2021 podcast documenting Mark Driscoll's arc as a Seattle megachurch pastor. The twelve episodes of *The Rise and Fall of Mars Hill* detail Driscoll's top-down leadership, his preoccupation with growth and his brand, and the reason his church ultimately closed. Cosper quoted *Jesus and John Wayne* and interviewed Du Mez to explain why Driscoll's aggressive alpha-male style was both popular with evangelicals and problematic for a man claiming to preach the word of God. The podcast was itself a phenomenon in 2021. *The Rise and Fall of Mars Hill* had over 2.5 million downloads, a #1 ranking on Apple's religion podcasts, and a brief spot as one of Apple's top three podcasts.[5] Cosper calls the story "painfully relevant" more than a decade after the events it chronicles. With his interviewees, he shows how Driscoll's rhetoric reverberates in a movement that holds up church growth, aggressive combativeness, and unwavering conservatism as evidence of Christian faith.

The Making of Biblical Womanhood by Beth Allison Barr also challenged twenty-first-century evangelical rhetoric and belief by chronicling historical events. Rather than looking at prior decades in the United States, though, Barr introduces evangelicals to evidence of patriarchy in ancient Mesopotamia, in Roman household codes, in medieval Europe, and in the Reformation. Barr asks, "Shouldn't the historical continuity of a practice that has caused women to fare much worse than men for thousands of years cause concern? Shouldn't Christians, who are called to be different from the world, treat women *differently*?"[6]

Barr weaves personal narrative with that historical evidence and textual analysis. Each chapter begins by recounting instances when she encountered patriarchal thought in the church, including the church where her husband was a pastor (and where she, despite her knowledge of Christian theology and history was not allowed to teach adult Sunday School). She writes:

> Listen not just to my experiences but also to the evidence I present as a historian. I am a historian who believes in the birth, death, and resurrection of Jesus. A historian who still identifies with the evangelical tradition—as a Baptist.
>
> I confess it was the experience in my life, my personal exposure to the ugliness and trauma inflicted by complementarian systems in the name of Jesus, that tipped me over the edge. I can no longer watch silently as gender hierarchies oppress and damage both women and men in the name of Jesus. But what brought me to this edge was not experience; it was historical evidence. It was historical evidence that showed me how biblical womanhood was constructed—brick by brick, century by century.
>
> This is what changed my mind.[7]

Passages like these were the context for seminary professor Denny Burk's criticism of Barr, Du Mez, and Byrd, which I quoted in chapter 2. Burk castigates their reliance on subjectivity, saying, "They believe they'll win the day by appealing not to Bible or to reason but to emotion and experience. It's what their books do." He calls this use of emotion and experience "a strategy of normalization then acceptance" and suggests that the practice is a shameful or sinful choice: "It's striking to me that Barr would be so open about this approach. Sincerely, it's how theological error always works: normalize it, and make it more appealing to people who otherwise ought to know better."[8] To me, however, the striking aspect of Barr's work is how personal narrative and research—two kinds of authority—animate one another. Historical evidence can validate and explain experience; experience can compel a turn away from documented patterns of history.

As I have researched, drafted, and revised this book, I have watched white Christian nationalism grow. Evangelicals attacked the Black Lives Matter and #MeToo movements, and the Supreme Court overturned Roe v. Wade protections for reproductive rights. I followed news of reformers in the SBC trying (and largely failing) to hold congregations accountable for hiring or shielding sexual abusers. In many ways, the evangelical movement became even more fractured, and some factions took a disturbing turn toward authoritarianism and violence. Some of my research subjects, who came across as tepid in their critiques even years before, now seem out of step with the pressing worries of people in the evangelical movement. However, they took on a new significance as an archive for emerging writers to consult as they crafted arguments and narratives for this time.

Personal narratives by Christian women have proliferated in the years following 2018. That includes new writers like Rachael Denhollander (author of *What Is a Girl Worth? My Story of Breaking the Silence and Exposing the Truth about Larry Nassar and USA Gymnastics*), Kaitlin Curtice (author of *Native: Identity, Belonging, and Rediscovering God*), and Julie Rodgers (author of *Outlove: A Queer Christian Survival Story*). Sarah McCammon, the NPR politics correspondent who covered Donald Trump's 2016 campaign, will publish *The Exvangelicals: Loving, Living, and Leaving the White Evangelical Church* in 2024. The form continues to offer an avenue for voices and messages not widely heard within the evangelical movement.

Well-known writers further explored how the form could confront blind spots in the movement. After decades of writing personal narratives in her blog, Bible studies, and social media, Beth Moore published a memoir in 2023. *All My Knotted-Up Life* reveals that she survived sexual abuse by her father, recounts her transcendent encounters with God, and describes her years in ministry.[9] She writes, too, about the failings of the Southern Baptist Convention in its treatment of women and its responses to documented patterns of sexual abuse by pastors. Moore drew national attention in 2021 when she declared that she could no longer call herself a Southern Baptist. After years when she had been one of the public faces and trusted voices of that denomination, her departure drew attention to how SBC leadership had dithered over how to handle abuse and overt sexism in the church and largely continued to defend abusers and entrenched power.

Toward the end of the period I studied, I saw a shift from winsome rhetoric and indirect comments on United States politics to explicit engagement with the rhetoric of church leaders and politicians. Rachel Held Evans, Natalia Kohn, Noemi Vega Quiñones, and Kristy Garza Robinson are all examples. Trillia Newbell is another example. In 2016 and 2018, Newbell had already begun to write in a more pointed and political way in her social media. After SBC leaders targeted her with racist rhetoric (which came to light in 2021), she tweeted:

> **Me**: minding my own business doing the good work the Lord planned for me
>
> **Them**: Revealing their racism because I'm a Black "girl" (cough, I'm a grown woman)
>
> **Me**: Keeping on doing the good work the Lord planned for me
>
> I've experienced racism my entire life. Not gonna stop me now.[10]

Like Beth Moore and Rachel Held Evans the decade before, she chose to leave. She left her position at the ERLC and later announced that her family began "a new season at a non-SBC church."[11] Newbell's public role began with visible leadership in the largest evangelical institution and led to a thoughtful exit from that denomination. She was not an outspoken reformer or a public figure whose following made her a target, like Beth Moore, but her modesty and orthodox faith did not make her immune to the demeaning rhetoric of male leaders.

I hesitate to argue that evangelical women writing personal narratives from 2008–2018 directly led to paradigm-influencing texts and events like *Jesus and John Wayne* or Moore's exit from the SBC. Such an argument would be beyond the scope of this project. However, I contend that personal narratives draw ire from figures like Burk because those men see women's writing changing the movement (in ways perhaps like the title of Burk's screed "How to Turn Complementarians into Egalitarians"). The attention that conservatives like Burk and Rod Dreher pay to evangelical women's writing, as well as the criticism of more moderate voices like Tish Harrison Warren, suggest to me that these texts matter quite a bit. They articulate new ways of being in the evangelical movement, or ways of reconstituting faith outside the movement.

The intertextual relationships between writing of 2008–2018 and 2019–2023 also suggest a trajectory of writing by evangelical women. I see a throughline connecting Rachel Held Evans and her denunciation of Mark Driscoll to Kristin Kobes Du Mez and her critique of militant evangelical masculinity. Jonna Petry and Wendy Alsup were crucial resources for *The Rise and Fall of Mars Hill.* When George Floyd was killed in May 2020, readers rediscovered *I'm Still Here* (published two years earlier) as a resource for coming to terms with white evangelical racism. I could draw other lines as well, all showing how texts looking to renovate evangelical rhetoric speak to and build upon one another. Personal narratives of 2008–2018 built a space for evangelical women to voice their situated and subjective experiences of the church. Subsequent writers wholeheartedly joined them in that mission.

Notes

Introduction

1 King 1998, 1.
2 Piper 2014.
3 Prior 2018a.
4 Enns and Byas 2017 (emphasis added).
5 Jones 2016.
6 In fact, most growth came from pulling attendees from other Christian denominations, not by reaching unchurched Americans.
7 Jones 2016, 52.
8 Mitchell 2019.
9 PRRI Staff 2021.
10 Jones 2016, 55.
11 Labberton 2018, 3.
12 Labberton 2018, 3–4.
13 Labberton 2018, 3.
14 Brown 2018, 170.
15 Evans 2010, 49.
16 Glenn 2018a, 4.
17 Evans 2018a, 170.
18 Gerson 2018.
19 Hatmaker 2016.
20 Moore 2018.
21 For example, Robert P. Jones weaves his own autobiography into *White Too Long*, and Alan Jacobs devotes two chapters of *Looking Before and After* to writing and then analyzing his own testimony. Journalist Jon Ward has written about his experience in the evangelical movement in *Testimony* (2023), as has Christian rapper Lecrae in *Unashamed* (2016). The tradition of evangelical writing includes Augustine's *Confessions* (397–400) and C. S. Lewis' *Surprised by Joy: The Shape of My Early Life* (1955).
22 Ryan, Myers, and Jones 2016, 2.
23 Crowley 2006; Gilyard 2008.
24 Glenn 2018a, 46.
25 Engels 2015, 14.
26 Bebbington 1989.

27 McLaren 2006, 129 (emphasis in original).
28 McLaren 2006, 130 (emphasis in original).
29 Kidd 2019, 1.
30 Kidd 2019, 2.
31 Martin 2021, 18.
32 Butler 2021, 12 (emphasis in original).
33 Young 2018, 55.
34 "Religious Landscape Study" 2015.
35 Bowler 2019, 7.
36 Tisby 2019b, 21–22.
37 Brown 2018, 20.
38 Jones 2016, 202.
39 Ingersoll 2003, 12.
40 Jones 2016, 58.
41 Pence 2019.
42 Pence 2019.
43 Jones et al. 2017.
44 Ingersoll 2003, 9.
45 1 Peter 3:15 NRSV.
46 Vander Lei 2014, xi.
47 Camper 2020, 104.
48 For evangelicals, that evolving context includes recurring culture wars, the scars of which distinguish evangelical culture and rhetoric from other religious practices in the United States. While this movement might have once distanced itself from fundamentalism, it perpetuates fundamentalist rhetoric, as Sharon Crowley argues in *Toward a Civil Discourse.* Crowley writes, "A cleavage between 'us' and 'them' motivates contemporary conservative rhetoric," and conservative evangelicals translate this dichotomy as "an absolute difference between the saved and the unsaved" (15). Evangelicals also rely on "revelation, faith, and biblical interpretation to ground claims" and do not particularly value "the tactics typically used in liberal argument—empirically based reason and factual evidence" (3). At the same time, evangelicalism fosters a fierce argument culture. In *Winsome Persuasion: Christian Influence in a Post-Christian World*, communication scholars Timothy M. Muehlhoff and Richard Langer describe a "culture war rhetoric" that trains many Christians "to interpret mere disagreement as personal attack" (34) and "stir up emotions by presenting the views of the other so simplistically as to foster disbelief and ridicule" (56). Personal narratives present a critique of this rhetoric and an alternative.
49 Muehlhoff and Langer 2017.
50 Prior 2018b.
51 Beitler 2019.
52 Evans 2015, 25; Merritt 2018, 9–10.

53 Ringer 2016, 11.
54 Foss and Griffin 1995, 13.
55 Buchanan and Ryan 2010, xiii.
56 Glenn 2018a, 9.
57 Glenn 2018b, 3–4 (emphasis in original).
58 Foss and Griffin 1995, 5.
59 Hogg 2015, 392.
60 Enoch and Gold 2019, 3.
61 Hogg 2015, 392.
62 Butler 2007, 10.
63 Fredlund 2020, 162.
64 Glenn 1997, 92.
65 Donawerth 2013, 75; see also Bizzell 2006.
66 Shaver 2012, 129.
67 Zimmerelli 2015, 187.
68 Gallagher 2003, 96.
69 Worthen 2014, 187.
70 Worthen 2014, 184.
71 Gerson 2018.
72 Stenberg and Hogg 2020, 12.
73 Smith and Watson 2010, 4.
74 Hindmarsh 2002.
75 Zimmerelli 2015, 187.
76 Peterson 2008, 13.
77 Rak 2013; Gilmore 2016.
78 Poletti 2011b, 81.
79 Poletti 2011a, 34.
80 Whitlock 2007, 3.
81 Stenberg and Hogg 2020, 11; see also Glenn 1997.
82 Mannon 2020.
83 Smith 1993, 20; see also Gilmore 2016 and Rak 2013.
84 Yagoda 2009, 28–29.
85 Moody 2003, xi–xii.
86 Robillard 2019, 186.
87 Newkirk 2014, 34.
88 Jurecic 2012, 11.
89 Robillard 2019, 187.
90 Jacobs 2008, 8.
91 DePalma and Ringer 2015, 5.
92 Ringer 2016, 11.
93 Glenn 2018a, 46.
94 Crowley 2006, 71.
95 Let me clarify that this group has no relationship to capital-O Orthodox Christianity. I use lower case *orthodox* when I discuss these women to

refer to their orthodox belief and distinguish it from conservative culture and politics.

96 Evans 2010, 201.
97 Adams-Roberts, Eves, and Rohan 2014, 46.
98 Crowley 2006, 197.
99 Jones 2016, 239.
100 Van Opstal 2018, 136.
101 Van Opstal 2018, 129.
102 Van Opstal 2018, 132.
103 Van Opstal 2018, 128.

1 A Rhetorical History of the Evangelical Movement in the United States

1 Turner 1998, 2.
2 Turner 1998, 2.
3 Engels 2015, 14.
4 Connors 1989, 232.
5 Cope and Ringer, 2015, 3.
6 See Fea 2018, Kidd 2019, Worthen 2014, Du Mez 2020, Hindmarsh 2002.
7 Du Mez 2020, 7.
8 Du Mez 2020, 5.
9 Du Mez 2020, 7.
10 Ingersoll 2003, 16.
11 Ingersoll 2003, 13.
12 Ingersoll 2003, 16.
13 Bowler 2019, xvi.
14 Worthen 2014, 4.
15 Noll 2008, 2.
16 "Religious Landscape Study" 2015.
17 Newport 2018.
18 Eskridge 2012.
19 Moore 2022.
20 Jones 2020, 12.
21 Jones 2020, 15.
22 Kidd 2019, 53.
23 Noll 2008, 102.
24 Jones 2020, 15.
25 Kidd 2019, 1.
26 Burge 2021.
27 These debates over definition are themselves a preoccupation of white evangelicals, maybe even a product of their anxiety over politicization. In "Black Religion and the Question of Evangelical Identity," professor of African American religious history Milton G. Sernett points out that

white Christians have been the ones most invested in debates over the term; "contemporary black theologians do not seem much interested in the question" (Sernett 1991, 137). However, the question matters to Black women like Austin Channing Brown, and other women of color, as they contemplate what keeps them in community with white evangelicals who share some of their beliefs but not their rhetoric, politics, or social location.

28 Pason, Foust, and Rogness 2017.
29 Pason, Foust, and Rogness 2017, 5
30 Chávez 2011, 3.
31 Pason 2017, 111.
32 Pason 2017, 112.
33 Du Mez 2020, 293.
34 Pason 2017, 111.
35 Slotkin 2020, 459.
36 Slotkin 2020, 459.
37 Crowley 2006, 70.
38 Hindmarsh 2017, 290.
39 Kidd 2019, 10.
40 Sernett 1991, 138.
41 Hindmarsh 2017, 290.
42 Kidd 2019, 15.
43 Kidd 2019, 27.
44 Martin 2021, 20.
45 Jones 2020, 100.
46 Kidd 2019, 4.
47 Cope and Ringer 2015, 3.
48 Mark Noll enumerates the growth of Methodist congregations (from about seven hundred to twenty thousand), Baptists (from fewer than nine hundred to more than twelve thousand), and Presbyterians (from seven hundred to over six thousand). Noll 2006.
49 Noll 2006, 27.
50 Lynerd 2014, 101.
51 Lynerd 2014, 110.
52 Lynerd 2014, 35.
53 Young 2018, 3.
54 Fea 2018, 87.
55 Fea 2018, 112.
56 In 2023, Lifeway Research found that "almost 7 in 10 U.S. Protestant pastors (69%) believe there is a growing sense of fear within their congregations about the future of the nation and world. Additionally, more than 3 in 5 (63%) say their churches have a similar increasing dread specifically about the future of Christianity in the U.S. and around the world." This fear was higher among white (71 percent) and Hispanic

pastors (62 percent); African American pastors were less likely to agree (42 percent) and more likely to disagree (55 percent). Earls 2023.

57 Jones 2020.
58 Kidd 2019, 49.
59 Kidd 2019, 50.
60 Jones 2020, 92.
61 Noll 2006, 74.
62 Noll 2006, 34–35.
63 Noll 2006, 45.
64 Noll 2006, 69.
65 Noll 2006, 49.
66 Noll 2006, 32–33.
67 Noll 2008, 86.
68 Jones 2020, 91.
69 Noll 2008, 59.
70 Kidd 2019, 52.
71 Noll 2006, 5.
72 Sullivan 1992, 321.
73 Sullivan 1992, 323.
74 Noll 2006, 86.
75 Noll 2006, 93.
76 Martin 2021, 30.
77 Martin 2021, 30.
78 Magnuson 2017, 819.
79 Bizzell 2006; Zimmerelli 2015; Shaver 2012.
80 Gerson 2018.
81 Magnuson 2017, 820.
82 Hardesty 1999, 7.
83 Worthen 2014, 19–20.
84 Worthen 2014, 19.
85 Sernett 1991, 142.
86 Borg 2001, 7.
87 Borg 2001, 9.
88 Cochran 2005, 108.
89 Worthen 2014, 24.
90 Crowley 2006, 74.
91 Noll 2008, 27.
92 McIntire 2017, 333.
93 Noll 2017, 788. When the state of Tennessee indicted John Scopes, a high school biology teacher who assigned his students a reading that treated evolution as fact, anti-evolution activist and politician William Jennings Bryan spoke on behalf of the prosecution and asserted the literal truth of the biblical account of creation. Bryan's appeal to the Bible and "simple facts," Noll writes, "gave fundamentalists a reputation for cultural backwardness."

94 Labberton 2018, 4.
95 Sernett 1991, 142.
96 McIntire 2017, 334.
97 Sire 2015, 24.
98 Sire 2015, 20.
99 Worthen 2014, 29.
100 Worthen 2014, 253.
101 Jones 2020, 104.
102 Jones 2020, 139.
103 Jones 2020, 140.
104 Jones 2020, 140.
105 Jones 2020, 142.
106 Enns 2016, 29.
107 Enns 2016, 30.
108 Enns 2016, 18.
109 Worthen 2014, 8.
110 Worthen 2014, 218; see also Fea 2018, 48.
111 Enns 2016, 21.
112 Jones 2020, 76.
113 Kidd 2019, 101.
114 Lynerd 2014, 175.
115 Kidd 2019, 99.
116 Butler 2021, 57; see also Tisby 2019b.
117 Kidd 2019, 101.
118 Demar 2007.
119 Demar 2007.
120 Jones 2020, 103.
121 Butler 2021, 49.
122 Harding 2001, 22.
123 Blumenthal 2007.
124 Tisby 2019a, 21.
125 Jones 2020, 21.
126 Kidd 2019, 23.
127 Jones 2020, 17.
128 Jones 2020, 6.
129 Jones 2020, 10.
130 Scanzoni and Hardesty 1974.
131 Cochran 2005, 8.
132 Cochran 2005, 77.
133 Kidd 2019, 123.
134 Kell 2006, xxxiii.
135 Foust 2004.
136 Emily Murphy Cope explains that complementarians interpret the Bible as saying men and women "share equally in God's image" but their different natures "suit them for distinct roles" (220) with women

submitting to male leadership. Denominations like the SBC use this reasoning to explicitly reject women's ordination and most SBC churches prohibit women from preaching. Cope 2013.

137 Du Mez 2020, 108.
138 Du Mez 2020, 109.
139 Du Mez 2020.
140 Marsden 2006, 159.
141 Bowler 2019, 75.
142 Jones 2020, 142.
143 Du Mez 2020.
144 Darsey and Ritter 2009.
145 Jones 2020, 74.
146 I omit the ones I see women using less often, like prophetic and apocalyptic rhetoric.
147 Weber 2017, 292.
148 Weber 2017, 293.
149 Weber 2017, 293.
150 Balmer 1999.
151 Balmer 1999, 56.
152 Cope 2013, 225.
153 Enns 2016, 30.
154 Sernett 1991, 144.
155 Mannon 2023.
156 Martin 2021, 8.
157 Mountford 2003, 45.
158 Cope 2013, 230.
159 Hayes and Kornfield 2020, 42.
160 Du Mez 2020, 7.
161 Cope 2013, 230.
162 Vidu 2017, 380.
163 Borg 2001, 8–9.
164 Worthen 2014, 257.
165 Du Mez 2020; Noll 2006, 32.
166 Jones 2020, 101–2.
167 Stackhouse 2017.
168 Stackhouse 2017, 71.
169 Worthen 2014, 21.
170 Root 2021.
171 Glenn 2018a, 12.
172 Hindmarsh 2002, 4.
173 Hindmarsh 2002, 8.
174 Hauerwas and Jones 1997, 5.
175 Hauerwas and Jones 1997, 4.
176 Jones 2021.

177 Scharold 2011.
178 Teasdale 2016.
179 Du Mez 2020, 8.
180 Campbell 1989, 14.
181 Jensen 2017, 747.
182 Johnson 2014, 13.
183 Crowley 2006, 4.

2 A Generous Evangelical Orthodoxy

1 Moore [@BethMoorePM] 2016a and 2016b.
2 Newbell [@trillianewbell] 2018.
3 In February 2018, fifty evangelical leaders, including Newbell, attended a two-day closed-door conference at Wheaton College to discuss the future of evangelicalism. Katelyn Beaty (who was invited because she had recently been managing editor of *Christianity Today*) wrote about the meeting for the *New Yorker*. In "At a Private Meeting in Illinois, a Group of Evangelicals Tried to Save Their Movement from Trumpism," she describes rifts over politics, gender, and racism that kept attendees from agreeing on a statement or course of action. She writes:

> With the bewildering skittishness about getting political, my time at Wheaton left me feeling deeply unsettled about the moral and political fortitude of my spiritual community in the era of Trump and beyond. Much of evangelicalism still functions with a spiritual-secular divide, as if the physical concerns of this world can be neatly fixed with worship and prayer. But worship and prayer are not the only things that this Trumpian moment demands of us. Rather, the moment calls for risk. (Beaty 2018)

4 Martin 2021, 150. In October 2016, a recording of Donald Trump behind the scenes on the set of *Access Hollywood* surfaced. The tape showed him referring to sexually assaulting women. Male evangelical leaders and politicians excused the remarks as "locker room talk," but evangelical women responded by publicly sharing that they had been the victims of similar violence and disrespect. Beth Moore's tweets quoted at the beginning of chapter 2 are one example. Moore and other women lamented that evangelical men did not take seriously Trump's blatant sexism and disregard for a Christian sexual ethic. For a longer analysis of this controversy, see Geiger 2022.
5 Frei 1987, 22.
6 Ryan, Myers, and Jones 2016, 3.
7 The Pelican Project 2018.
8 Newbell 2014, 15.
9 Newbell 2020.
10 Shellnutt 2019.

11 Griswold 2019.
12 Donawerth 2013, 75.
13 Donawerth 2013, 75.
14 Hogg 2015, 394.
15 Mahmood 2012, 5.
16 Ingersoll 2003, 1; 1–2.
17 Mahmood 2012, 9.
18 Mahmood 2012, x.
19 Mahmood 2012, 1–2.
20 Mahmood 2012, 5.
21 Alsup 2008a, 13.
22 Alsup 2008a, 13.
23 Alsup 2008a, 14.
24 Alsup 2008a, 14.
25 My goal in studying this sprawling story is to show how feminism and feminist rhetoric reckon with evangelical commonplaces of combat, authority, and divine providence. To that end, I focus on women and on personal testimony and say less about church elders, their business decisions, or their critiques of Driscoll's rhetoric. I largely omit other texts, like legal documents, that do not foreground personal experience. I also focus on Mark Driscoll rather than Mars Hill Church because, in my interpretation, he was responsible for the authoritarian and misogynistic rhetoric that many women want to remove from orthodox belief.
26 Johnson 2018, 23.
27 Cosper 2021a.
28 Evans 2014. When she writes this on her blog, Evans includes hyperlinks to Driscoll's social media posts, Seattle local news, Driscoll's writing on sites like The Resurgence, and national media covering Driscoll. These statements are corroborated and documented by Johnson, Du Mez, Alsup, and *Christianity Today*.
29 Evans 2014.
30 Evans 2014.
31 Johnson 2018, 4.
32 Cosper 2021c.
33 Johnson 2018, 30.
34 Johnson 2018, 30.
35 Cosper 2021c. Such origin stories are not an evangelical phenomenon. In this episode, Cosper talks about the "garage mythology" of many Silicon Valley tech firms. He also notes that these stories of a company's founders building transformative new technology in their garages is rarely entirely true.
36 Cosper 2021c.
37 Johnson 2018, 24.
38 Du Mez 2020, 197.

39 Du Mez 2020, 204.
40 Du Mez 2020, 204.
41 Du Mez 2020, 194.
42 Du Mez 2020, 196.
43 Petry 2012, 5.
44 Petry 2012, 6.
45 Evangelical media has covered these incidents in some depth, as in the May 25, 2018 episode of the *Christianity Today* podcast *Quick to Listen*, titled "Are Southern Baptists Experiencing a #MeToo Moment?" T. J. Geiger II examines case studies of evangelical women's responses to sexual abuse in *Faithful Deliberation* (2022).
46 Petry 2012, 10.
47 Petry 2012, 14.
48 Petry 2012, 14.
49 Alsup 2008a, 15.
50 Alsup 2008a, 16.
51 Cosper 2021b.
52 Cosper 2021b.
53 Cosper 2021b. These are my own transcriptions of *Rise and Fall* episodes.
54 Peterson 2020, xxi. Peterson ends his introduction by musing about the "the stability of the generously orthodox approach" (xxxiv). He asks, "Can it withstand the criticisms from conservative voices, who claim that it is a heterodox and revisionist betrayal, or from progressive voices, who claim that it is still stuck in dogmatism?" (xxxiv). The diversification of Christianity from immigration and globalization and the decline of white Christian America all keep these questions relevant in the twenty-first century.
55 Alsup 2017, 127–28.
56 Alsup 2017, 128.
57 Alsup 2017, 129.
58 Griswold 2019.
59 Prior 2018a.
60 Prior 2018a.
61 Alsup 2017, 1–2.
62 Newbell 2014, 19–20.
63 Newbell 2014, 24. Newbell became a Christian as an adult—she writes "I didn't grow up in church" (Newbell 2014, 36).
64 Newbell 2014, 39.
65 Newbell 2014, 33.
66 Newbell 2014, 55.
67 Newbell 2014, 61.
68 Vischer and Jethani 2023.
69 Tisby 2019b.
70 Newbell [@trillianewbell] 2016.

71 Newbell [@trillianewbell] 2018.
72 Jacobs 2008, 10.
73 Peterson 2020, xxi.
74 Byrd 2013, 32.
75 Jacobs 2008, 35.
76 Jacobs 2008, 34.
77 Alsup 2008a, 13.
78 Alsup 2008a, 14.
79 Alsup 2008a, 24.
80 Alsup 2008a, 20.
81 Hindmarsh 2002.
82 Clark 2016.
83 Worthen 2014, 17.
84 Anderson 2016, 124.
85 Ratcliffe 2005.
86 Anderson 2016, 123.
87 Anderson 2016, 123.
88 Anderson 2016, 124.
89 Alsup 2008a, 4; 6.
90 Alsup 2008b.
91 Burk 2021. After writing books like *Housewife Theologian* that did not overtly confront complementarian and patriarchal ideologies, Byrd published *Recovering from Biblical Manhood and Womanhood* in 2020. The book's title signals its explicit break from and rejection of Wayne Grudem, John Piper, the CBMW, and their influential 1991 book *Recovering Biblical Manhood and Womanhood.*
92 Alsup 2017, 46.
93 Ingersoll 2003, 17.
94 Ingersoll 2003, 22.
95 Alsup 2021.
96 Prior 2018a.
97 Anderson 2016, 111.
98 Anderson 2016, 112.

3 Storytelling as Verbal Hospitality

1 Evans 2010, 77.
2 Evans 2010, 204.
3 Merritt 2015.
4 Horner 2011, 190.
5 Ringer 2016, 21.
6 Bailey 2015.
7 Evans 2010, 30–31.
8 Graham 2019.

9 Graham 2019.
10 Beaty 2019.
11 Beaty 2019.
12 Stetzer 2019.
13 Robillard 2019, 187.
14 Gubar 2011, xv.
15 Glenn 2018a, 78.
16 Stenberg and Hogg 2020, 14.
17 Evans 2015, xii.
18 Evans 2015, xiii.
19 Cordova 2012, 148.
20 See Jarratt and Reynolds 1994.
21 Ryan, Myers, and Jones 2016, 5.
22 Robillard 2019, 186.
23 Evans 2013.
24 Evans 2018a, 170.
25 Warren 2017.
26 Worthen 2014, 257.
27 Evans 2010, 42.
28 Evans 2015, 218.
29 Muehlhoff and Langer 2017, 34.
30 Guinness 2015.
31 Beitler 2019, 4.
32 Root 2021.
33 Chatraw 2018.
34 Evans 2015, 50.
35 Evans 2015, 51.
36 "Six Reasons Young Christians Leave Church" 2011.
37 Evans 2010, 75.
38 Evans 2010, 68.
39 Evans 2010, 78.
40 Evans 2010, 94.
41 Crowley 2006, 15.
42 Evans 2010, 71.
43 Evans 2010, 67.
44 Evans 2010, 78.
45 Evans 2010, 79.
46 Evans 2010, 203.
47 Evans 2010, 102.
48 Evans 2010, 77.
49 Evans 2010, 186.
50 Evans 2010, 186.
51 Evans 2015, 8.
52 Evans 2010, 78.

53 Evans 2010, 201.
54 Crowley 2006, 15.
55 Evans 2010, 29.
56 Evans 2010, 41.
57 Evans 2010, 184.
58 Evans 2010, 185.
59 Evans 2012a, xx (emphasis in original).
60 Evans 2012a, 1.
61 Evans 2012a, xx.
62 Evans 2012a, 60.
63 Evans 2012a, 16.
64 Evans 2012a, 16.
65 Evans 2012a, 43.
66 Evans 2012a, 179.
67 Evans 2012a, 180.
68 Evans 2012a, 66.
69 Evans 2012a, 65.
70 Evans 2012a, 295.
71 Evans 2018b.
72 Evans 2011.
73 Evans 2012b.
74 Evans 2012a, 295.
75 Evans 2012a, 296.
76 Newbell 2012.
77 Newbell 2012.
78 Keller 2017.
79 Keller 2017 (emphasis in original).
80 Evans 2012c (emphasis in original).
81 Evans 2012c.
82 Evans 2010, 187.
83 Evans 2015, 215.
84 Evans 2015, 215.
85 Robillard 2019, 191.
86 Evans 2015, 31.
87 Evans 2015, 33.
88 Evans 2015, 51.
89 Evans 2015, 51–52.
90 Evans 2015, 62.
91 Mannon 2020, 232.
92 Evans 2015, 83.
93 Beaty 2019.
94 Beaty 2019.
95 Whitlock 2007, 3.

96 Lee 2015, 3.
97 Lee 2015, 23.
98 Lee 2015, 24.
99 Lee 2015, 13.
100 Lee 2015, 13.
101 Evans 2015, 258.
102 Glenn 2018a, 73.
103 Evans 2018a, xviii.
104 Gold and Hobbs 2013, 3–4.
105 Logan 2008; Donawerth 2013; Garrison 2013.
106 Evans 2018a, xvi–xvii.
107 Miller 1984, 152.
108 Evans 2018a, xxii.
109 Miller 1984, 165.
110 Evans 2018a, 201–2.
111 Evans 2018a, 204.
112 Evans 2018a, 75.
113 Evans 2018a, 131.
114 Evans 2018a, xvii.
115 Evans 2018a, 219.
116 Evans 2018a, 43.
117 Enns and Byas 2019b.
118 Evans 2018a, 33.
119 Evans 2018a, 141.
120 Evans 2018a, 69.
121 Evans 2018a, xv.
122 Evans 2018a, 79.
123 Royster and Kirsch 2012, 71; 72.
124 Cited in Evans 2018a, 23.
125 Royster and Kirsch 2012, 71.
126 Chapter 1 and chapter 2 of this book and discussions of *A Year of Biblical Womanhood* show how conservatives like the CBMW resist historical or metaphorical approaches to the Bible. They allege that these pose a "threat to Biblical authority as the clarity of Scripture is jeopardized and the accessibility of its meaning to ordinary people is withdrawn into the restricted realm of technical ingenuity" (CBMW "Core Beliefs," quoted in *A Year of Biblical Womanhood*, xix).
127 Evans 2018a, xxi–xxii.
128 Evans 2018a, 25.
129 Evans 2018a, 125.
130 Evans 2018a, 68.
131 Evans 2008.

4 The "Resisterhood" of Progressive Evangelical Women

1 Brown 2016.
2 Bessey 2013c.
3 Bessey 2015b.
4 Hatmaker 2014, xxxi.
5 Beaty 2013.
6 Hatmaker 2015, 18.
7 Gerson 2018.
8 Gerson 2018.
9 Bizzell 2006; Shaver 2012, 128–29.
10 Bessey 2013a, 25.
11 Hatmaker 2015, 199.
12 Bessey 2013a, 16.
13 Bessey 2013a, 73.
14 Bessey 2013a, 74.
15 Bessey 2013a, 26 (emphasis in original).
16 Bessey 2013a, 16.
17 Bessey 2013a, 26.
18 Bessey 2013a, 18–20.
19 Mountford 2003 12–13; 45.
20 Cope 2013, 218.
21 Brown 2018, 183.
22 Brown 2018, 23.
23 Brown 2018, 15.
24 Brown 2018, 15.
25 Brown 2018, 17 (emphasis and interjection in the original).
26 Brown 2018, 43.
27 Brown 2018, 44.
28 Brown 2018, 73; 76 (emphasis in the original).
29 Hatmaker 2017a, 74.
30 Hatmaker 2015, 203; 201.
31 Cope 2013, 230.
32 Crowley 2006, 117; 131.
33 Lee 2015, 121.
34 Petersen 2016.
35 Petersen 2016.
36 Lee 2015, 211.
37 Worthen 2014, 187.
38 Worthen 2014, 184; 187.
39 Hatmaker 2015, 200.
40 Bessey 2013a, 14.
41 Bessey 2013a, 12.
42 Merritt 2016.

43 Jen Hatmaker 2016.
44 Brandon Hatmaker 2016.
45 Brandon Hatmaker 2016.
46 Brandon Hatmaker 2016.
47 Hatmaker 2017a, 208.
48 Dreher 2017.
49 Butterfield 2016.
50 Hatmaker 2017b.
51 Merritt 2017.
52 Warren 2017.
53 Warren 2017.
54 Hatmaker 2017b.
55 Glenn 2018a, 93.
56 Hatmaker 2017b.
57 Stanley 2017.
58 Hatmaker 2012, 23.
59 Glenn 2018a, 9.
60 Worthen 2014, 187.
61 Ringer 2013, 361.
62 Cope 2013, 221.
63 Bessey 2015a, 68.
64 Bessey 2013a, 16.
65 Bessey 2015a, 6.
66 Bessey 2015a, 58.
67 Bessey 2015a, 57.
68 Bessey 2015a, 59.
69 Bessey 2013a, 17.
70 Bessey 2013a, 18.
71 Marinelli 2016, 473.
72 Hatmaker 2015, 202.
73 Petersen 2016.
74 Hatmaker 2015, 90–91.
75 Hatmaker 2015, 91.
76 Enns 2016, 30.
77 Hatmaker 2015, 194.
78 Bessey 2015a, 59.
79 Bessey 2015a, 76.
80 Brown 2018, 35 (brackets in original).
81 Brown 2018, 37.
82 Brown 2018, 37.
83 Brown 2018, 38.
84 Ringer 2013, 350.
85 Brown 2018, 22.

86 Bessey 2013b.
87 Bessey 2013b (emphasis in original).
88 Donawerth 2013, 4.
89 Beaty 2017.
90 Brown 2018, 20.
91 Brown 2018, 20.
92 Brown 2018, 23.
93 Brown 2018, 98.
94 Brown 2018, 110.
95 Brown 2018, 170.
96 Brown 2018, 123.
97 Hatmaker 2017a, 80.
98 Hatmaker 2017a, 80.
99 Bessey 2015a, 3.
100 Hatmaker 2017a, 80.
101 Nadeem 2021. Pew exit polls do not break down by race, gender, and religion, but I draw this conclusion from looking at the trends in white evangelicals and white women together. Moreover, an ABC exit poll found that in the 2018 midterm election, 72 percent of white evangelical women voted for conservative House candidates (compared to 78 percent of white evangelical men). "White Evangelical Gender Gap?" 2018.
102 "Six Reasons Young Christians Leave Church" 2011.
103 "What Millennials Want When They Visit Church" 2015.
104 Hatmaker 2017a, 80.
105 Glenn 2018a, 23.
106 Glenn 2018a, 46.
107 Vander Lei 2014; DePalma and Ringer 2015.

5 The Rhetorical Leadership of Contemporary *Evangélicas*

1 Enoch and Gold 2019, 5; 15.
2 Other evangelical women who have written personal narratives about their experiences in leadership include Katelyn Beaty, Beth Moore, Julie Rodgers, and Sandra Maria Van Opstal:

- From 2007 to 2016, Beaty worked at *Christianity Today*, where she was the magazine's first female managing editor and its youngest. She recounts some of this experience in her 2017 memoir, *A Woman's Place*.
- Moore is a writer and Bible teacher, and Cope describes her ubiquity: "Today she teaches the Bible to millions through best-selling books, conferences, multimedia Bible-study packages, a blog, weekly television and radio broadcasts, and invited speaking appearances at churches and conferences around the world" (Cope 2013, 217).

- Julie Rodgers served on staff at Wheaton College from 2014 to 2015, when controversy surrounding her sexual orientation forced her to resign. After leaving Wheaton, Rodgers served as a Teaching Fellow at The Faith and Justice Network. She has published narratives of her experiences as a gay Christian in the *Washington Post*, *Time Magazine*, and the *New York Times*. Rodgers published her memoir *Outlove: A Queer Christian Survival Story* in 2021.
- Sandra Maria Van Opstal leads Grace and Peace Community Church in Chicago as a Preaching Pastor. She has written or contributed to five books, including *The Next Worship: Glorifying God in a Diverse World* and *Still Evangelical?*

3 Kohn, Vega Quiñones, and Robinson 2019, 102.
4 Kohn, Vega Quiñones, and Robinson 2019, 5.
5 Kohn, Vega Quiñones, and Robinson 2019, 2.
6 Kohn, Vega Quiñones, and Robinson 2019, 47.
7 Bowler 2019, xvi–xvii.
8 *Hermanas* itself is an example of the work parachurches do. The book came out through InterVarsity Press (IVP), a branch of InterVarsity Christian Fellowship, which publishes Bible studies, fiction, Bibles, textbooks, academic monographs, podcasts, and popular nonfiction in categories like "Christian Living" and "Politics & Government." IVP has a wide reach. It publishes over one hundred books each year and several of its authors, like J. I. Packer and Dallas Willard, are household names among evangelicals. The press uses its status and reach to promote women, authors from diverse backgrounds, young authors, and texts on race and ethnicity.
9 Kohn, Vega Quiñones, and Robinson 2019, 2.
10 My chapter "The Persuasive Power of Individual Stories: The Rhetoric in Narrative Archives," in the edited collection *Feminist Connections: Rhetoric and Activism across Time, Space, and Place*, reads compilations of personal narratives as archives that put forth "a feminist rhetoric of personal narrative" and create an avenue for "addressing homophobia, classism, and racism within existing feminist discourses and movements" (232). In such archives, "the individuality of each writer matters less than do the similarities, intersections, and points of contact that emerge from reading many stories together" (242). Alan Jacobs makes a related point when he reminds Christians that "testimony is an intrinsically communal enterprise—as is the use of any genre" (2008, 35).
11 Kohn, Vega Quiñones, and Robinson 2019, 11.
12 Kohn, Vega Quiñones, and Robinson 2019, 5.
13 Kohn, Vega Quiñones, and Robinson 2019, 6.
14 Kohn, Vega Quiñones, and Robinson 2019, 6.
15 Robillard 2019, 187.

16 Bratta and Powell 2016, para. 9.
17 Kohn, Vega Quiñones, and Robinson 2019, 10.
18 Martell-Otero 2013, 8.
19 Van Opstal 2018, 133.
20 Van Opstal 2018, 133.
21 Rhetorical leadership remains an understudied area of feminist rhetorical scholarship. In their overview of feminist research methodologies Elizabeth Tasker and Francis B. Holt-Underwood only discuss leadership as tangential to the larger field of rhetoric and composition. Case studies of women's rhetorical leadership, like Cristy Beemer's analysis of Queen Mary and Queen Elizabeth I or Bligh and Kohles' study of women in the United States Senate, tend to analyze the gendered rhetoric that a leader must use to be perceived as such. Tasker and Holt-Underwood 2008; Beemer 2016; Bligh and Kohles 2008.
22 Zarefsky 2000, 6; Gaffey 2017, 1499.
23 Riley 2016, 299.
24 Kohn, Vega Quiñones, and Robinson 2019, 163 (emphasis in original).
25 Bratta and Powell 2016, para. 9.
26 Jacobs 2008, 10.
27 Jacobs 2008, 10.
28 Jacobs 2008, 12.
29 1 Peter 3:15 NRSV.
30 Jacobs 2008, 8.
31 Jacobs 2008, 9.
32 Jacobs 2008, 8.
33 Jacobs 2008, 35.
34 Jacobs 2008, 34.
35 Jacobs 2008, 39.
36 Jacobs 2008, 39.
37 Kohn, Vega Quiñones, and Robinson 2019, 41 (emphasis in original).
38 Kohn, Vega Quiñones, and Robinson 2019, 42.
39 Kohn, Vega Quiñones, and Robinson 2019, 46.
40 Kohn, Vega Quiñones, and Robinson 2019, 49.
41 Kohn, Vega Quiñones, and Robinson 2019, 49.
42 Kohn, Vega Quiñones, and Robinson 2019, 56.
43 Jacobs 2008, 6.
44 Cruz-Malavé 2017, 228.
45 Cobos et al. 2018, 150.
46 Delgado Bernal, Burciaga, and Flores Carmona 2012, 364.
47 Delgado Bernal, Burciaga, and Flores Carmona 2012, 364.
48 Kohn, Vega Quiñones, and Robinson 2019, 45.
49 Kohn, Vega Quiñones, and Robinson 2019, 43.
50 Delgado Bernal, Burciaga, and Flores Carmona 2012, 363.
51 Kohn, Vega Quiñones, and Robinson 2019, 57.

52 Kohn, Vega Quiñones, and Robinson 2019, 58.
53 Conde-Frazier 2013, 66.
54 Jones 2020, 6.
55 Kidd 2019, 49.
56 Butler 2021, 10.
57 The history of white evangelical racism toward Black Americans is well documented by writers like Jones, Tisby, Noll, and Brown, but information on evangelical racism toward other groups is not as easy to locate. The PRRI 2018 American Values Survey found attitudes toward demographic change and immigration that might point to evangelical attitudes toward Latinos. PRRI found that 55 percent of white Americans say that the impact of the U.S. becoming a majority-non-white country by 2045 will be mostly positive (compared to 80 percent of Hispanics and 79 percent of Black Americans). A majority (54 percent) of white evangelical Protestants say that this change will be mostly negative. Further, 57 percent of white evangelical Protestants say that immigrants threaten American society; they are the only major religious group in which a majority believe this (Vandermaas-Peeler et al. 2018).
58 Kohn, Vega Quiñones, and Robinson 2019, 19.
59 Kohn, Vega Quiñones, and Robinson 2019, 17.
60 Kohn, Vega Quiñones, and Robinson 2019, 20.
61 Kohn, Vega Quiñones, and Robinson 2019, 18.
62 Kohn, Vega Quiñones, and Robinson 2019, 24.
63 Kohn, Vega Quiñones, and Robinson 2019, 23.
64 Kohn, Vega Quiñones, and Robinson 2019, 18.
65 Kohn, Vega Quiñones, and Robinson 2019, 22.
66 Sipiora 2012, 115.
67 Kohn, Vega Quiñones, and Robinson 2019, 20.
68 Kohn, Vega Quiñones, and Robinson 2019, 20.
69 Kohn, Vega Quiñones, and Robinson 2019, 22.
70 Kohn, Vega Quiñones, and Robinson 2019, 22.
71 Kohn, Vega Quiñones, and Robinson 2019, 23.
72 Kohn, Vega Quiñones, and Robinson 2019, 54.
73 Kohn, Vega Quiñones, and Robinson 2019, 17.
74 Kohn, Vega Quiñones, and Robinson 2019, 11.
75 Cruz-Malavé 2017, 228; 229.
76 Kohn, Vega Quiñones, and Robinson 2019, 24.
77 Conde-Frazier 2013, 74.
78 Conde-Frazier 2015, 79.
79 Martell-Otero 2013, 6.
80 Kohn, Vega Quiñones, and Robinson 2019, 163 (emphasis in original).
81 Martell-Otero 2013, 4.
82 Conde-Frazier 2015, 66.
83 Moraga and Anzaldúa 1981, 23.

84 Kurtyka 2017, 110.
85 Kurtyka 2017, 102.
86 Martell-Otero 2013, 12.
87 Conde-Frazier 2015, 79.
88 Kohn, Vega Quiñones, and Robinson 2019, 25.
89 Kohn, Vega Quiñones, and Robinson 2019, 25–26.
90 Kohn, Vega Quiñones, and Robinson 2019, 62.
91 Kohn, Vega Quiñones, and Robinson 2019, 62.
92 Kohn, Vega Quiñones, and Robinson 2019, 60.
93 Kurtyka 2017, 116.
94 Kohn, Vega Quiñones, and Robinson 2019, 84.
95 Kohn, Vega Quiñones, and Robinson 2019, 85.
96 Kohn, Vega Quiñones, and Robinson 2019, 85.
97 Kohn, Vega Quiñones, and Robinson 2019, 85.
98 Kohn, Vega Quiñones, and Robinson 2019, 90.
99 Kohn, Vega Quiñones, and Robinson 2019, 95.
100 Kohn, Vega Quiñones, and Robinson 2019, 93.
101 Kohn, Vega Quiñones, and Robinson 2019, 94.
102 Kohn, Vega Quiñones, and Robinson 2019, 94.
103 Kohn, Vega Quiñones, and Robinson 2019, 92.
104 Kohn, Vega Quiñones, and Robinson 2019, 42–43.
105 Kohn, Vega Quiñones, and Robinson 2019, 96.
106 Kohn, Vega Quiñones, and Robinson 2019, 96.
107 Kohn, Vega Quiñones, and Robinson 2019, 166.
108 Kohn, Vega Quiñones, and Robinson 2019, 164.
109 Kohn, Vega Quiñones, and Robinson 2019, 168.
110 Kohn, Vega Quiñones, and Robinson 2019, 164–65.
111 Kohn, Vega Quiñones, and Robinson 2019, 176.
112 Jones 2020, 100.
113 "The Statement on Social Justice & the Gospel" n.d.
114 Kohn, Vega Quiñones, and Robinson 2019, 132.
115 Kohn, Vega Quiñones, and Robinson 2019, 131.
116 Kohn, Vega Quiñones, and Robinson 2019, 132.
117 Kohn, Vega Quiñones, and Robinson 2019, 134.
118 Kohn, Vega Quiñones, and Robinson 2019, 135; 166.
119 Mannon 2020, 242.

Conclusion

1 A line from the 2006 worship song "In Christ Alone" by Keith and Kristyn Getty.
2 Matthew 13:1–8 NRSV.
3 Matthew 13:18–23 NRSV.
4 Pason 2017, 111.
5 Pason 2017, 112.

6 Matthew 13:23 NRSV.
7 Miller 2005, 6.
8 Miller 2005, 16.
9 Miller 2005, 20.
10 Glenn 2018a, 201.
11 Hatmaker 2017b.
12 Glenn 2018a, 4.
13 Brown 2018, 178.
14 Brown 2018, 178.
15 Brown 2018, 179.
16 Brown 2018, 181.

Epilogue

1 Du Mez 2020, 13.
2 Du Mez 2020, 3.
3 McKnight 2020.
4 Bailey 2021.
5 "Christianity Today's New Hit Podcast" 2021.
6 Barr 2021, 25.
7 Barr 2021, 9–10.
8 Burk 2021.
9 Moore 2023.
10 Newbell [@trillianewbell] 2021a.
11 Newbell [@trillianewbell] 2021b.

Bibliography

Adams-Roberts, Aesha, Rosalyn Collings Eves, and Liz Rohan. 2014. "'With the Tongue of [Wo]men and Angels': Apostolic Rhetorical Practices among Religious Women." In *Renovating Rhetoric in Christian Tradition*, edited by Elizabeth Vander Lei, Thomas Amorose, Beth Daniell, and Anne Ruggles Gere, 45–58. Pittsburgh: University of Pittsburgh Press.

Alsup, Wendy. 2008a. *Practical Theology for Women: How Knowing God Makes a Difference in Our Daily Lives*. Wheaton, Ill.: Crossway.

———. 2008b. "On Lament, Hope, and Divorce." *Practical Theology for Women* (blog), May 14. https://theologyforwomen.org/2017/07/lament-hope-divorce.html.

———. 2017. *Is the Bible Good for Women? Seeking Clarity and Confidence Through a Jesus-Centered Understanding of Scripture*. New York: Multnomah.

———. 2021. "The Model for Christian Manhood: Introduction." Modern Reformation, June 16. https://www.modernreformation.org/resources/articles/the-model-for-christian-manhood.

Anderson, Hannah. 2016. *Humble Roots: How Humility Grounds and Nourishes Your Soul*. Chicago: Moody.

———. 2018. *All That's Good: Recovering the Lost Art of Discernment*. Chicago: Moody.

Bailey, Sarah Pulliam. 2015. "How Rachel Held Evans Became the Most Polarizing Woman in Evangelicalism." *Washington Post*, April 25. www.washingtonpost.com/news/acts-of-faith/wp/2015/04/16/how-rachel-held-evans-became-the-most-polarizing-woman-in-evangelicalism/.

———. 2021. "How a Book about Evangelicals, Trump and Militant Masculinity Became a Surprise Bestseller." *Washington Post*, July 19. https://www.washingtonpost.com/religion/2021/07/16/jesus-and-john-wayne-evangelicals-surprise-bestseller/.

Balmer, Randall Herbert. 1999. *Blessed Assurance: A History of Evangelicalism in America*. Boston: Beacon.

Barr, Beth Allison. 2021. *The Making of Biblical Womanhood: How the Subjugation of Women Became Gospel Truth*. Grand Rapids: Brazos.

Beaty, Katelyn. 2013. "'I'm a Feminist Because I Love Jesus So Much.'" *Christianity Today*, November 4. https://www.christianitytoday.com/ct/2013/november-web-only/sarah-bessey-feminist-because-i-love-jesus-so-much.html.

———. 2017. "Why Evangelical Women Leaders Don't Talk about Politics." Religion & Politics, December 19. https://religionandpolitics.org/2017/12/19/why-evangelical-women-leaders-dont-talk-about-politics/.

———. 2018. "At a Private Meeting in Illinois, a Group of Evangelicals Tried to Save Their Movement from Trumpism." *The New Yorker*, April 26. https://www.newyorker.com/news/on-religion/at-a-private-meeting-in-illinois-a-group-of-evangelicals-tried-to-save-their-movement-from-trumpism.

———. 2019. "Instead of Throwing out God or Church, Rachel Held Evans Demonstrated a Robust Christian Faith." *Washington Post*, May 4. https://www.washingtonpost.com/religion/2019/05/05/instead-throwing-out-god-or-church-rachel-held-evans-demonstrated-robust-christian-faith/.

Bebbington, David. 1989. *Evangelicalism in Modern Britain: A History from the 1730s to the 1980s*. London: Unwin Hyman.

Beemer, Cristy. 2016. "God Save the Queen: Kairos and the Mercy Letters of Elizabeth I and Mary, Queen of Scots." *Rhetoric Review* 35 (2): 75–90.

Beitler, James Edward. 2019. *Seasoned Speech: Rhetoric in the Life of the Church*. Downers Grove, Ill.: IVP Academic.

Bessey, Sarah. 2013a. *Jesus Feminist: An Invitation to Revisit the Bible's View of Women*. New York: Howard.

———. 2013b. "I Am Damaged Goods." *Reform Magazine*, April 24. https://www.reform-magazine.co.uk/2013/04/i-am-damaged-goods/.

———. 2013c. "Jesus Feminist." https://www.sarahbessey.com/books/jesus-feminist.

———. 2015a. *Out of Sorts: Making Peace with an Evolving Faith*. New York: Howard.

———. 2015b. "Out of Sorts." https://www.sarahbessey.com/books/out-of-sorts.

Bizzell, Patricia. 2006. "Frances Willard, Phoebe Palmer, and the Ethos of the Methodist Woman Preacher." *Rhetoric Society Quarterly* 36 (4): 377–98.

Bligh, Michelle C., and Jeffrey C. Kohles. 2008. "Negotiating Gender Role Expectations: Rhetorical Leadership and Women in the US Senate." *Leadership* 4 (4): 381–402.

Blumenthal, Max. 2007. "Agent of Intolerance." *The Nation*, May 16. https://www.thenation.com/article/archive/agent-intolerance/.

Borg, Marcus J. 2001. *Reading the Bible Again for the First Time: Taking the Bible Seriously but Not Literally*. San Francisco: HarperCollins.

Bowler, Kate. 2019. *The Preacher's Wife: The Precarious Power of Evangelical Women Celebrities*. Princeton: Princeton University Press.

Bratta, Phil, and Malea Powell. 2016. "Introduction to the Special Issue: Entering the Cultural Rhetorics Conversations." *Enculturation: A Journal of Rhetoric, Writing, and Culture* 21. https://enculturation.net/entering-the-cultural-rhetorics-conversations.

Brown, Austin Channing. 2016. "How the Hell Did We Get Here?" *Austin Channing* (blog), March 8. http://austinchanning.com/blog/2016/3/how-the-hell-did-we-get-here.

———. 2018. *I'm Still Here: Black Dignity in a World Made for Whiteness*. New York: Convergent.

Buchanan, Lindal, and Kathleen J. Ryan. 2010. Introduction to *Walking and Talking Feminist Rhetorics: Landmark Essays and Controversies*, edited by Lindal Buchanan and Kathleen J. Ryan, xiii–xx. West Lafayette, Ind.: Parlor Press.

Burge, Ryan. 2021. "Are We All Evangelicals Now? How the Term Has Grown to Blur Theology and Ideology." Religion Unplugged, March 11. https://religionunplugged.com/news/2021/3/11/are-we-all-evangelicals-now-how-the-term-has-grown-to-blur-theology-and-ideology.

Burk, Denny. 2021. "How to Turn Complementarians into Egalitarians." May 18. https://www.dennyburk.com/how-to-turn-complementarians-into-egalitarians/.

Butler, Anthea D. 2007. *Women in the Church of God in Christ: Making a Sanctified World*. Chapel Hill: University of North Carolina Press.

———. 2021. *White Evangelical Racism: The Politics of Morality in America*. Chapel Hill: University of North Carolina Press.

Butterfield, Rosaria. 2016. "Love Your Neighbor Enough to Speak Truth." The Gospel Coalition, June 15. https://www.thegospelcoalition.org/article/love-your-neighbor-enough-to-speak-truth/.

Byrd, Aimee. 2013. *Housewife Theologian: How the Gospel Interrupts the Ordinary*. Phillipsburg, N.J.: P&R.

Campbell, Karlyn Kohrs. 1989. Introduction to *Man Cannot Speak for Her*, edited by Karylyn Kohrs Campbell, 1–16. Westport, Conn.: Greenwood Press.

Camper, Martin. 2018. *Arguing over Texts: The Rhetoric of Interpretation*. Oxford: Oxford University Press.

———. 2020. "The Future of the History of Rhetoric Is Religious." *Journal for the History of Rhetoric* 23 (1): 104–5.

Chatraw, Joshua. 2018. "Stop Apologizing for Apologetics." *Christianity Today*, April 18. https://www.christianitytoday.com/ct/2018/may/stop-apologizing-for-apologetics.html.

Chávez, Karma R. 2011. "Counter-Public Enclaves and Understanding the Function of Rhetoric in Social Movement Coalition-Building." *Communication Quarterly* 59 (1): 1–18. https://doi.org/10.1080/01463373.2010.541333.

"Christianity Today's New Hit Podcast, 'The Rise and Fall of Mars Hill,' Stirs Evangelical Soul-Searching." 2021. *Christianity Today*, August 13. https://www.christianitytoday.org/media-room/news/2021/christianity-todays-new-hit-podcast-rise-and-fall-of-mars-h.html.

Clark, Richard. 2016. "Trillia Newbell: 'Everything Can't Be Your Ministry.'" *The Calling* (podcast), June 2. *Christianity Today*. https://www.christianitytoday.com/ct/podcasts/calling/everything-cant-be-your-ministry.html.

Cobos, Casie, Gabriela Raquel Ríos, Donnie Johnson Sackey, Jennifer Sano-Franchini, and Angela M. Haas. 2018. "Interfacing Cultural Rhetorics: A History and a Call." *Rhetoric Review* 37 (2): 139–54. https://doi.org/10.1080/07350198.2018.1424470.

Cochran, Pamela. 2005. *Evangelical Feminism: A History*. New York: New York University Press.

Conde-Frazier, Elizabeth. 2013. "*Evangélicas* Reading Scriptures: Readings from Within and Beyond the Tradition." In *Latina Evangélicas: A Theological Survey from the Margins*, edited by Loida I. Martell-Otero, Zaida Maldonado Pérez, and Elizabeth Conde-Frazier, 73–89. Eugene, Ore.: Cascade.

———. 2015. "Latina Evangélicas: A New Voice in Hispanic-Latina Theology." *Journal of Latin American Theology* 10 (1): 63–84. http://www.repci.co/repositorio/handle/123456789/471.

Connors, Robert J. 1989. "Rhetorical History as a Component of Composition Studies." *Rhetoric Review* 7 (2): 230–40.

Cope, Emily Murphy. 2013. "Learning Not to Preach: Evangelical Speaker Beth Moore and the Rhetoric of Constraint." In *Rhetoric, History, and Women's Oratorical Education: American Women Learn to Speak*, edited by David Gold and Catherine Hobbs, 217–38. New York: Routledge.

Cope, Emily Murphy, and Jeffrey M. Ringer. 2015. "Coming to (Troubled) Terms: Methodology, Positionality, and the Problem of Defining 'Evangelical Christian.'" In *Mapping Christian Rhetorics: Connecting Conversations, Charting New Territories*, edited by Michael-John DePalma and Jeffrey M. Ringer, 103–24. New York: Routledge.

Cordova, Nathaniel I. 2012. "Invention, Ethos, and New Media in the Rhetoric Classroom: The Storyboard as Exemplary Genre." In *Multimodal Literacies and Emerging Genres*, edited by Tracey Bowen and Carl Whithaus, 143–63. Pittsburgh: University of Pittsburgh Press.

Cosper, Mike. 2021a. "Who Killed Mars Hill?" *The Rise and Fall of Mars Hill* (podcast), June 21. Episode 1. *Christianity Today*. https://www.christianitytoday.com/ct/podcasts/rise-and-fall-of-mars-hill/who-killed-mars-hill-church-mark-driscoll-rise-fall.html.

———. 2021b. "'I Am Jack's Raging Bile Duct.'" *The Rise and Fall of Mars Hill* (podcast), July 14. Episode 4. *Christianity Today*. https://www.christianitytoday.com/ct/podcasts/rise-and-fall-of-mars-hill/mars-hill-mark-driscoll-podcast-jacks-raging-bile.html.

———. 2021c. "Questioning the Origin Myth: A Rise and Fall Short Story." *The Rise and Fall of Mars Hill* (podcast), August 20. Bonus Episode. *Christianity Today*. https://www.christianitytoday.com/ct/podcasts/rise-and-fall-of-mars-hill/mars-hill-podcast-driscoll-origin-myth.html.

Crowley, Sharon. 2006. *Toward a Civil Discourse: Rhetoric and Fundamentalism*. Pittsburgh: University of Pittsburgh Press.

Cruz-Malavé, Arnaldo. 2017. "Testimonio." In *Keywords for Latina/o Studies*, edited by Deborah R. Vargas, Lawrence La Fountain-Stokes, and Nancy Racquel Mirabal, 228–31. New York: New York University Press.

Darsey, James, and Joshua R. Ritter. 2009. "Religious Voices in American Public Discourse." In *The SAGE Handbook of Rhetorical Studies*, edited by Andrea A. Lunsford, Kirt H. Wilson, and Rosa A. Eberly, 553–86. SAGE Publications.

Delgado Bernal, Dolores, Rebeca Burciaga, and Judith Flores Carmona. 2012. "Chicana/Latina Testimonios: Mapping the Methodological, Pedagogical, and Political." *Equity & Excellence in Education* 45 (3): 363–72.

Demar, Gary. 2007. "The Old and the New Jerry Falwell." The American Vision, May 21. https://americanvision.org/1288/old-jerry-falwell/.

DePalma, Michael-John, and Jeffrey M. Ringer, eds. 2015. *Mapping Christian Rhetorics: Connecting Conversations, Charting New Territories*. New York: Routledge.

Donawerth, Jane. 2013. *Conversational Rhetoric: The Rise and Fall of a Women's Tradition, 1600–1900*. Carbondale: Southern Illinois University Press.

Dreher, Rod. 2017. "Of Hatmaker and Heresy." The American Conservative, December 18. https://www.theamericanconservative.com/jen-hatmaker-heresy-evangelical/.

Du Mez, Kristin Kobes. 2020. *Jesus and John Wayne: How White Evangelicals Corrupted a Faith and Fractured a Nation*. New York: Liveright.

Earls, Aaron. 2023. "Fear Prevalent in Pews, According to Protestant Pastors." Lifeway Research, August 8. https://research.lifeway.com/2023/08/08/fear-prevalent-in-pews-according-to-protestant-pastors/.

Engels, Jeremy. 2015. *The Politics of Resentment: A Genealogy*. University Park: Pennsylvania State University Press.

Enns, Peter. 2016. *The Sin of Certainty: Why God Desires Our Trust More Than Our "Correct Beliefs."* San Francisco: HarperCollins.

Enns, Peter, and Jared Byas. 2017. "Carolyn Custis James—Moving Beyond the Patriarchy." *The Bible for Normal People* (podcast), December 11. Episode 32. https://thebiblefornormalpeople.com/b4np-podcast-episode-32-moving-beyond-patriarchy-carolyn-custis-james/.

———. 2019a. "Austin Channing Brown—Preaching the Bible in the Black Church." *The Bible for Normal People* (podcast), March 18. Episode 79. https://thebiblefornormalpeople.com/preaching-the-bible-in-the-black-church/.

———. 2019b. "Rachel Held Evans—Reading the Bible Creatively." *The Bible for Normal People* (podcast), May 20. Episode 88. https://thebiblefornormalpeople.com/reading-the-bible-creatively/.

Enoch, Jessica, and David Gold. 2019. "Working Women In[to] Rhetorical History." In *Women at Work: Rhetorics of Gender and Labor*, edited by Jessica Enoch and David Gold, 3–16. Pittsburgh: University of Pittsburgh Press.

Eskridge, Larry. 2012. "Defining the Term in Contemporary Times." Institute for the Study of American Evangelicals. https://web.archive.org/web/20170805202658/http://www.wheaton.edu/ISAE/Defining-Evangelicalism/Defining-the-Term.

Evans, Rachel Held. 2008. "Book Club Discussion: Confronting Our 'Situatedness'." *Rachel Held Evans* (blog), March 24. https://rachelheldevans.com/blog/article-1205119927.

———. 2010. *Evolving in Monkey Town: How a Girl Who Knew All the Answers Learned to Ask the Questions*. Grand Rapids: Zondervan.

———. 2011. "Blessed Are the Un-cool." *Rachel Held Evans* (blog), June 15. https://rachelheldevans.com/blog/blessed-are-the-uncool.

———. 2012a. *A Year of Biblical Womanhood: How a Liberated Woman Found Herself Sitting on Her Roof, Covering Her Head, and Calling Her Husband "Master."* Nashville: Thomas Nelson.

———. 2012b. "Christian Bookstores and Their Chokehold on the Industry." *Rachel Held Evans* (blog), July 6. https://rachelheldevans.com/blog/christian-bookstores-chokehold.

———. 2012c. "'Biblical Womanhood' and the Illusion of Clarity: A Response to Kathy Keller." *Rachel Held Evans* (blog), November 7. https://rachelheldevans.com/blog/biblical-womanhood-and-the-illusion-of-clarity-a-response-to-kathy-keller.

———. 2013. "Ask a Racial Reconciler. . . . (Response)." *Rachel Held Evans* (blog), September 26. https://rachelheldevans.com/blog/ask-a-racial-reconcilerresponse.

———. 2014. "Inside Mark Driscoll's Disturbed Mind." *Rachel Held Evans* (blog), July 29. https://rachelheldevans.com/blog/driscoll-troubled-mind-william-wallace.

———. 2015. *Searching for Sunday: Loving, Leaving, and Finding the Church*. Nashville: Thomas Nelson.

———. 2018a. *Inspired: Slaying Giants, Walking on Water, and Loving the Bible Again*. Nashville: Thomas Nelson.

———. 2018b. "Patriarchy Doesn't 'Protect' Women: A Response to John Piper." *Rachel Held Evans* (blog), March 20. https://rachelheldevans.com/blog/me-too-john-piper.

Fea, John. 2018. *Believe Me: The Evangelical Road to Donald Trump*. Grand Rapids: Eerdmans.

Foss, Sonja K., and Cindy L. Griffin. 1995. "Beyond Persuasion: A Proposal for an Invitational Rhetoric." *Communication Monographs* 62: 2–18.

Foust, Michael. 2004. "25 Years Ago, Conservative Resurgence Got Its Start." Baptist Press, June 15. https://www.baptistpress.com/resource-library/news/25-years-ago-conservative-resurgence-got-its-start/.

Fredlund, Katherine. 2020. "Response Rhetorics." In *Feminist Connections: Rhetoric and Activism across Time, Space, and Place*, edited by

Katherine Fredlund, Kerri Hauman, and Jessica Ouellette, 161–66. Tuscaloosa: University of Alabama Press.

Frei, Hans W. 1987. "Response to [C. F. H. Henry] 'Narrative Theology, an Evangelical Appraisal.'" *Trinity Journal* 8 (1): 21–24.

Gaffey, Adam. 2017. "Rhetorical Leadership." In *The SAGE Encyclopedia of Communication Research Methods*, edited by Mike Allen, 1499–502. SAGE Publications.

Gallagher, Sally K. 2003. *Evangelical Identity and Gendered Family Life*. New Brunswick: Rutgers University Press.

Garrison, Kristen. 2013. "Margaret Fuller's Boston Conversations as Hybrid Rhetorical Practice." In *Rhetoric, History, and Women's Oratorical Education: American Women Learn to Speak*, edited by David Gold and Catherine L. Hobbs, 96–115. New York: Routledge.

Geiger, T. J., II. 2022. *Faithful Deliberation: Rhetorical Invention, Evangelicalism, and #MeToo Reckonings*. *Rhetoric, Culture, and Social Critique*. Tuscaloosa: University of Alabama Press.

Gerson, Michael. 2018. "The Last Temptation." *The Atlantic*, March 11. https://www.theatlantic.com/magazine/archive/2018/04/the-last-temptation/554066/.

Gilmore, Leigh. 2016. *Tainted Witness: Why We Doubt What Women Say About Their Lives*. New York: Columbia University Press.

Gilyard, Keith. 2008. *Composition and Cornel West: Notes Toward a Deep Democracy*. Carbondale: Southern Illinois University Press.

Glenn, Cheryl. 1997. *Rhetoric Retold: Regendering the Rhetorical Tradition from Antiquity to the Renaissance*. Carbondale: Southern Illinois University Press.

———. 2018a. *Rhetorical Feminism and This Thing Called Hope*. Carbondale: Southern Illinois University Press.

———. 2018b. "A Feminist Tactic of Hope." Conference on College Composition and Communication, Kansas City, Mo.

Gold, David, and Catherine L. Hobbs, eds. 2013. *Rhetoric, History, and Women's Oratorical Education: American Women Learn to Speak*. New York: Routledge.

Graham, Ruth. 2019. "Rachel Held Evans, the Hugely Popular Christian Writer Who Challenged the Evangelical Establishment, Is Dead at 37." Slate, May 4. https://slate.com/human-interest/2019/05/rachel-held-evans-the-hugely-popular-evangelical-writer-is-dead-at-37.html.

Griswold, Eliza. 2019. "Conservative Evangelicals Attempt to Disentangle Their Faith from Trumpism." *The New Yorker*, January 8.

https://www.newyorker.com/news/on-religion/conservative-evangelicals-attempt-to-disentangle-their-faith-from-trumpism.

Gubar, Susan. 2011. "Introduction." In *True Confessions: Feminist Professors Tell Stories out of School*, edited by Susan Gubar, ix–xviii. New York: W. W. Norton.

Guinness, Os. 2015. "Os Guinness: Welcome to the 'Grand Age of Apologetics.'" Interview by Tim Stafford. *Christianity Today*, July 23. https://christianitytoday.com/ct/2015/july-web-only/os-guinness-interview-welcome-grand-age-apologetics.html.

Hardesty, Nancy. 1999. *Women Called to Witness: Evangelical Feminism in the Nineteenth Century*. 2nd ed. Knoxville: University of Tennessee Press.

Harding, Susan F. 2001. *The Book of Jerry Falwell: Fundamentalist Language and Politics*. Princeton: Princeton University Press.

Hatmaker, Brandon. 2016. "Where I Stand on LGBTQ." Facebook, November 1. https://www.facebook.com/HatmakerBrandon/posts/where-i-stand-on-lgbtq-as-you-read-this-and-consider-responding-please-also-reme/661677820673474/.

Hatmaker, Jen. 2012. *7: An Experimental Mutiny Against Excess*. Nashville: B&H.

———. 2014. *Interrupted: When Jesus Wrecks Your Comfortable Christianity*. Colorado Springs: NavPress.

———. 2015. *For the Love: Fighting for Grace in a World of Impossible Standards*. Nashville: Thomas Nelson.

———. 2016. "A couple of quick thoughts on all these tender things." Facebook, October 31. https://www.facebook.com/jenhatmaker/posts/1083375421761452.

———. 2017a. *Of Mess and Moxie: Wrangling Delight out of This Wild and Glorious Life*. Nashville: Thomas Nelson.

———. 2017b. "My Saddest Good Friday in Memory: When Treasured Things Are Dead." *JenHatmaker* (blog), April 14. https://jenhatmaker.com/my-saddest-good-friday-in-memory-when-treasured-things-are-dead.

Hauerwas, Stanley, and L. Gregory Jones. 1997. *Why Narrative? Readings in Narrative Theology*. Eugene, Ore.: Wipf and Stock.

Hayes, Lindsay, and Sarah Kornfield. 2020. "Prophesying a Feminist Story: Sarah Bessey and the Evangelical Pulpit." *Journal of Communication & Religion* 43 (2): 33–54.

Hindmarsh, D. Bruce. 2002. "The Antecedents of Evangelical Conversion Narrative: Spiritual Autobiography and the Christian Tradition." *Crux: A Quarterly Journal of Christian Thought and Opinion* 38 (4): 4–13.

———. 2017. "Evangelicalism." In *Evangelical Dictionary of Theology*, edited by Daniel J. Treier and Walter A. Elwell, 290–92. Grand Rapids: Baker Academic.

Hogg, Charlotte. 2015. "Including Conservative Women's Rhetorics in an 'Ethics of Hope and Care.'" *Rhetorical Review* 34 (4): 391–408.

Horner, David A. 2011. *Mind Your Faith: A Student's Guide to Thinking and Living Well*. Downers Grove, Ill.: InterVarsity Press.

Ingersoll, Julie. 2003. *Evangelical Christian Women: War Stories in the Gender Battles*. New York: New York University Press.

Jacobs, Alan. 2008. *Looking Before and After: Testimony and the Christian Life*. Grand Rapids: Eerdmans.

Jarratt, Susan C., and Nedra Reynolds. 1994. "The Splitting Image: Contemporary Feminisms and the Ethics of Ethos." In *Ethos: New Essays in Rhetorical and Critical Theory*, edited by James S. Baumlin and Tita French Baumlin, 37–64. University Park, Tex.: Southern Methodist University Press.

Jensen, Peter F. 2017. "Revelation." In *Evangelical Dictionary of Theology*, edited by Daniel J. Treier and Walter A. Elwell, 747–48. Grand Rapids: Baker Academic.

Johnson, Jenell. 2014. *American Lobotomy: A Rhetorical History*. Ann Arbor: University of Michigan Press.

Johnson, Jessica. 2018. *Biblical Porn: Affect, Labor, and Pastor Mark Driscoll's Evangelical Empire*. Durham: Duke University Press.

Jones, Robert P. 2016. *The End of White Christian America*. New York: Simon and Schuster.

———. 2020. *White Too Long: The Legacy of White Supremacy in American Christianity*. New York: Simon & Schuster.

———. 2021. "The Unmaking of the White Christian Worldview." *Time*, September 29. https://time.com/6102117/white-christian-americans-sins/.

Jones, Robert P., Daniel Cox, Betsy Cooper, and Rachel Lienesch. 2017. "Majority of Americans Oppose Transgender Bathroom Restrictions." *PRRI* (blog), March 10. https://www.prri.org/research/lgbt-transgender-bathroom-discrimination-religious-liberty/

Jurecic, Ann. 2012. *Illness as Narrative*. Pittsburgh: University of Pittsburgh Press.

Kell, Carl L. 2006. *Exiled: Voices of the Southern Baptist Convention Holy War*. Knoxville: University of Tennessee Press.

Keller, Kathy. 2017. "A Year of Biblical Womanhood." The Gospel Coalition, June 16. https://www.thegospelcoalition.org/reviews/year-biblical-womanhood/.

Kidd, Thomas S. 2019. *Who Is an Evangelical? The History of a Movement in Crisis*. New Haven: Yale University Press.

King Jr., Martin Luther. 1998. *Autobiography of Martin Luther King Jr.* Ed. Clayborne Carson. New York: Warner Books.

Kohn, Natalia, Noemi Vega Quiñones, and Kristy Garza Robinson. 2019. *Hermanas: Deepening Our Identity and Growing Our Influence*. Downers Grove, Ill.: InterVarsity Press.

Kurtyka, Faith M. 2017. "Learning How to Feel: Conversion Narratives and Community Membership in First-year Composition." *Composition Studies* 45 (1): 99–121.

Labberton, Mark, ed. 2018. *Still Evangelical? Insiders Reconsider Political, Social, and Theological Meaning*. Downers Grove, Ill.: InterVarsity Press.

Lee, Deborah Jian. 2015. *Rescuing Jesus: How People of Color, Women, and Queer Christians Are Reclaiming Evangelicalism*. New York: Beacon.

Logan, Shirley W. 2008. *Liberating Language: Sites of Rhetorical Education in Nineteenth-Century Black America*. Carbondale: Southern Illinois University Press.

Lynerd, Benjamin T. 2014. *Republican Theology: The Civil Religion of American Evangelicals*. Oxford: Oxford University Press.

Maddux, Kristy. 2010. *The Faithful Citizen: Popular Christian Media and Gendered Civic Identities*. Waco: Baylor University Press.

Magnuson, Norris A. 2017. "Social Gospel." In *Evangelical Dictionary of Theology*, edited by Daniel J. Treier and Walter A. Elwell, 819–20. Grand Rapids: Baker Academic.

Mahmood, Saba. 2012. *The Politics of Piety: The Islamic Revival and the Feminist Subject*. Princeton: Princeton University Press.

Mannon, Bethany Ober. 2020. "The Persuasive Power of Individual Stories: The Rhetoric in Narrative Archives." In *Feminist Connections: Rhetoric and Activism across Time, Space, and Place*, edited by Katherine Fredlund, Kerri Hauman, and Jessica Ouellette, 230–45. Tuscaloosa: University of Alabama Press.

———. 2023. "Evangelical Rhetoric in College Students' Writing Practice." *College Composition and Communication* 74 (4): 618–45.

Marsden, George M. 2006. *Fundamentalism and American Culture*. 2nd ed. Oxford: Oxford University Press.

Marinelli, Kevin. 2016. "Revisiting Edwin Black: Exhortation as a Prelude to Emotional–Material Rhetoric." *Rhetoric Society Quarterly* 46 (5): 465–485.

Martell-Otero, Loida I. 2013. "Introduction: Abuelita Theologies." In *Latina Evangélicas: A Theological Survey from the Margins*, edited by Loida I. Martell-Otero, Zaida Maldonado Pérez, and Elizabeth Conde-Frazier, 1–13. Eugene, Ore.: Cascade Books.

Martin, Stephanie A. 2021. *Decoding the Digital Church: Evangelical Storytelling and the Election of Donald Trump*. Tuscaloosa: University of Alabama Press.

McIntire, C. T. 2017. "Fundamentalism." In *Evangelical Dictionary of Theology*, edited by Daniel J. Treier and Walter A. Elwell, 333–35. Grand Rapids: Baker Academic.

McKnight, Scot. 2020. "What to Call the 20%?" *Jesus Creed* (blog), July 29. https://www.christianitytoday.com/scot-mcknight/2020/july/what-to-call-20.html.

McLaren, Brian. 2006. *A Generous Orthodoxy*. Grand Rapids: Zondervan.

Merritt, Jonathan. 2015. "Rachel Held Evans Defends Exit from Evangelicalism, Calls Christians to Celebrate Sacraments." Religion News Service, March 9. https://religionnews.com/2015/03/09/rachel-held-evans-defends-exit-evangelicalism-calls-christians-celebrate-sacraments/.

———. 2016. "The Politics of Jen Hatmaker: Trump, Black Lives Matter, Gay Marriage and More." Religion News Service, October 25. https://religionnews.com/2016/10/25/the-politics-of-jen-hatmaker-trump-black-lives-matter-gay-marriage-and-more/.

———. 2017. "Why I'll Take Courageous Jen Hatmaker over Her Cowardly Critics Any Day." May 16. https://www.jonathanmerritt.com/article/ill-take-courageous-jen-hatmaker-cowardly-critics-day.

———. 2018. *Learning to Speak God from Scratch: Why Sacred Words are Vanishing–and How We Can Revive Them*. New York: Convergent.

Miller, Carolyn. 1984. "Genre as Social Action." *Quarterly Journal of Speech* 70: 151–67.

Miller, Richard. 2005. *Writing at the End of the World*. Pittsburgh: University of Pittsburgh Press.

Mitchell, Travis. 2019. "In U.S., Decline of Christianity Continues at Rapid Pace." *Pew Research Center's Religion & Public Life Project* (blog), October 17. https://www.pewresearch.org/religion/2019/10/17/in-u-s-decline-of-christianity-continues-at-rapid-pace/.

Moody, Joycelyn K. 2003. *Sentimental Confessions: Spiritual Narratives of Nineteenth-Century African American Women*. Athens: University of Georgia Press.

Moore, Beth (@BethMooreLPM). 2016a. "Try to absorb how acceptable the disesteem and objectifying of women has been when some Christian leaders don't think it's that big a deal." Twitter, October 9. https://twitter.com/BethMooreLPM/status/785123300636667905.

———. 2016b. "Wake up, Sleepers, to what women have dealt with all along in environments of gross entitlement & power. Are we sickened? Yes. Surprised? NO." Twitter, October 9. https://twitter.com/BethMooreLPM/status/785119502769852418.

———. 2018. "A Letter to My Brothers." *Living Proof Ministries Blog* (blog), May 3. https://blog.lproof.org/2018/05/a-letter-to-my-brothers.html.

———. 2023. *All My Knotted-Up Life: A Memoir.* Carol Stream, Ill.: Tyndale.

Moore, Russell. 2022. "When the South Loosens Its Bible Belt." *Christianity Today*, August 11. https://www.christianitytoday.com/ct/2022/august-web-only/russell-moore-white-evangelicals-bible-belt-south-church.html.

Moraga, Cherríe, and Gloria Anzaldúa. 1981. "Entering the Lives of Others: Theories in the Flesh." In *This Bridge Called My Back: Writings by Radical Women of Color*, edited by Cherríe Moraga and Gloria Anzaldúa. Latham, N.Y.: Kitchen Table Press.

Mountford, Roxanne. 2003. *The Gendered Pulpit. Preaching in American Protestant Spaces.* Carbondale: Southern Illinois University Press.

Muehlhoff, Timothy M., and Richard Langer. 2017. *Winsome Persuasion: Christian Influence in a Post-Christian World.* Downers Grove, Ill.: InterVarsity Press.

Nadeem, Reem. 2021. "Behind Biden's 2020 Victory." *Pew Research Center—U.S. Politics & Policy* (blog), June 30. https://www.pewresearch.org/politics/2021/06/30/behind-bidens-2020-victory/.

Newbell, Trillia. 2012. "A Year of Biblical Womanhood: A Review." Desiring God, October 12. www.desiringgod.org/articles/a-year-of-biblical-womanhood-a-review.

———. 2014. *United: Captured by God's Vision for Diversity.* Chicago: Moody Publishers.

——— (@trillianewbell). 2016. "Actually in tears after seeing someone I love post that they are voting for Trump. I can take the Christian celebrities but friends are hard." Twitter, October 15. https://twitter.com/trillianewbell/status/791108418866151424.

——— (@trillianewbell). 2018. "Because racism is on display from national leaders, no one can now say 'racism would go away if you'd stop talking about it.' Perhaps now, especially for the church, we can face realities, confess, repent, and actually move towards true harmony and reconciliation." Twitter, January 12. https://twitter.com/trillianewbell/status/951802227391385605.

———. 2020. "A Personal Update." *Trillia Newbell* (blog). https://www.trillianewbell.com/blog/joining-moody-publishers.

——— (@trillianewbell). 2021a. "Me: minding my own business doing the good work the Lord planned for me Them: Revealing their racism because I'm a Black 'girl' (cough, I'm a grown woman) Me: Keeping on doing the good work the Lord planned for me I've experienced racism my entire life. Not gonna stop me now." Twitter, June 2. https://twitter.com/trillianewbell/status/1400167530572963846.

——— (@trillianewbell). 2021b. "For clarity and for those confused: I do not work at the ERLC and haven't for over a year. And we have been in a new season at a non-SBC church. I will not be at the SBC convention because I'm not associated. I hope this clarity is helpful. Have a blessed and wonderful weekend!!" Twitter, June 5. https://twitter.com/trillianewbell/status/1401176364062027785.

Newkirk, Thomas. 2014. *Minds Made for Stories: How We Really Read and Write Informational and Persuasive Texts*. Portsmouth, N.H.: Heinemann.

Newport, Frank. 2018. "5 Things to Know About Evangelicals in America." Gallup, May 31. https://news.gallup.com/opinion/polling-matters/235208/things-know-evangelicals-america.aspx.

Noll, Mark A. 2006. *The Civil War as a Theological Crisis*. Chapel Hill: University of North Carolina Press.

———. 2008. *God and Race in American Politics: A Short History*. Princeton: Princeton University Press.

———. 2017. "Scopes Trial." In *Evangelical Dictionary of Theology*, edited by Daniel J. Treier and Walter A. Elwell, 788–89. Grand Rapids: Baker Academic.

Pason, Amy. 2017. "Phenomenon or Meaning? A Tale of Two Occupies." In *What Democracy Looks Like: The Rhetoric of Social Movements and Counterpublics*, edited by Amy Pason, Christina R. Foust, and Kate Zittlow Rogness, 107–28. Tuscaloosa: University of Alabama Press.

Pason, Amy, Christina R. Foust, and Kate Zittlow Rogness. 2017. "Introduction: Rhetoric and the Study of Social Change." In *What Democracy Looks Like: The Rhetoric of Social Movements and Counterpublics*, edited by Amy Pason, Christina R. Foust, and Kate Zittlow Rogness, 1–26. Tuscaloosa: University of Alabama Press.

The Pelican Project. 2018. "The Pelican Project." https://thepelicanproject.com/.

Pence, Mike. 2019. "Liberty University Commencement 2019—Vice President Mike Pence" (video). Liberty University. https://www.youtube.com/watch?v=3XwJ_xgRliE.

Petersen, Anne Helen. 2016. "The New Evangelical Woman Vs. Trump." BuzzFeed News, November 7. https://www.buzzfeednews.com/article/annehelenpetersen/the-new-evangelical-woman-vs-trump.

Peterson, Eugene H. 2008. *Christ Plays in Ten Thousand Places: A Conversation in Spiritual Theology*. Grand Rapids: Eerdmans.

Peterson, Paul Silas. 2020. Introduction to *Generous Orthodoxies: Essays on the History and Future of Ecumenical Theology*, edited by Paul Silas Peterson, xvii–xxxiv. Eugene, Ore.: Pickwick Publications.

Petry, Jonna. 2012. "My Story." *Joyful Exiles* (blog), March 19. https://joyfulexiles.com/2012/03/19/my-story-by-jonna-petry/.

Piper, Barnabas. 2014. "Why You Shouldn't Give Up on the Church." *Relevant*, August 14. https://relevantmagazine.com/faith/why-you-shouldnt-give-church/.

Piper, John, and Wayne Grudem. 1991. *Recovering Biblical Manhood and Womanhood: A Response to Evangelical Feminism*. Wheaton, Ill.: Crossway.

Poletti, Anna. 2011a. "Intimate Economies: PostSecret and the Affect of Confession." *Biography* 34 (1): 25–36.

———. 2011b. "Coaxing an Intimate Public: Life Narrative in Digital Storytelling." *Continuum* 25 (1): 73–83.

Prior, Karen Swallow. 2018a. "Practice the Christian Virtue of Reading Promiscuously." The Gospel Coalition, October 11. https://www.thegospelcoalition.org/article/virtue-reading/.

———. 2018b. *On Reading Well: Finding the Good Life through Great Books*. Grand Rapids: Brazos.

PRRI Staff. 2021. "The 2020 Census of American Religion." Public Religion Research Institute, August 7. https://www.prri.org/research/2020-census-of-american-religion/.

Rak, Julie. 2013. *Boom! Manufacturing Memoir for the Popular Market*. Waterloo, Ont.: Wilfrid Laurier University Press.

Ratcliffe, Krista. 2005. *Rhetorical Listening: Identification, Gender, Whiteness*. Carbondale: Southern Illinois University Press.

"Religious Landscape Study." 2015. *Pew Research Center's Religion & Public Life Project* (blog), May 15. https://www.pewresearch.org/religion/2015/05/12/americas-changing-religious-landscape.

Riley, Catherine L. 2016. "Rhetorical Leadership and the Black Church: Revisiting 1940s' Durham." *Howard Journal of Communications* 27 (4): 291–310. https://doi.org/10.1080/10646175.2016.1194788.

Ringer, Jeffrey M. 2013. "The Dogma of Inquiry: Composition and the Primacy of Faith." *Rhetoric Review* 32 (3): 349–65. https://doi.org/10.1080/07350198.2013.797880.

———. 2016. *Vernacular Christian Rhetoric and Civil Discourse*. New York: Routledge.

Robillard, Amy. 2019. "Seeking Adequate Rhetorical Witnesses for Life Writing." *Rhetoric Society Quarterly* 49 (2): 185–92.

Root, Jerry. 2021. "Apologetics." Personal website. June 10. www.drjerryroot.com/post/apologetics.

Royster, Jacqueline Jones, and Gesa Kirsch. 2012. *Feminist Rhetorical Practices: New Horizons for Rhetoric, Composition, and Literacy Studies*. Carbondale: Southern Illinois University Press.

Ryan, Kathleen J., Nancy Myers, and Rebecca Jones. 2016. "Introduction: Identifying Feminist Ecological Ethe." In *Rethinking Ethos: A Feminist Ecological Approach to Rhetoric*, edited by Kathleen J. Ryan, Nancy Myers, and Rebecca Jones, 1–22. Carbondale: Southern Illinois University Press.

Scanzoni, Letha, and Nancy Hardesty. 1974. *All We're Meant to Be: A Biblical Approach to Women's Liberation*. Waco, Tex.: Word.

Scharold, Kristen. 2011. "Testify!" *Christianity Today*, January 2. https://www.christianitytoday.com/ct/2011/januaryweb-only/testify.html.

Sernett, Milton G. 1991. "Black Religion and the Question of Evangelical Identity." In *The Variety of American Evangelicalism*, edited by Donald W. Dayson and Robert K. Johnson, 135–47. Knoxville: University of Tennessee Press.

Shaver, Lisa J. 2012. *Beyond the Pulpit: Women's Rhetorical Roles in the Antebellum Religious Press*. Pittsburgh: University of Pittsburgh Press.

Shellnutt, Kate. 2019. "Longtime Liberty Prof Karen Swallow Prior Leaving for Southeastern." *Christianity Today*, October 24. https://www.christianitytoday.com/news/2019/october/karen-swallow-prior-sebts-southeastern-liberty-university.html.

Sipiora, Phillip. 2012. "Kairos: The Rhetoric of Time and Timing in the New Testament." In *Rhetoric and Kairos: Essays in History, Theory, and Praxis*, edited by Phillip Sipiora and James S. Baumlin, 114–27. Albany: State University of New York Press.

Sire, James W. 2015. *Naming the Elephant: Worldview as a Concept*. 2nd ed. Downers Grove, Ill.: IVP Academic.

"Six Reasons Young Christians Leave Church." 2011. Barna Group, September 27. https://www.barna.com/research/six-reasons-young-christians-leave-church/.

Slotkin, Alexander. 2020. "'The Woman Who Talks': A Qualitative Case Study in Feminist Jewish Rhetorics." *Rhetoric Review* 39 (4): 457–70.

Smith, Sidonie. 1993. *Subjectivity, Identity, and the Body: Women's Autobiographical Practices in the Twentieth Century*. Bloomington: Indiana University Press.

Smith, Sidonie, and Julia Watson. 2010. *Reading Autobiography: A Guide for Interpreting Life Narratives*. 2nd ed. Minneapolis: University of Minnesota Press.

Stackhouse, J. G. 2017. "Apologetics." In *Evangelical Dictionary of Theology*, edited by Daniel J. Treier and Walter A. Elwell, 71–72. Grand Rapids: Baker Academic.

Stanley, Tiffany. 2017. "This Evangelical Leader Denounced Trump. Then the Death Threats Started." *Politico*, December 17. https://www.politico.com/magazine/story/2017/12/17/is-jen-hatmaker-the-conscious-of-evangelical-christianity-216068/.

"The Statement on Social Justice & the Gospel." N.d. https://statementonsocialjustice.com.

Stenberg, Sheri J., and Charlotte Hogg. 2020. "Introduction: Gathering Women's Rhetorics for the Twenty-First Century." In *Persuasive Acts: Women's Rhetorics in the Twenty-First Century*, edited by Sheri J. Stenberg and Charlotte Hogg, 3–21. Pittsburgh: University of Pittsburgh Press.

Stetzer, Ed. 2019. "Reflecting on Rachel: Why She Mattered." *Outreach Magazine*, May 6. https://outreachmagazine.com/features/discipleship/42703-why-rachel-held-evans-mattered.html.

Sullivan, Dale. 1992. "Kairos and the Rhetoric of Belief." *Quarterly Journal of Speech* 78: 317–32.

Tasker, Elizabeth, and Frances B. Holt-Underwood. 2008. "Feminist Research Methodologies in Historic Rhetoric and Composition: An Overview of Scholarship from the 1970s to the Present." *Rhetoric Review* 27 (1): 54–71.

Tisby, Jemar. 2019a. *The Color of Compromise: The Truth about the American Church's Complicity in Racism*. Grand Rapids: Zondervan.

———. 2019b. "Are Black Christians Evangelical?" In *Evangelicals: Who They Have Been, Are Now, and Could Be*, edited by Mark A. Noll, David W. Bebbington, and George M. Marsden, 262–72. Grand Rapids: Eerdmans.

Teasdale, Mark. 2016. "Evangelism, Without the Weird Aftertaste." Interview by Joshua Ryan Butler. *Christianity Today*, October 21.

https://www.christianitytoday.com/ct/2016/november/evangelism-without-weird-aftertaste.html.

Turner, Kathleen J. 1998. *Doing Rhetorical History: Concepts and Cases.* Tuscaloosa: University of Alabama Press.

Van Opstal, Sandra Maria. 2018. "Remaining to Reform." In *Still Evangelical? Insiders Reconsider Political, Social, and Theological Meaning*, edited by Mark Labberton, 120–37. Downers Grove, Ill.: InterVarsity.

Vander Lei, Elizabeth. 2014. Introduction to *Renovating Rhetoric in Christian Tradition*, edited by Elizabeth Vander Lei, Thomas Amorose, Beth Daniell, and Anne Ruggles Gere, ix–xviii. Pittsburgh: University of Pittsburgh Press.

Vandermaas-Peeler, Alex, Daniel Cox, Maxine Najle, Molly Fisch-Friedman, Rob Griffin, and Robert P. Jones. 2018. "Partisan Polarization Dominates Trump Era: Findings from the 2018 American Values Survey." PRRI, October 29. https://www.prri.org/research/partisan-polarization-dominates-trump-era-findings-from-the-2018-american-values-survey/.

Vidu, Adonis. 2017. "Hermeneutics." In *Evangelical Dictionary of Theology*, edited by Daniel J. Treier and Walter A. Elwell, 378–80. Grand Rapids: Baker Academic.

Vischer, Phil, and Skye Jethani. 2023. "Why I'm Still a Christian with Jemar Tisby." *The Holy Post* (podcast), October 9. https://www.holypost.com/post/why-i-m-still-a-christian-with-jemar-tisby.

Warren, Tish Harrison. 2017. "Who's in Charge of the Christian Blogosphere?" *Christianity Today*, April 27. https://www.christianitytoday.com/women/2017/april/whos-in-charge-of-christian-blogosphere.html.

Weber, Timothy P. 2017. "Evangelism." In *Evangelical Dictionary of Theology*, edited by Daniel J. Treier and Walter A. Elwell, 292–93. Grand Rapids: Baker Academic.

"What Millennials Want When They Visit Church." 2015. Barna Group, March 4. https://www.barna.com/research/what-millennials-want-when-they-visit-church/.

"White Evangelical Gender Gap?" 2018. ABC News, November 7. https://abcnews.go.com/Politics/white-evangelical-gender-gap/story?id=59036921.

Whitlock, Gillian. 2007. *Soft Weapons: Autobiography in Transit.* Chicago: University of Chicago Press.

Worthen, Molly. 2014. *Apostles of Reason: The Crisis of Authority in American Evangelicalism*. Oxford: Oxford University Press.

Yagoda, Ben. 2009. *Memoir: A History.* New York: Riverhead.

Young, Mark. 2018. "Recapturing Evangelical Identity and Mission." In *Still Evangelical? Insiders Reconsider Political, Social, and Theological Meaning*, edited by Mark Labberton, 46–65. Downers Grove, Ill.: InterVarsity Press.

Zarefsky, David. 2000. "Lincoln's 1862 Annual Message: A Paradigm of Rhetorical Leadership." *Rhetoric and Public Affairs* 3 (1): 5–14.

Zimmerelli, Lisa. 2015. "'Heaven-Touched Lips and Pent-up Voices': The Rhetoric of Female Preaching Apologia, 1820–1930." In *Mapping Christian Rhetorics: Connecting Conversations, Charting New Territories*, edited by Michael-John DePalma and Jeffrey M. Ringer, 180–202. New York: Routledge.

Index